ARGENTINE INDIAN ART

BY

Alejandro Eduardo Fiadone

I0474383

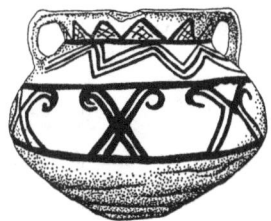

DOVER PUBLICATIONS, INC.
Mineola, New York

Bibliographical Note

Argentine Indian Art is a new work, first published by Dover Publications, Inc., in 1997.

DOVER *Pictorial Archive* SERIES

Library of Congress Cataloging-in-Publication Data

Fiadone, Alejandro Eduardo.
    Argentine Indian art / by Alejandro Eduardo Fiadone.
        p. cm.
    Includes bibliographical references.
    ISBN-13: 978-0-486-29896-2 (pbk.)
    ISBN-10: 0-486-29896-5 (pbk.)
     1. Indian art—Argentina.   2. Art—Argentina—Themes, motives. I. Title.
F2821.3.A8F53   1997
704.03'98082—dc21   97-30218
                                                          CIP

www.doverpublications.com

INTRODUCTION

The first signs of humanity in what is today Argentina date from about 9000 B.C. From that time until the Spanish conquest, different cultures developed in different geographical areas, each possessing its own characteristics, but also absorbing influences from various neighboring cultures, including the Inca Empire in the northwest.

The designs used by these cultures in ceramics, leather work, stone artifacts, textiles and on other materials are symbols of indigenous knowledge which today we find difficult to understand. While some visible manifestations of these early cultures persist to this day in Argentine language, religion, folklore, fashion, and custom ("Cha," for instance, is a Mapuche word; the gaucho clothing has incorporated many garments of Indian origin, etc.), these designs reflect ideas lost to cultural change. Their meaning is bound up in the cultural practices and experiences of the times. These symbols comprised a code that communicated a wide array of information. Some of them, owing to migrations, trade, wars, and shared religious beliefs, were common to the whole continent (such as the two-headed serpent, the large cat, the cross, terraces, the "greca") with stylistic variations in each region. These and other symbols, such as supernatural birds, spirals, fantastic beings and animals, reflect a mythology necessary to the various cultures to explain their cosmos and the meaning of life. Footprints and fragments of animal figures suggested the existence of things not known through direct knowledge, but only through intuition. The many representations of animals, birds and sea creatures reflect an acute awareness and knowledge of nature and its essential relationship to food, clothing, medicine and all aspects of life and culture.

The native American iconography was no mere product of absurd pagan beliefs, as was the hasty conclusion of many Europeans who first came into contact with it. The work *The Interior Castle* by Saint Teresa of Jesus (1515–1582), widely-known during the time of the conquest, exemplifies such misconceptions in its interpretation of toads, snakes, serpents, and lizards as symbols of sin. The true symbolic meaning of these creatures in American iconography was vastly different and more complex. What was seen as superstition and demonic falsehood by the Europeans was in actuality a rich symbolic system intended to communicate life and existence as perceived by these cultures. Much suffering, abuse and misfortune could have been avoided had the Europeans understood and appreciated this.

The intrinsic interest, strength and beauty of the designs in this copyright-free treasury make them ideal for use by artists and craftspeople, whether as design inspiration or for direct application.

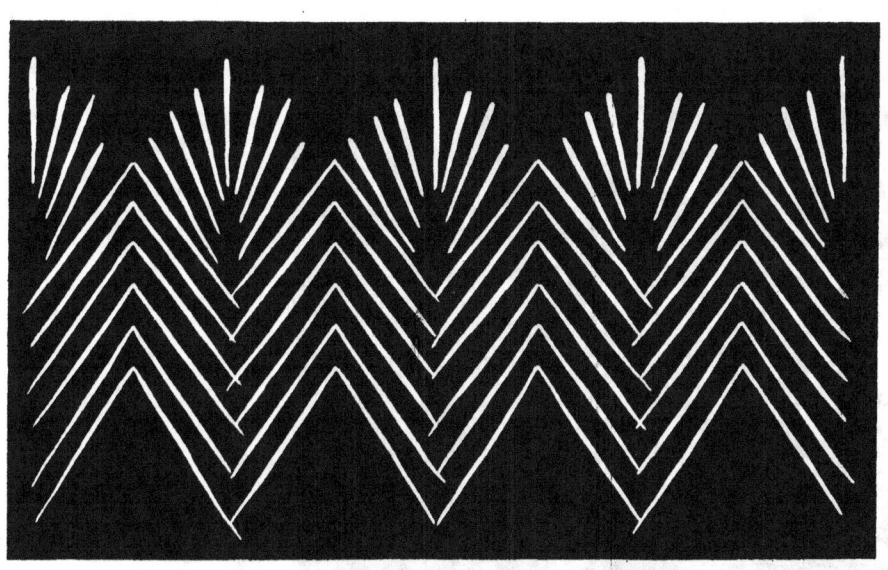

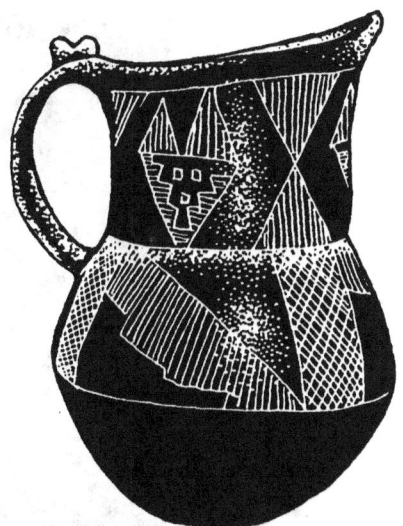

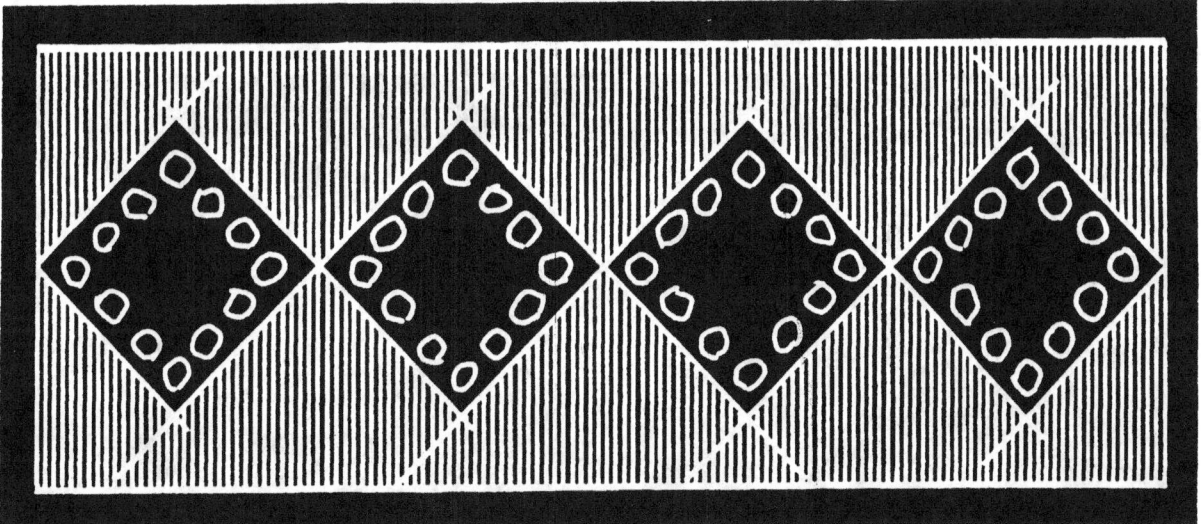

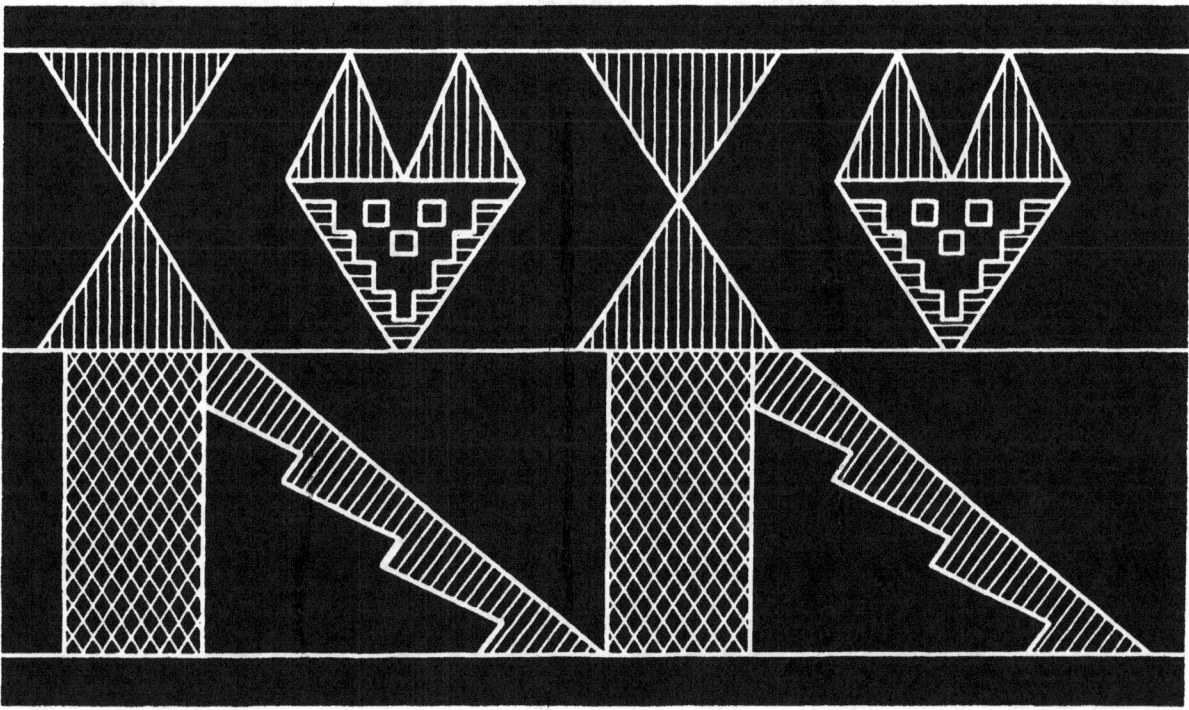

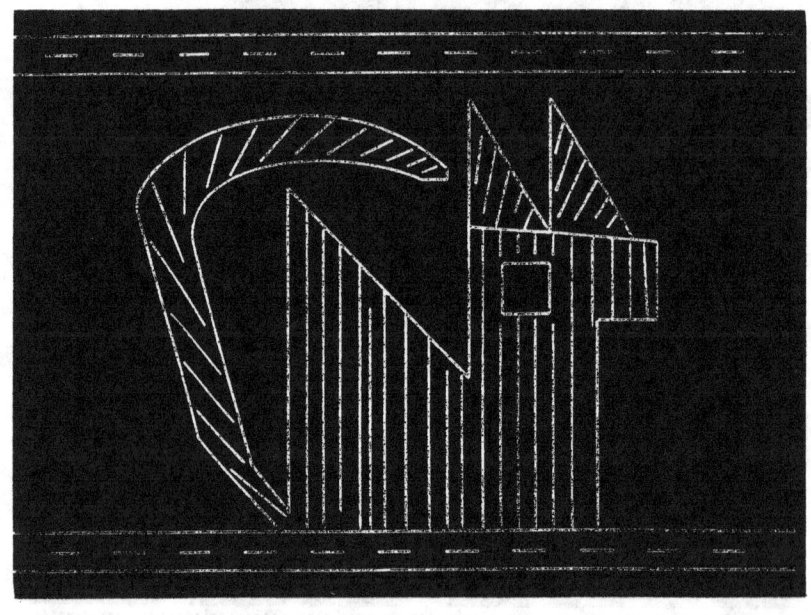

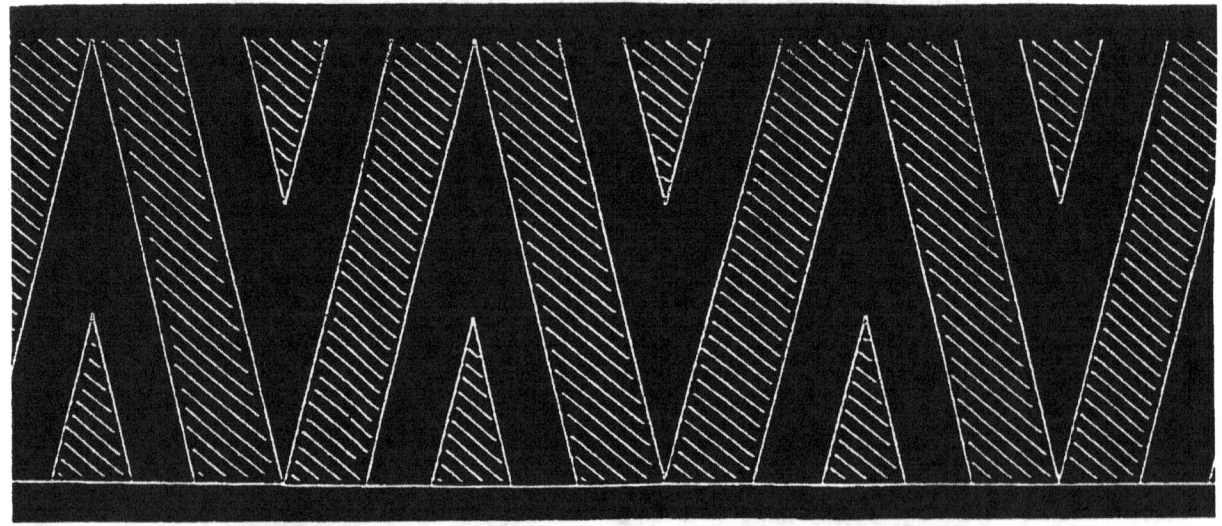

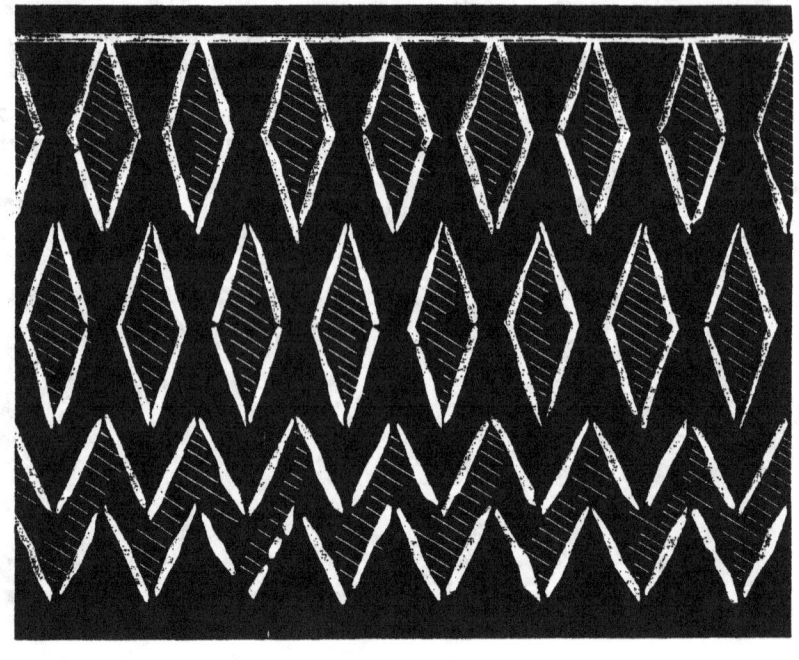

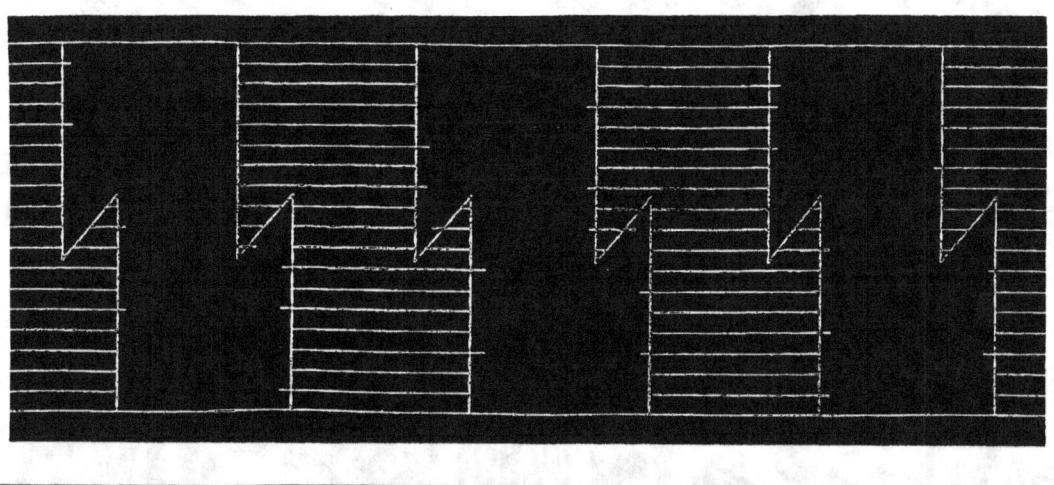

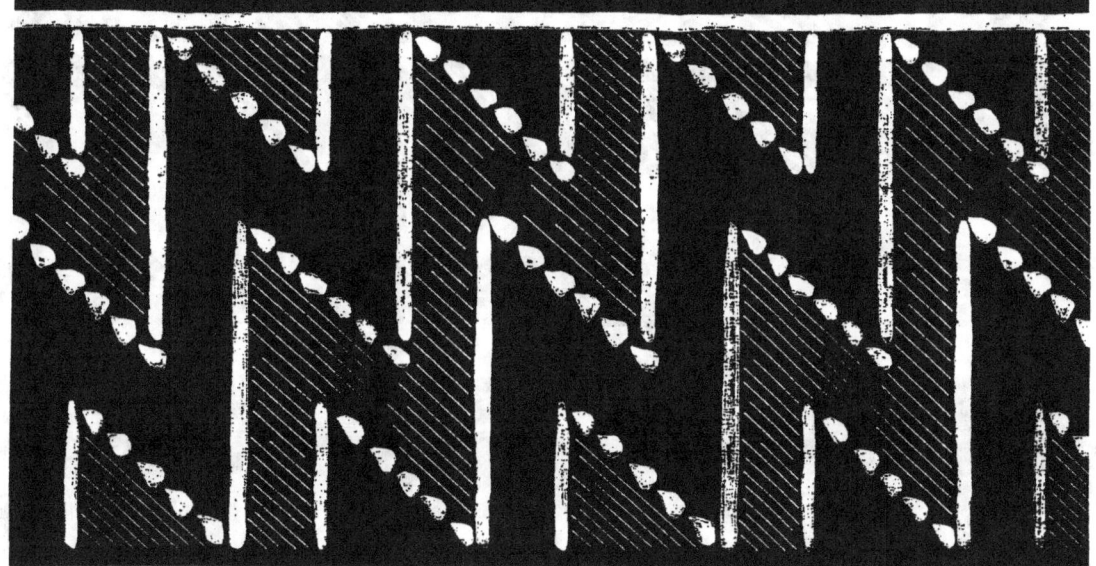

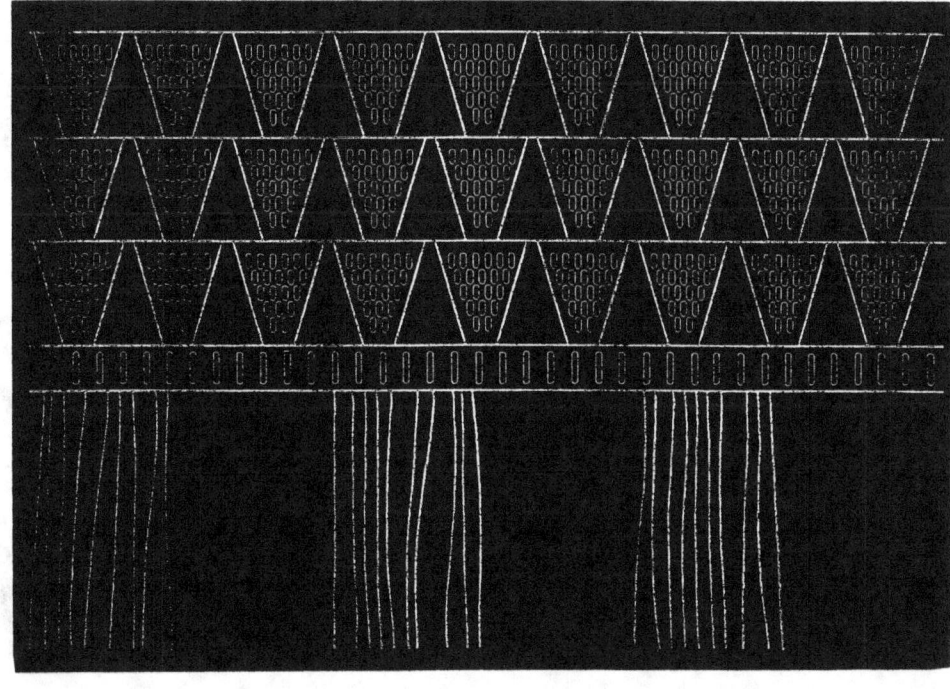

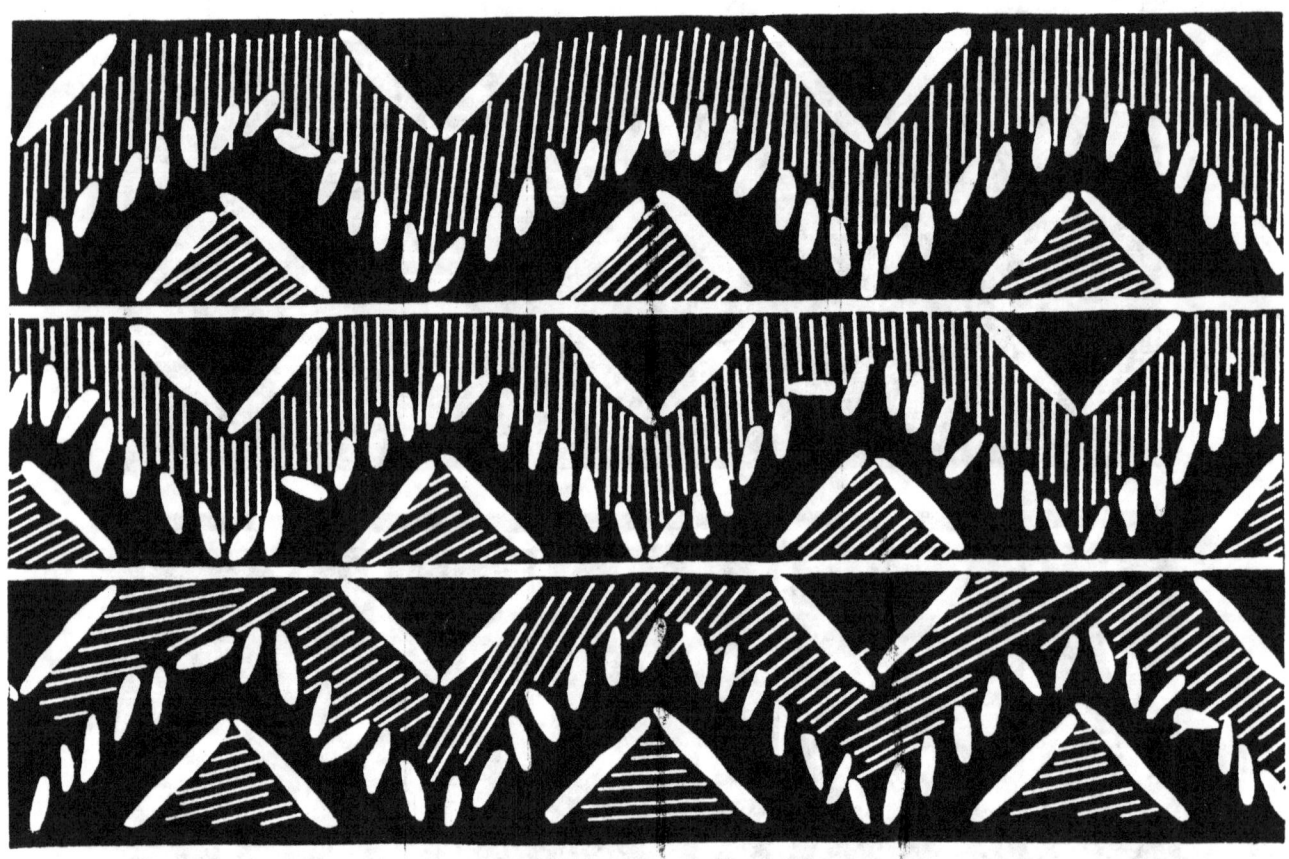

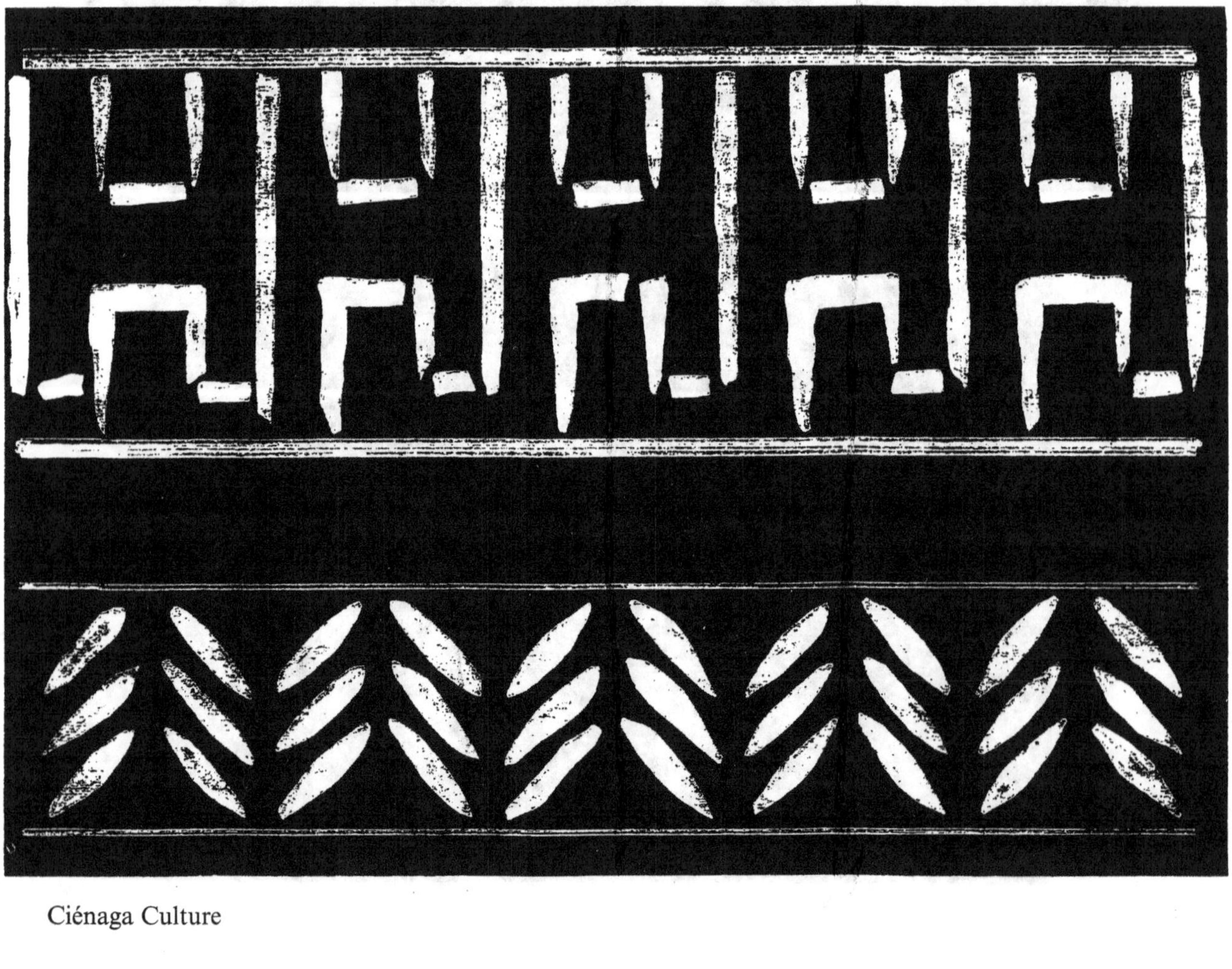

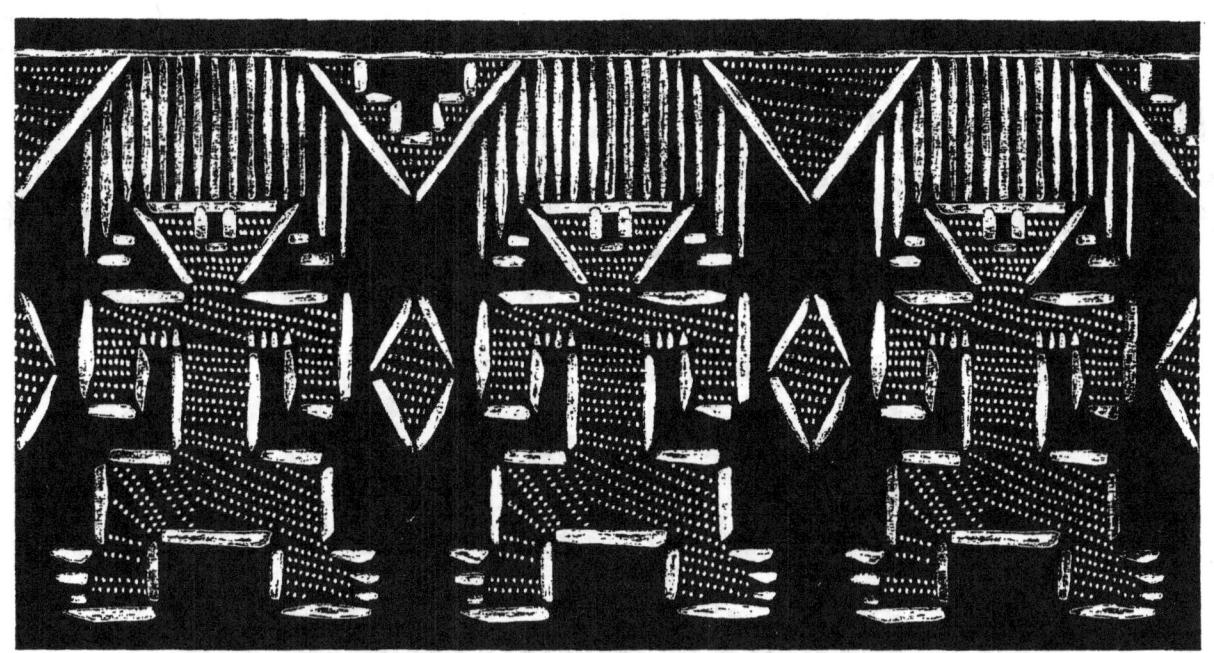

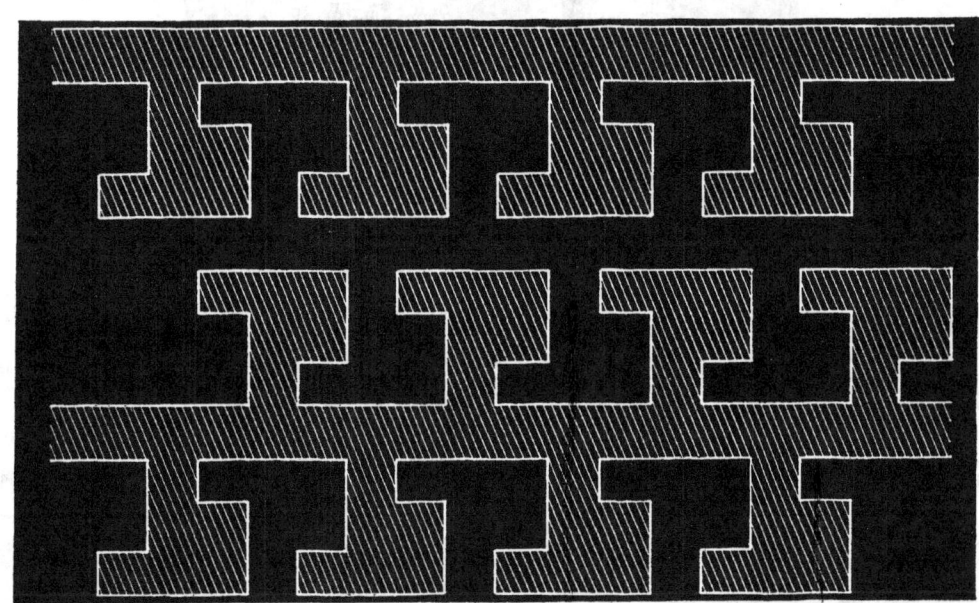

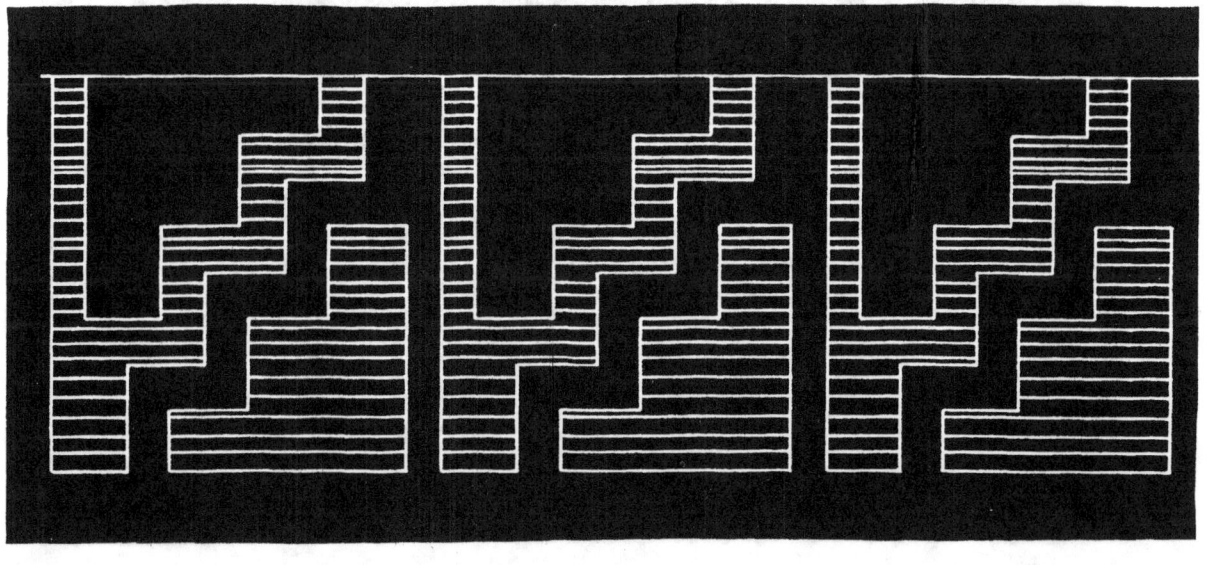

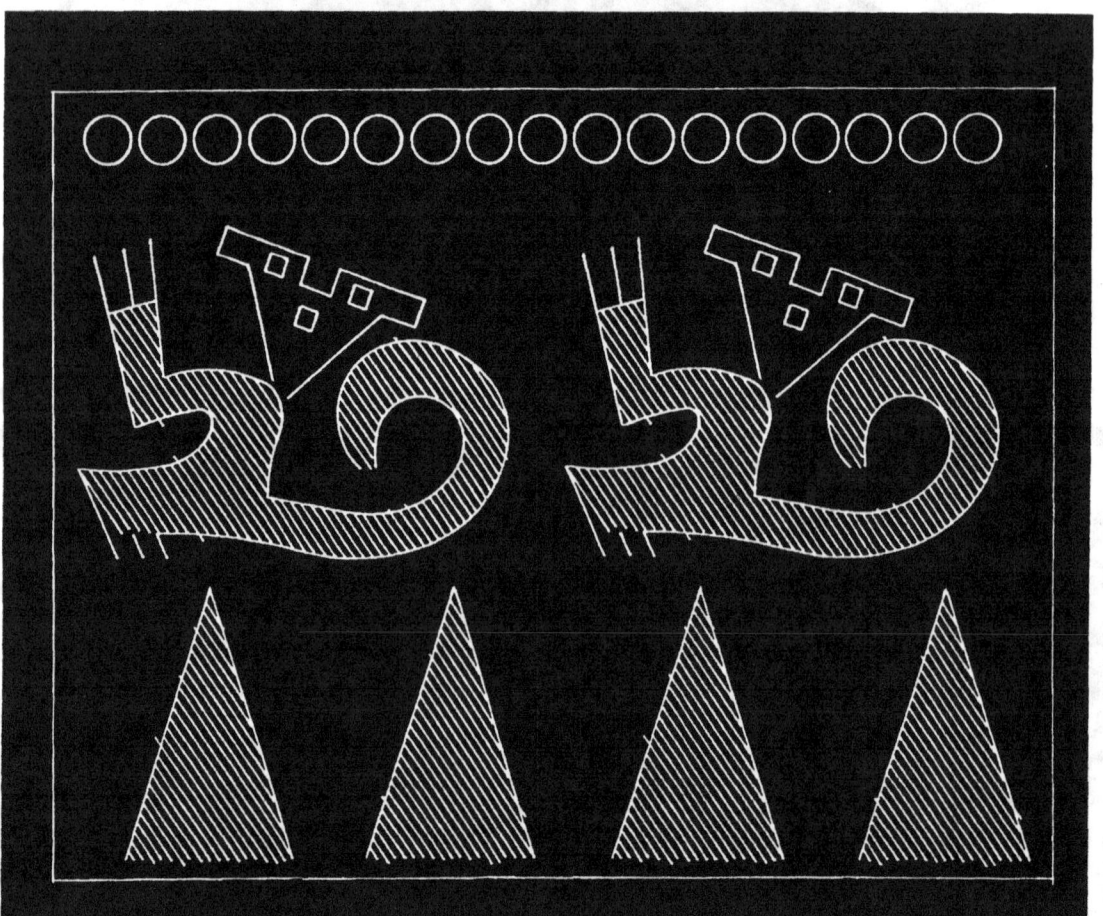

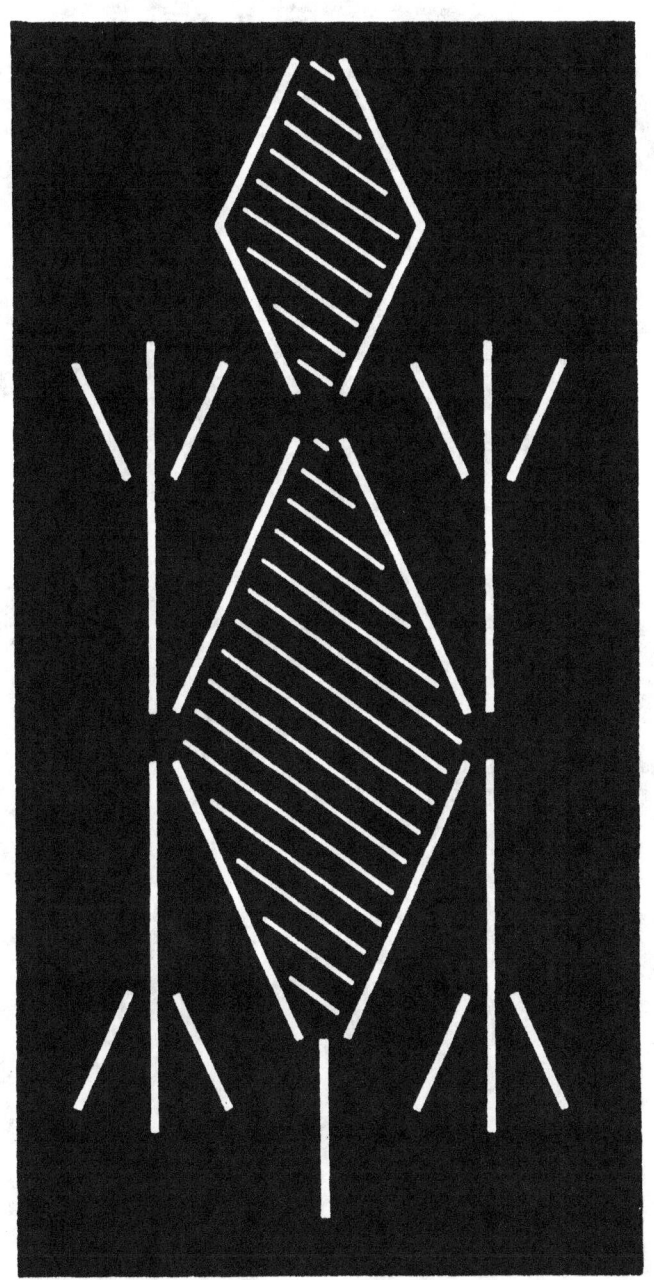

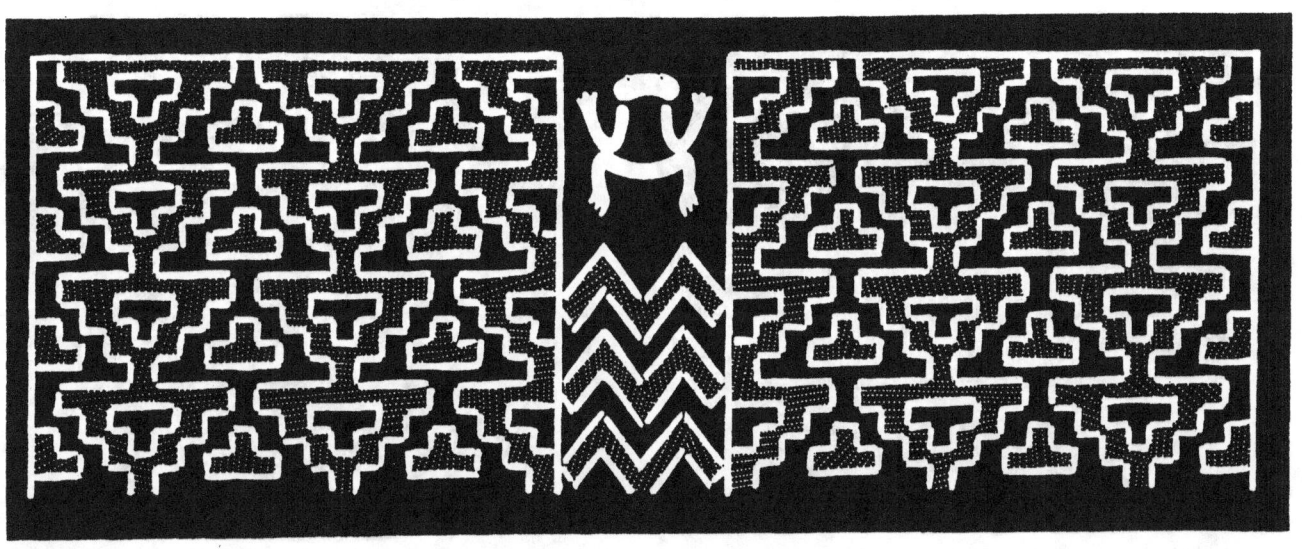

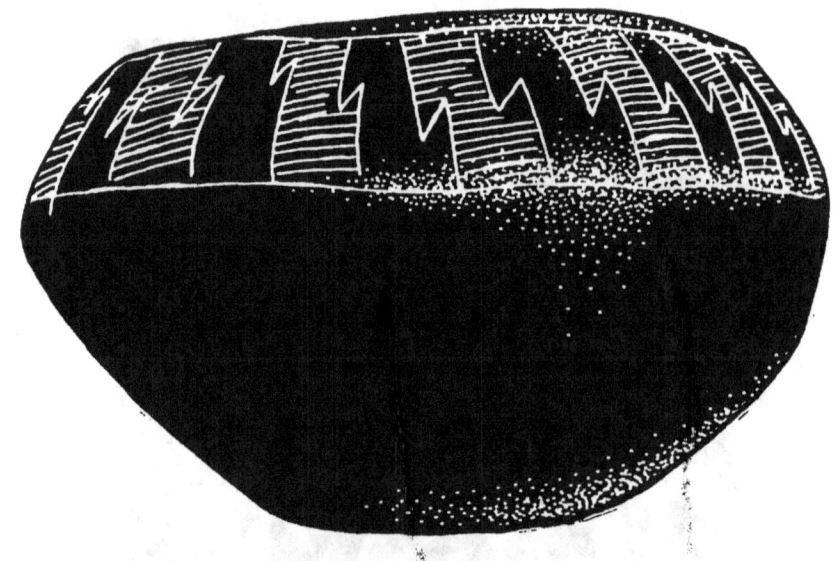

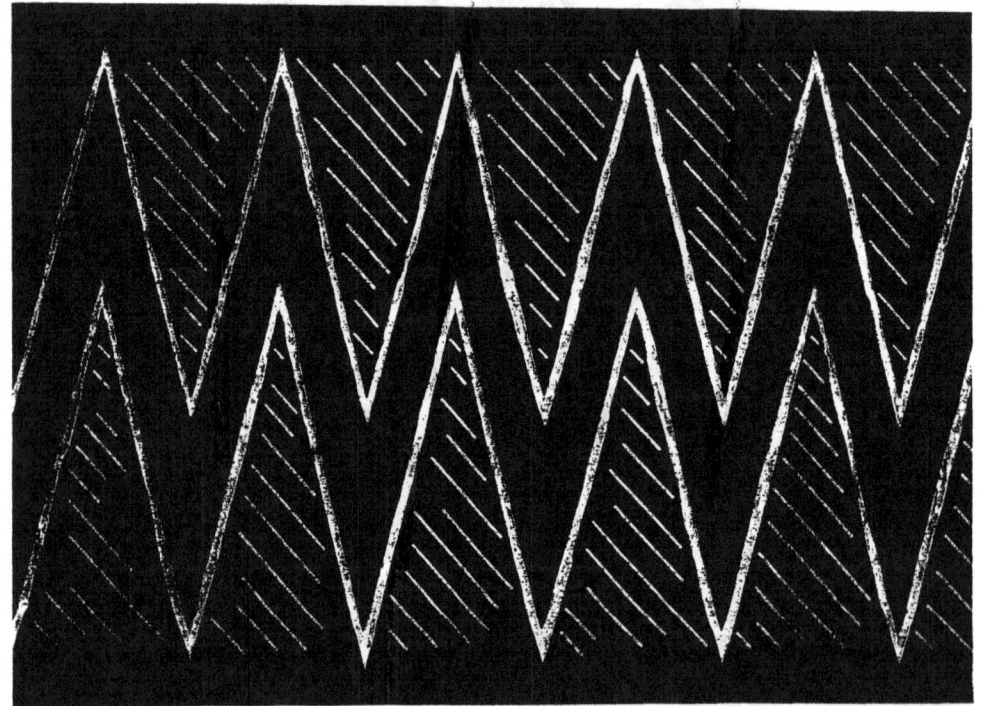

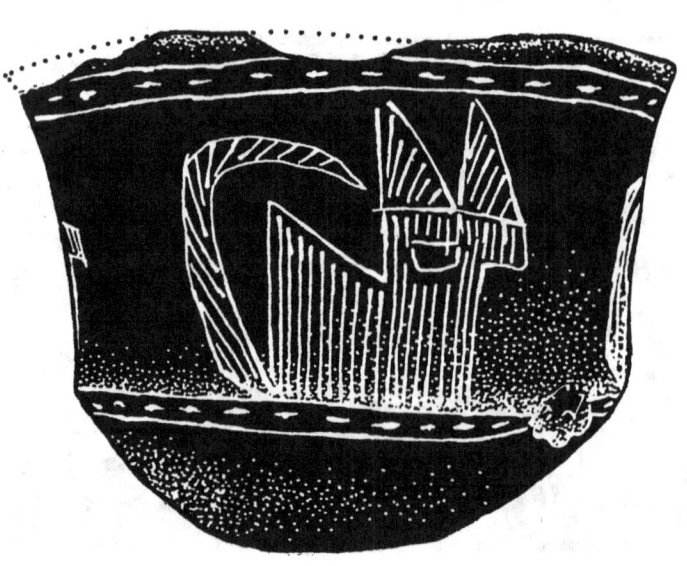

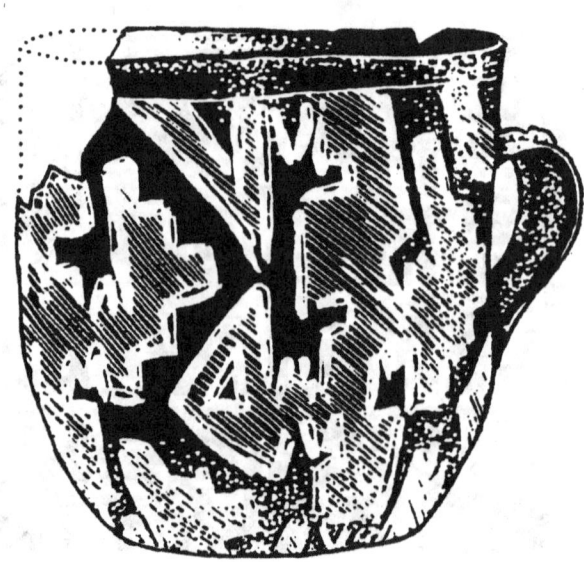

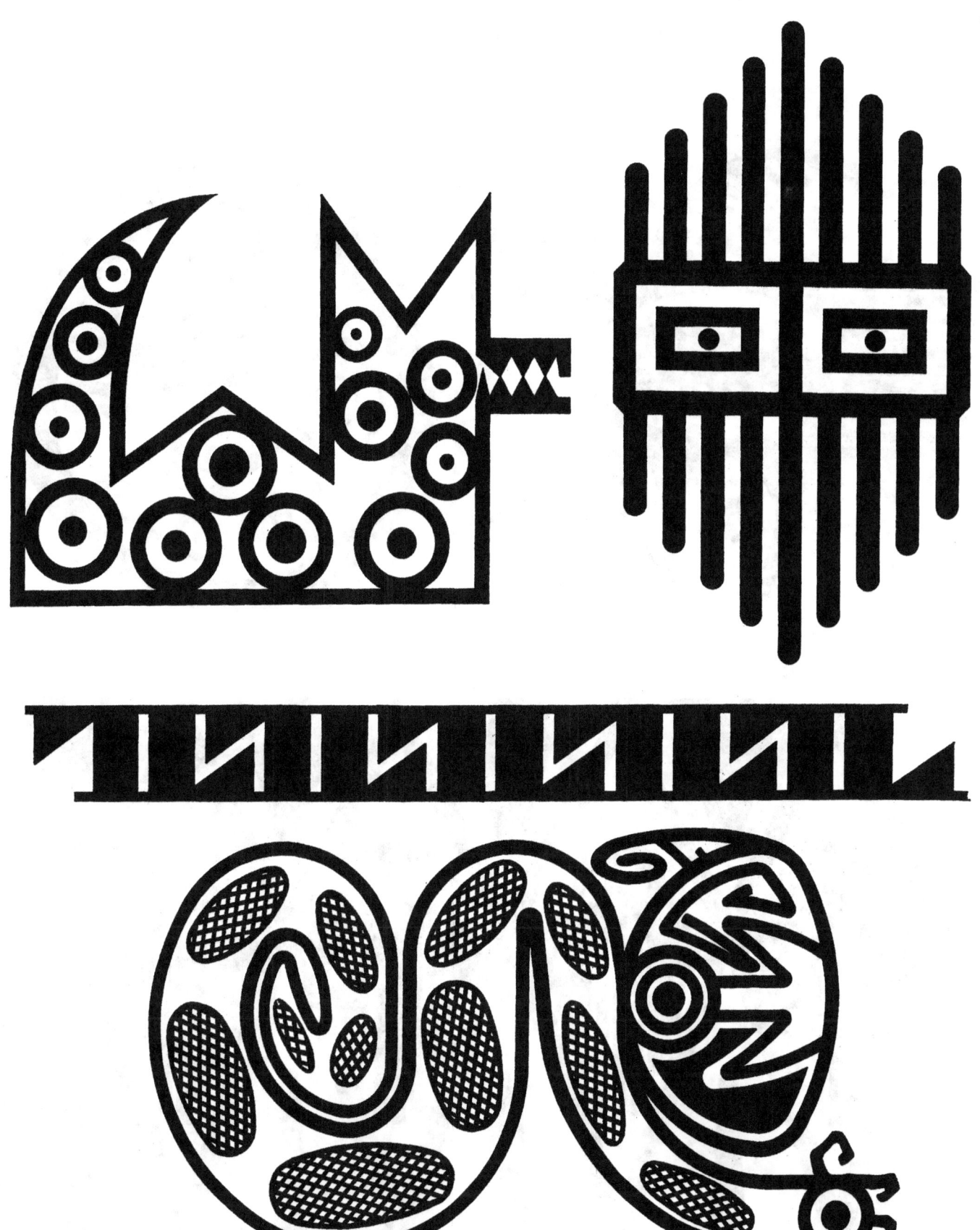

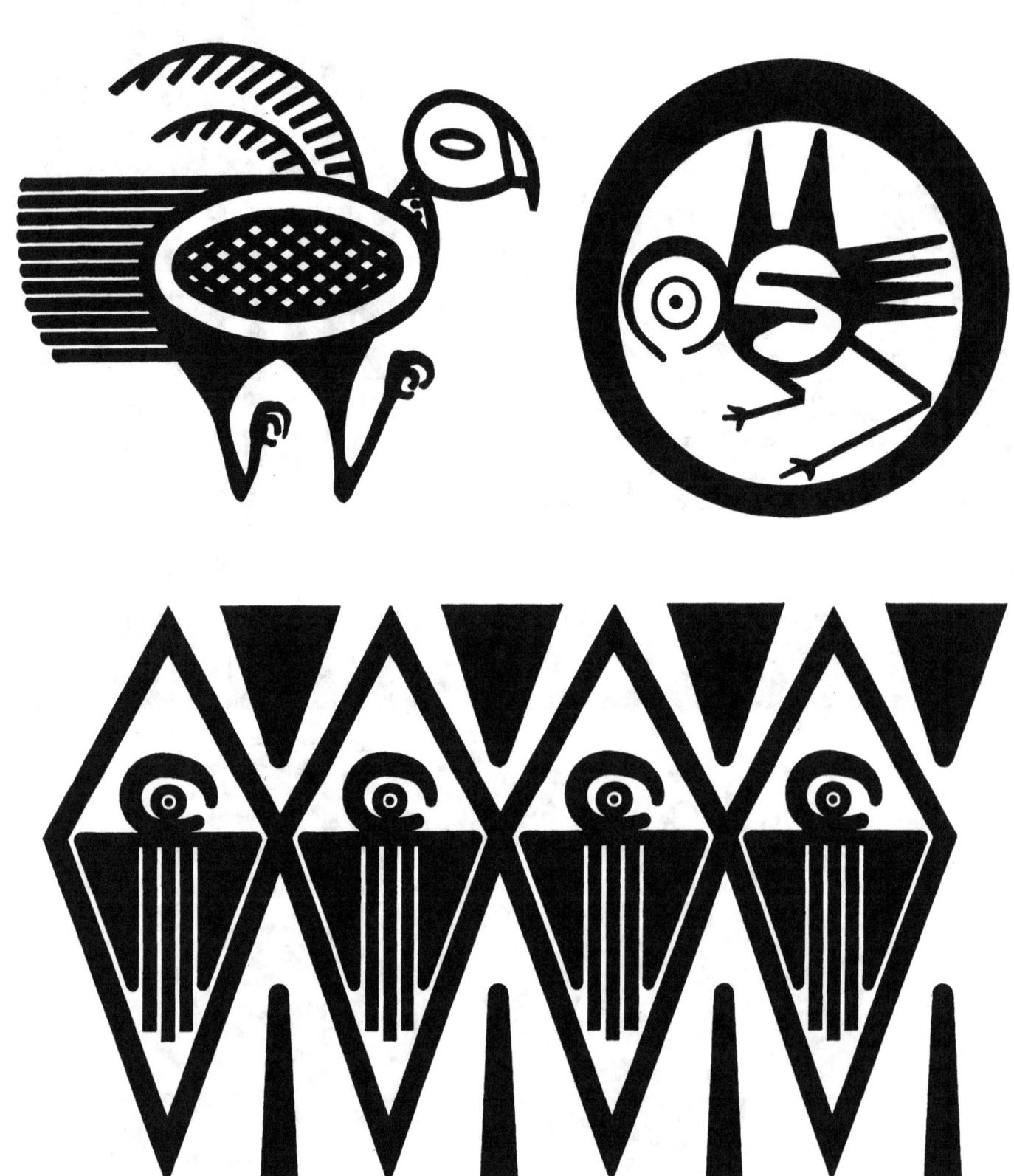

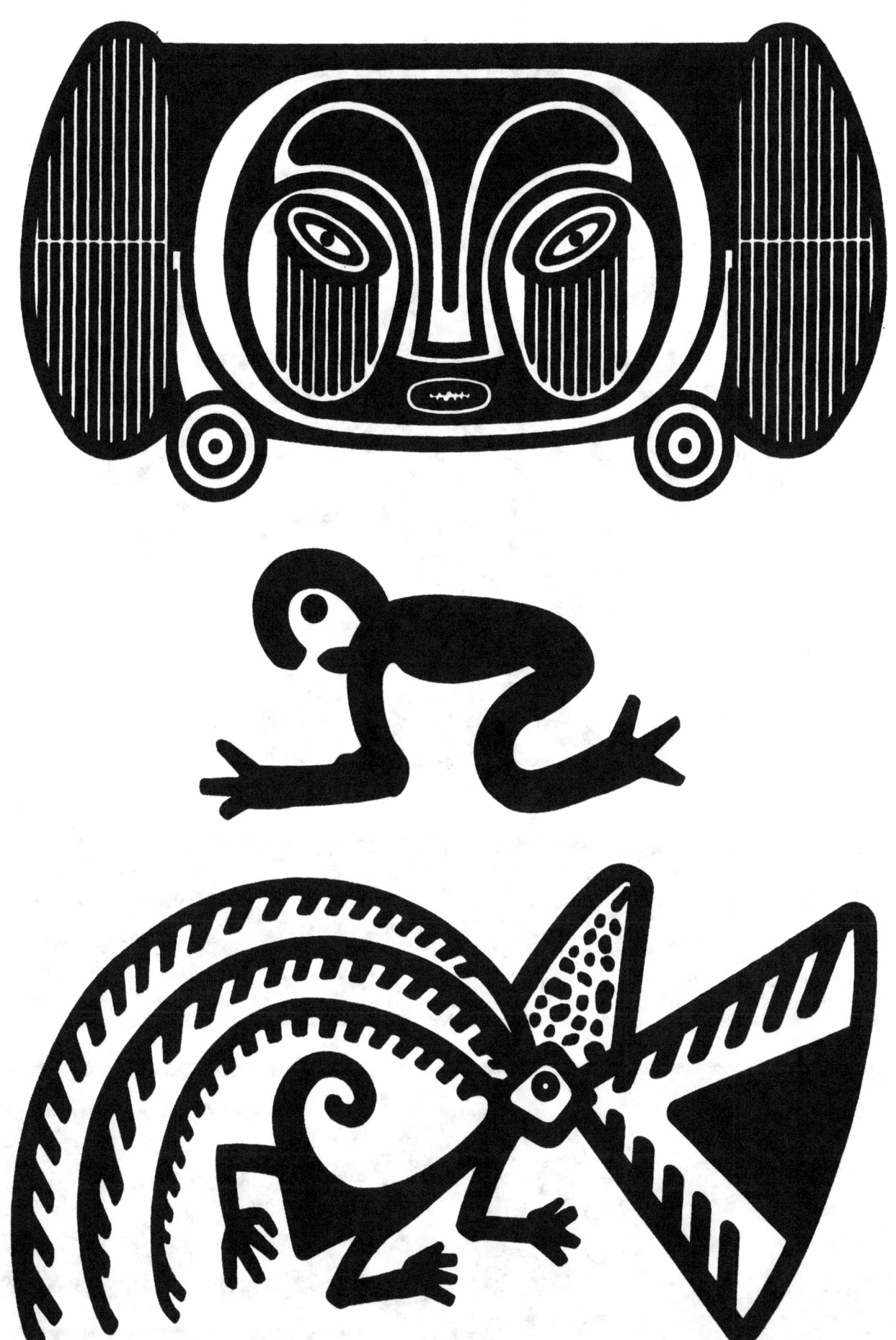

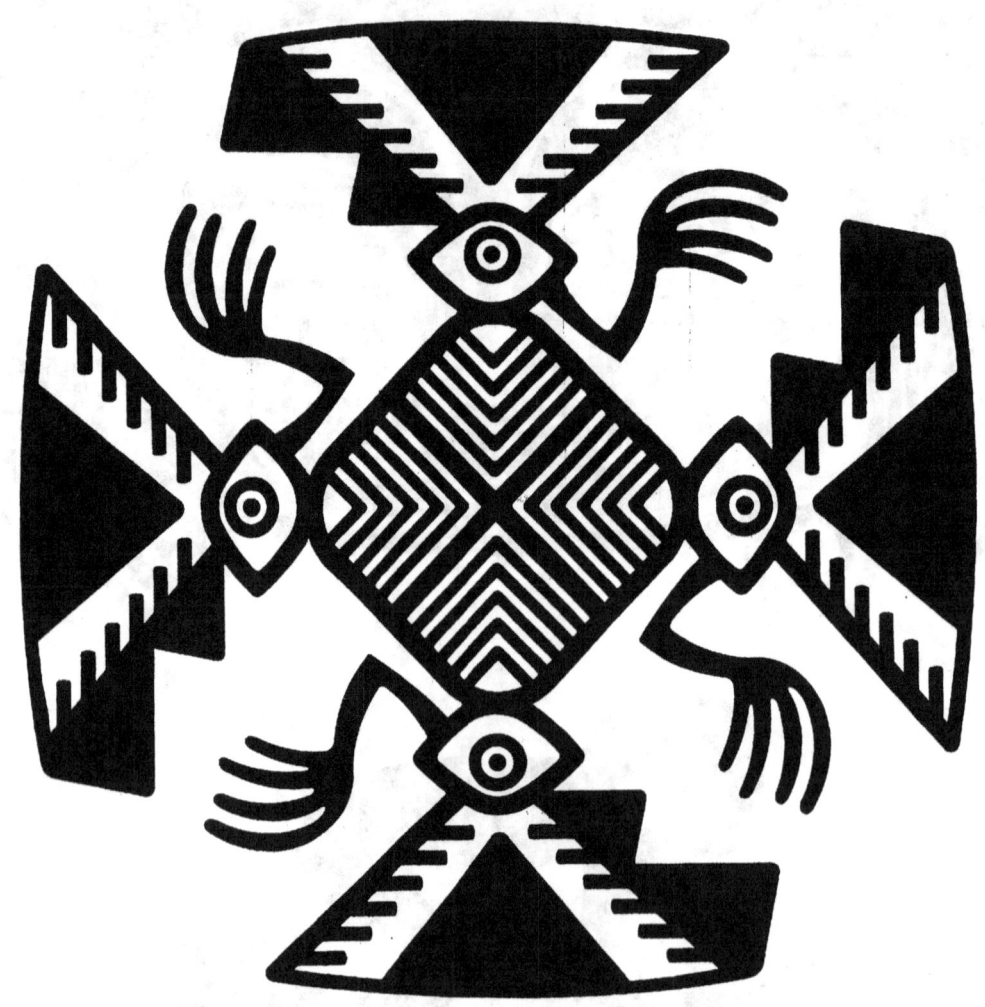

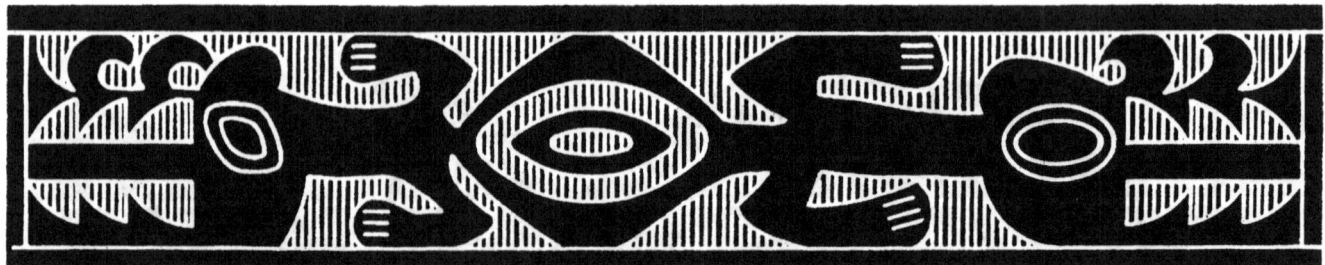

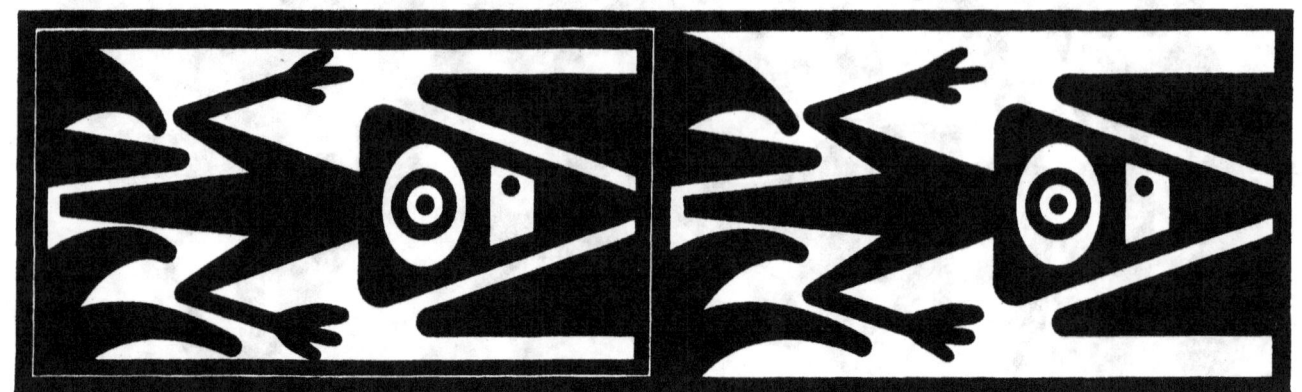

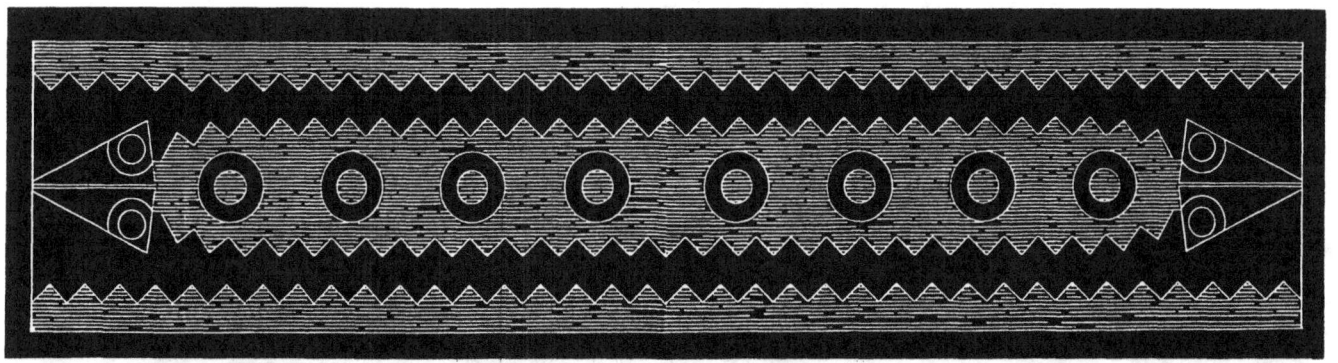

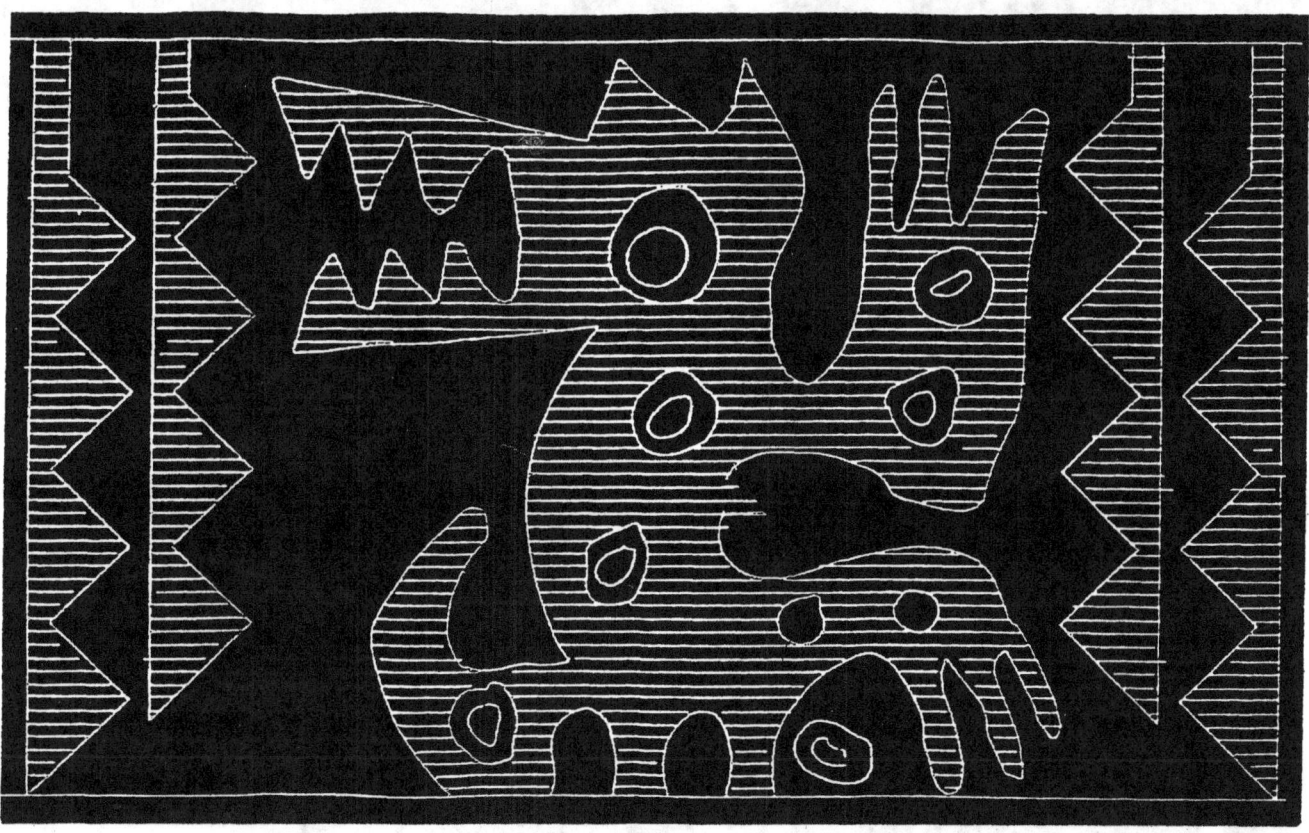

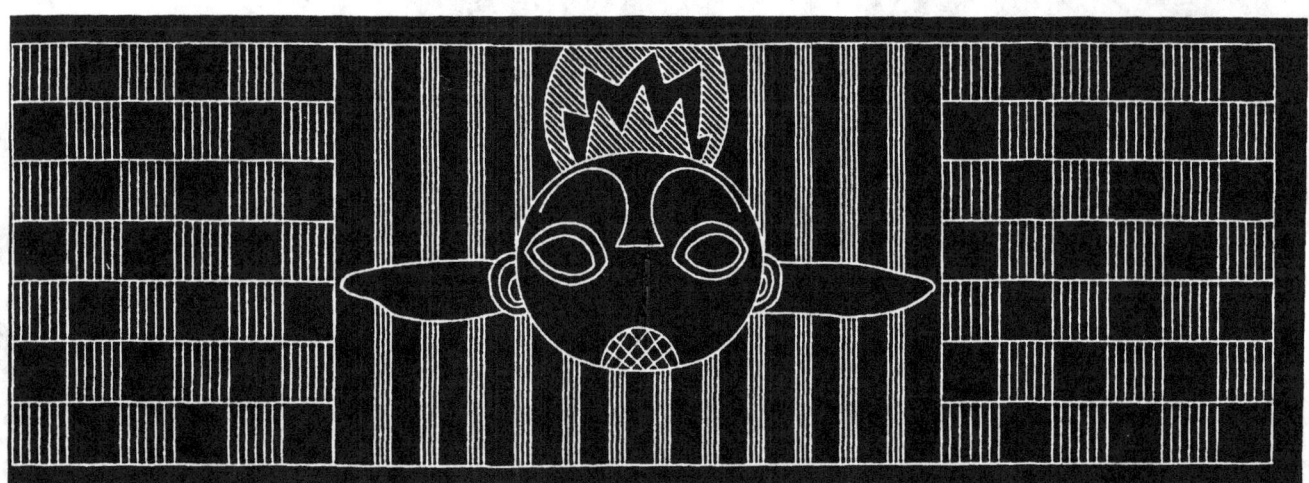

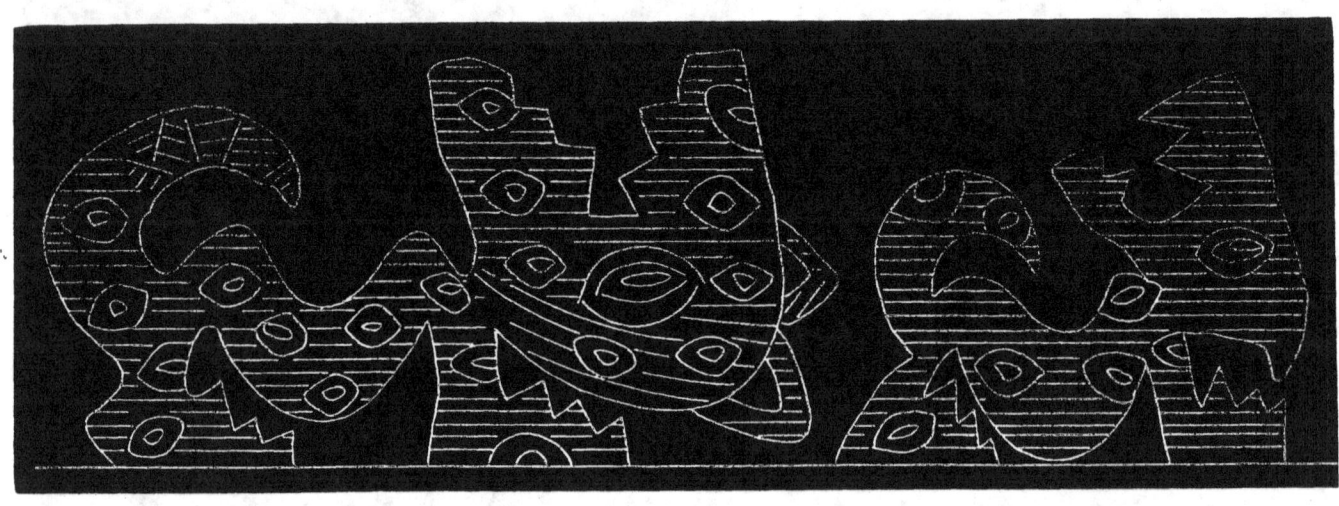

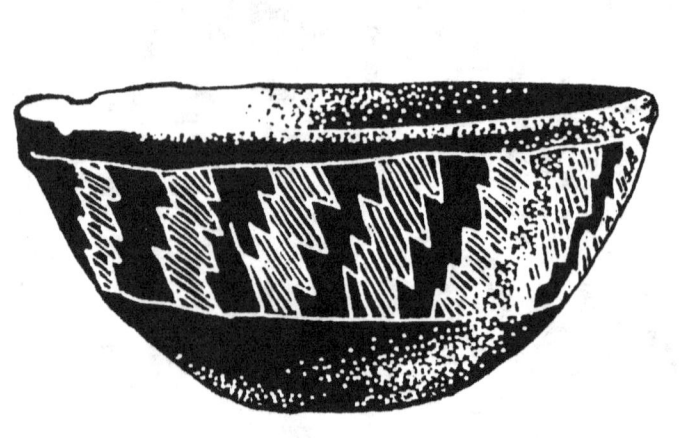

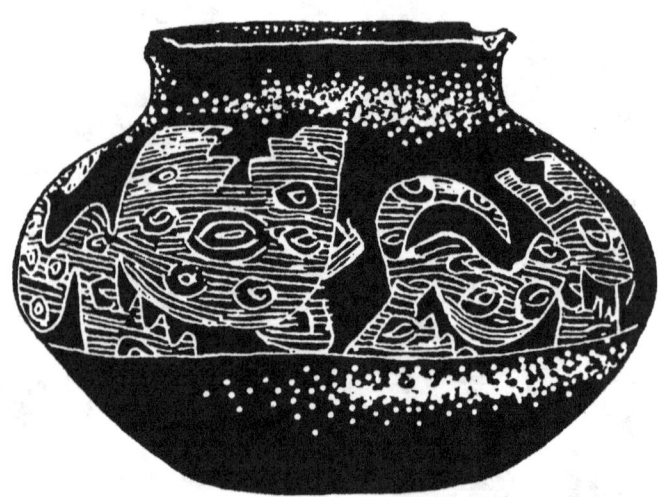

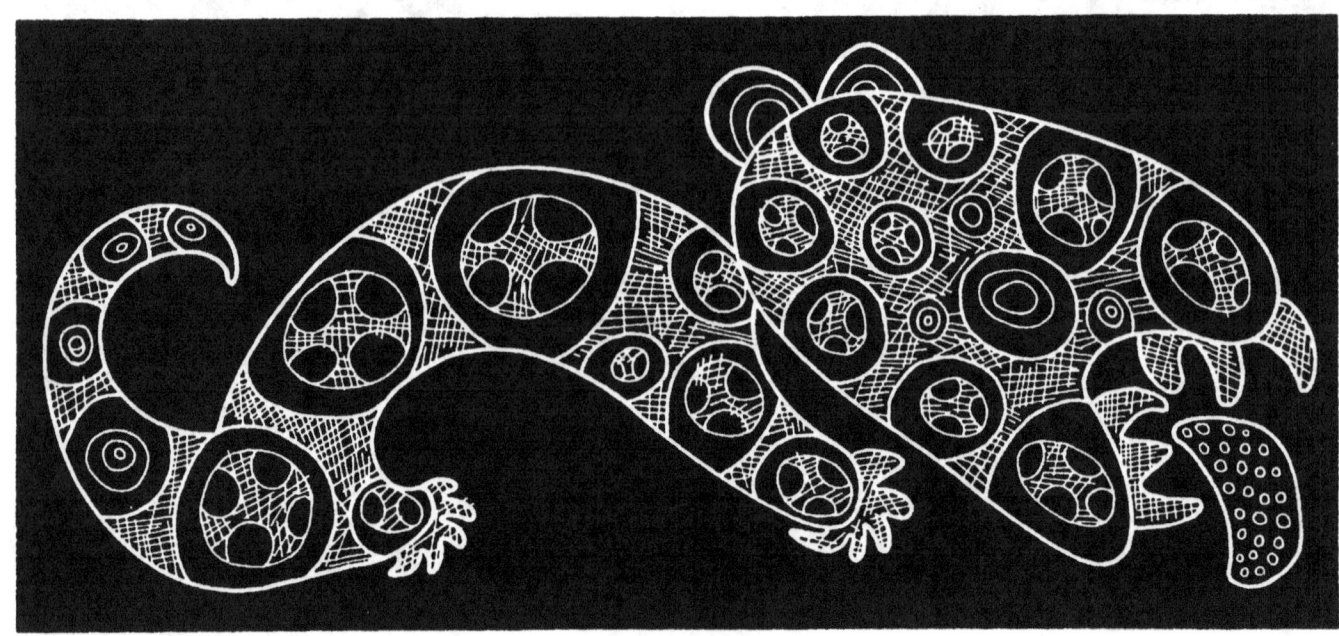

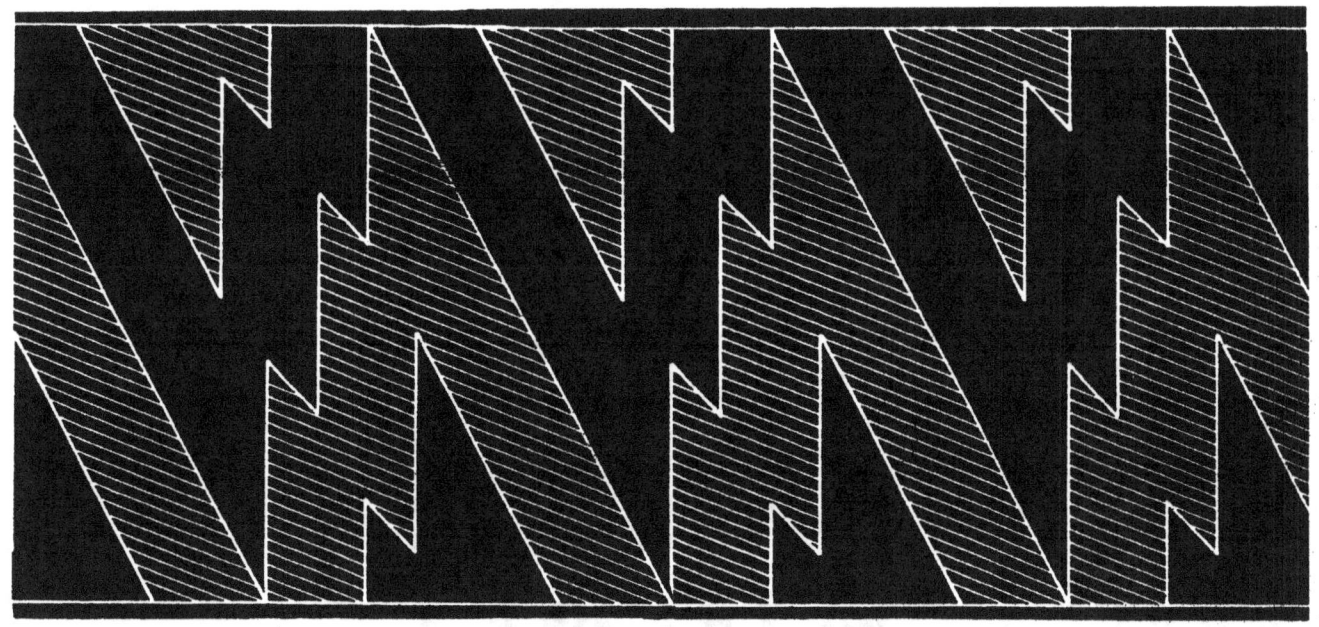

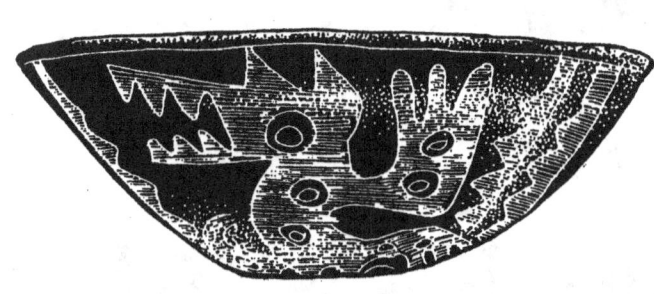

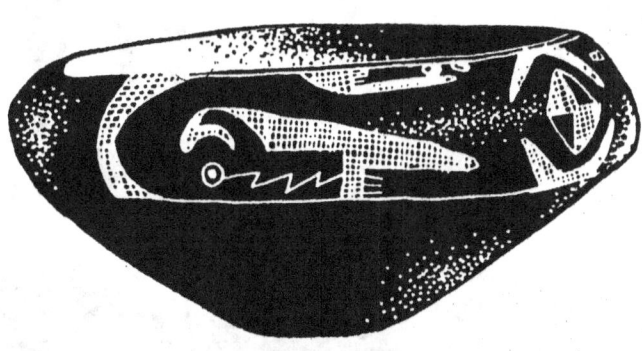

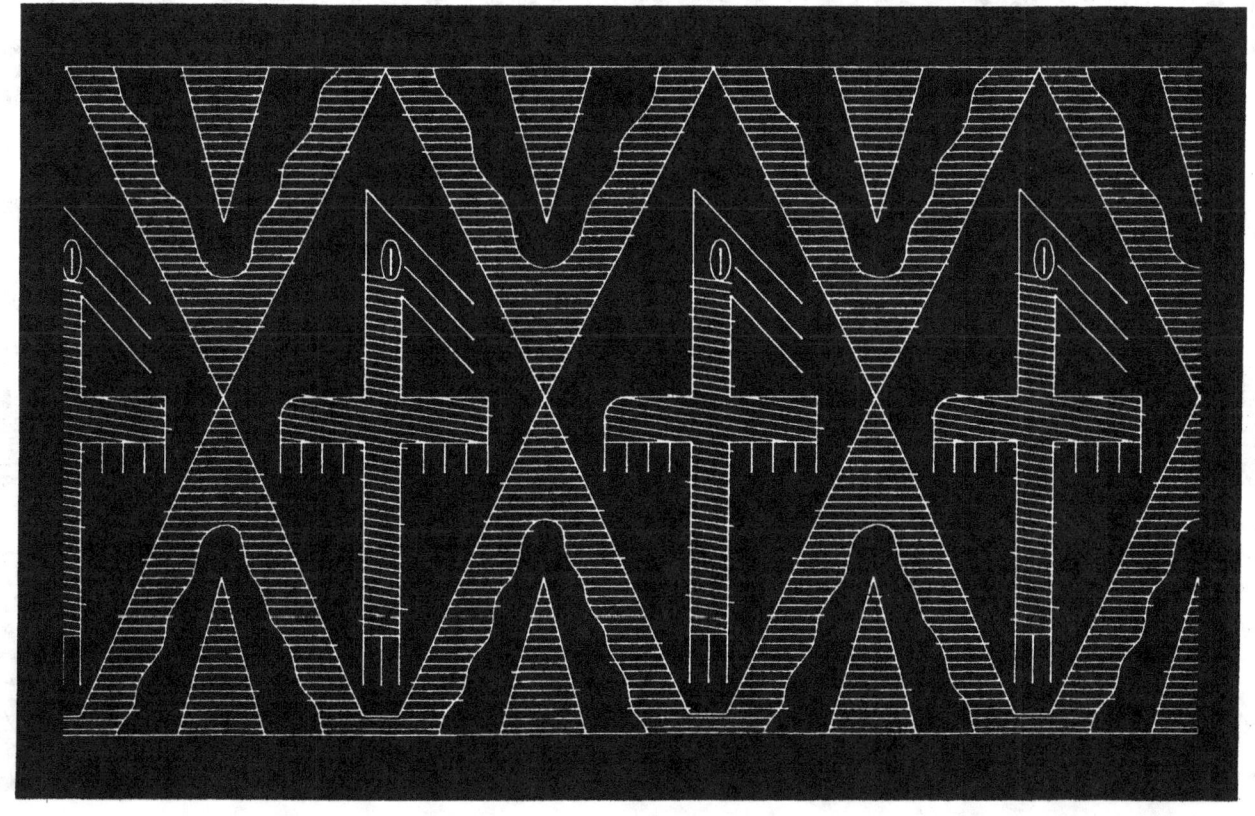

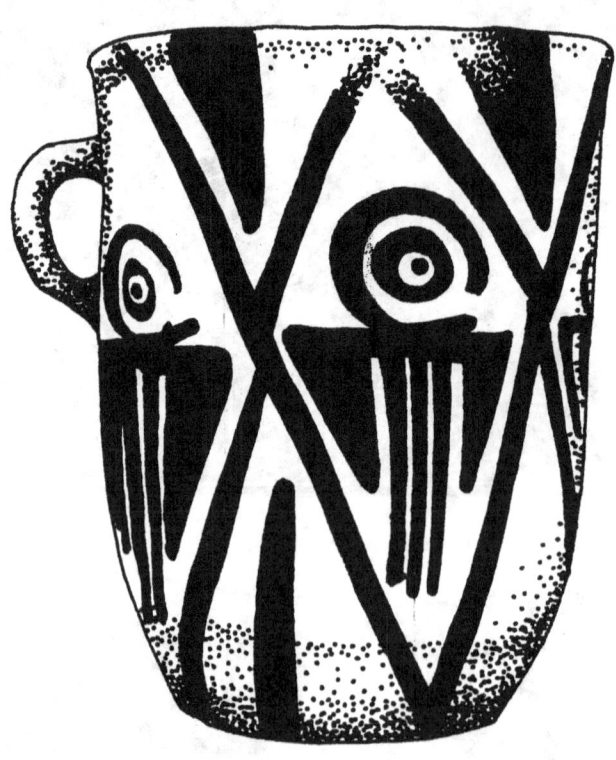

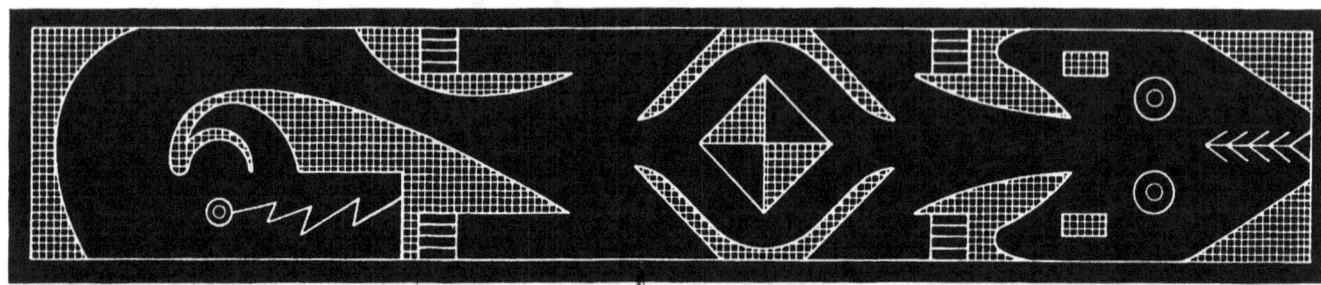

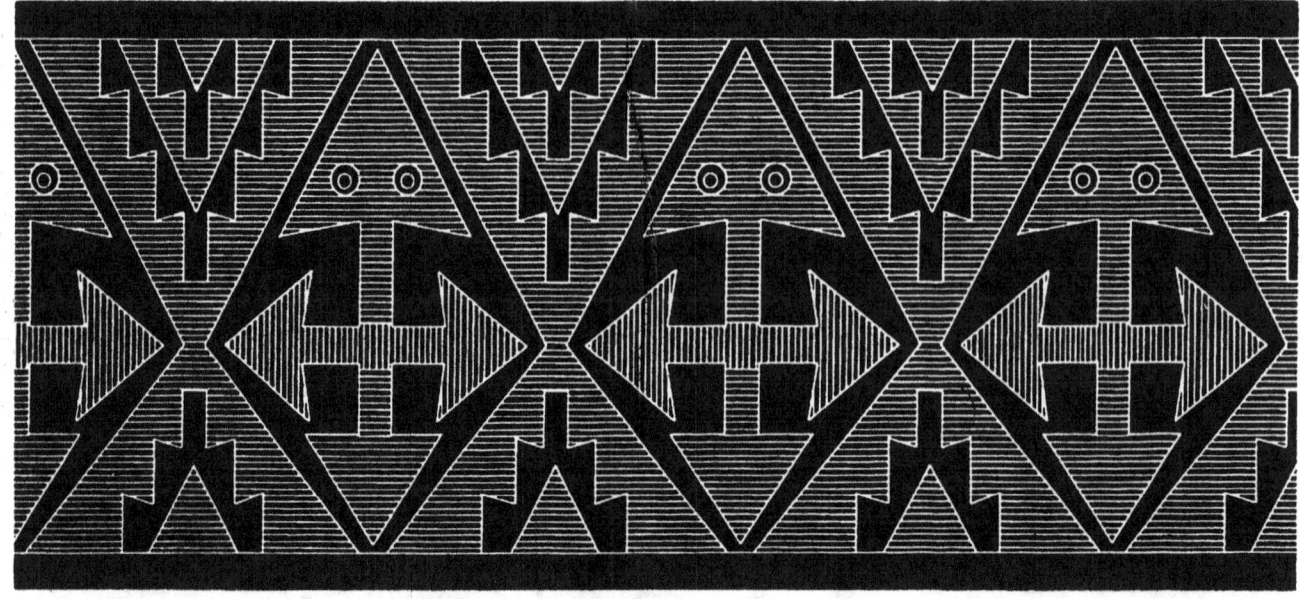

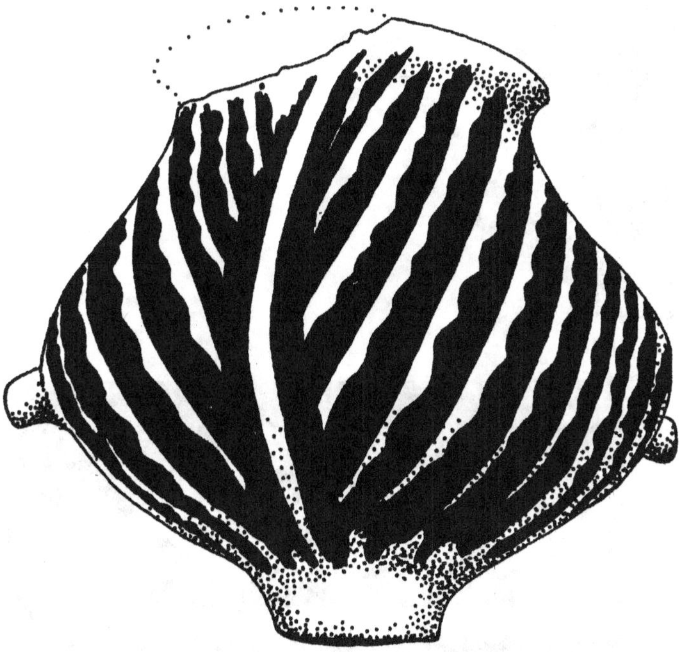

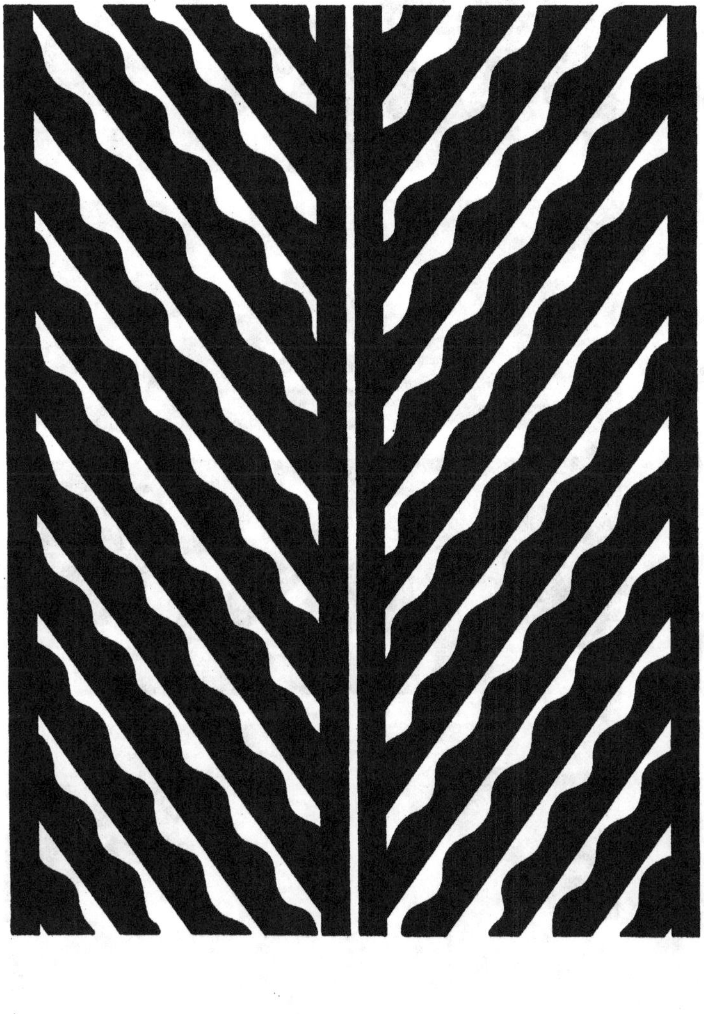

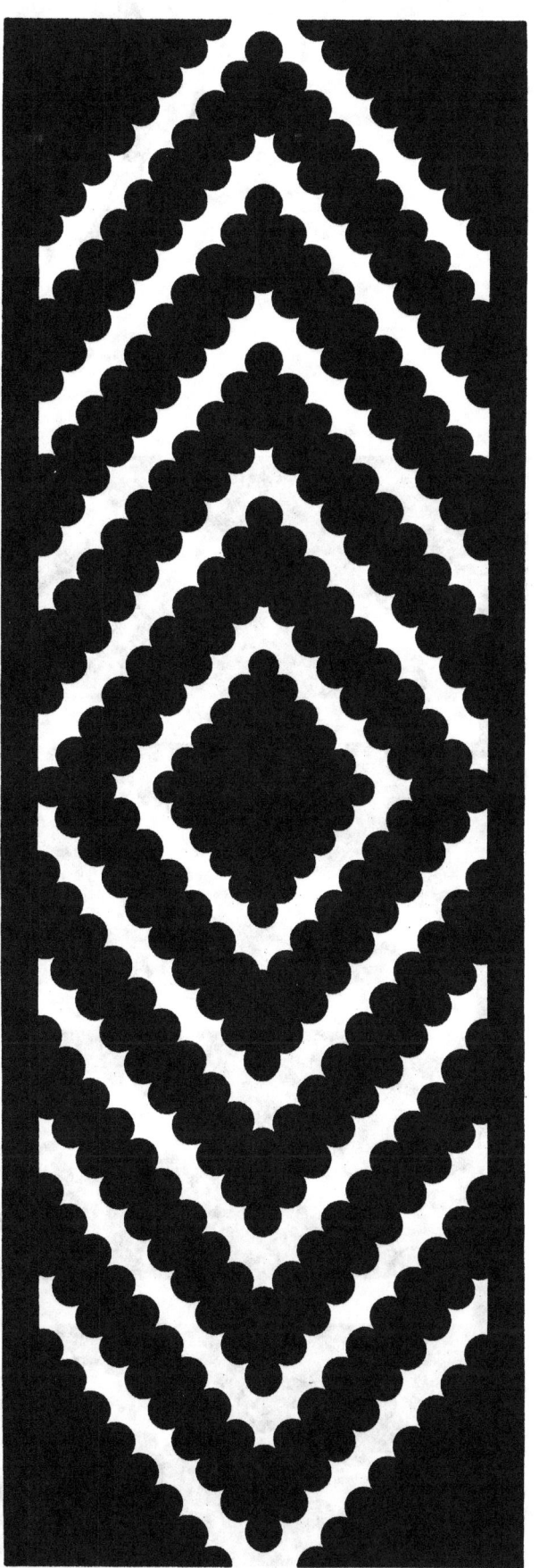

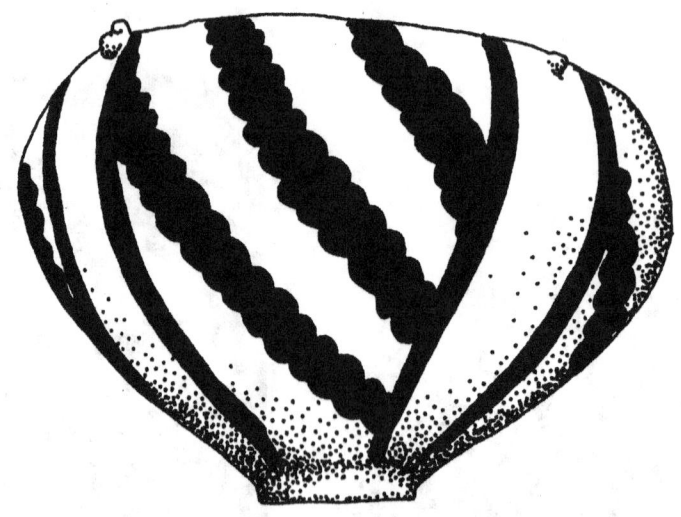

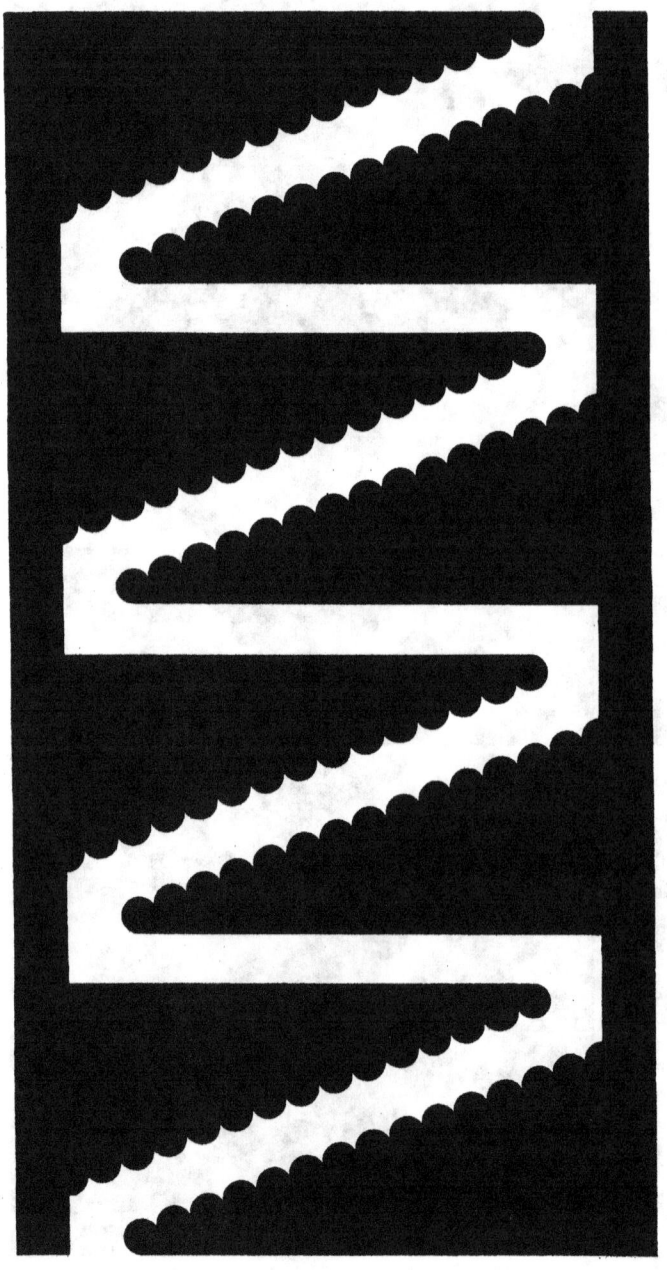

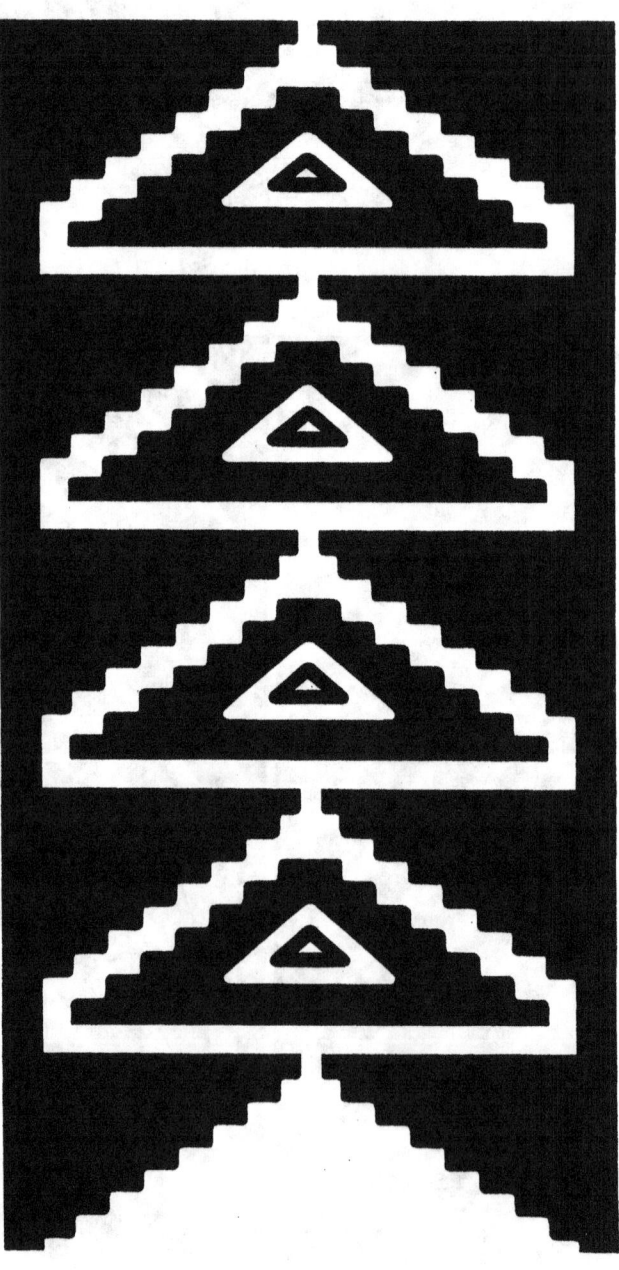

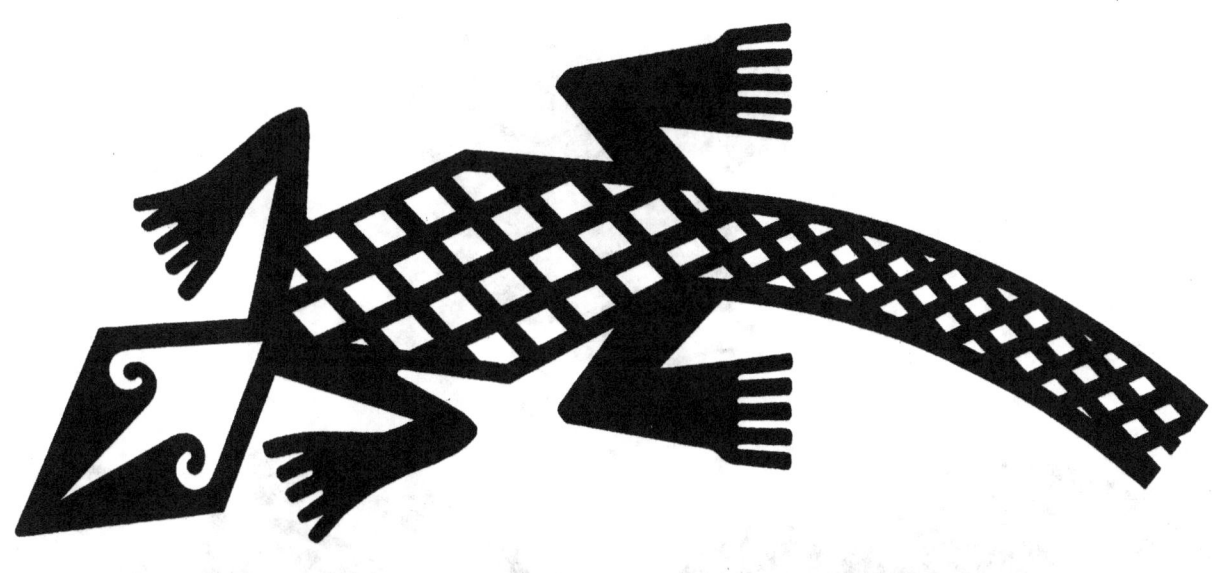

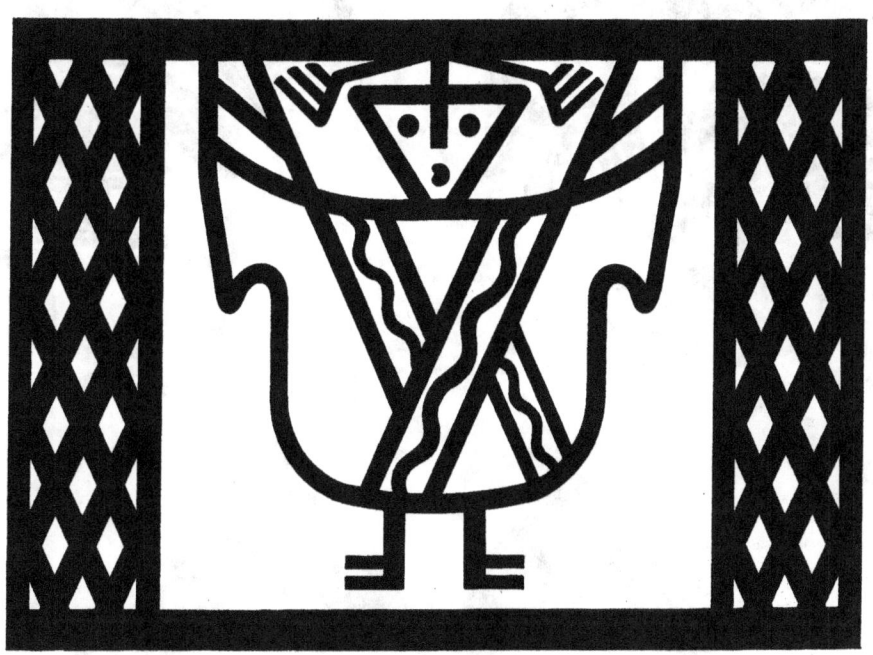

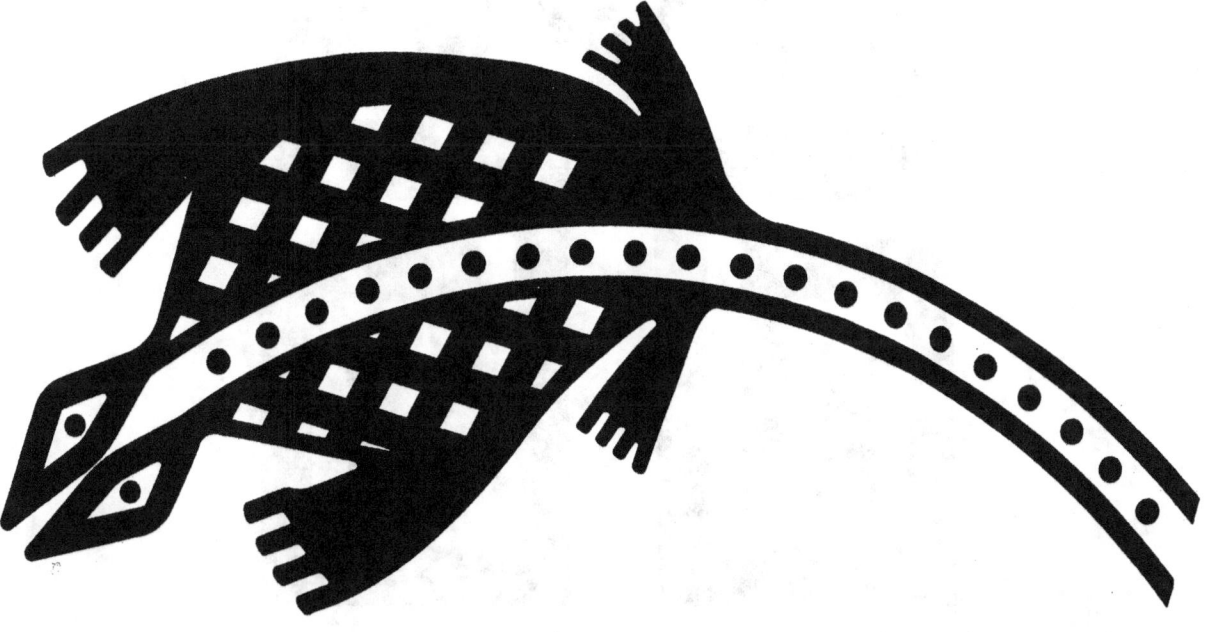

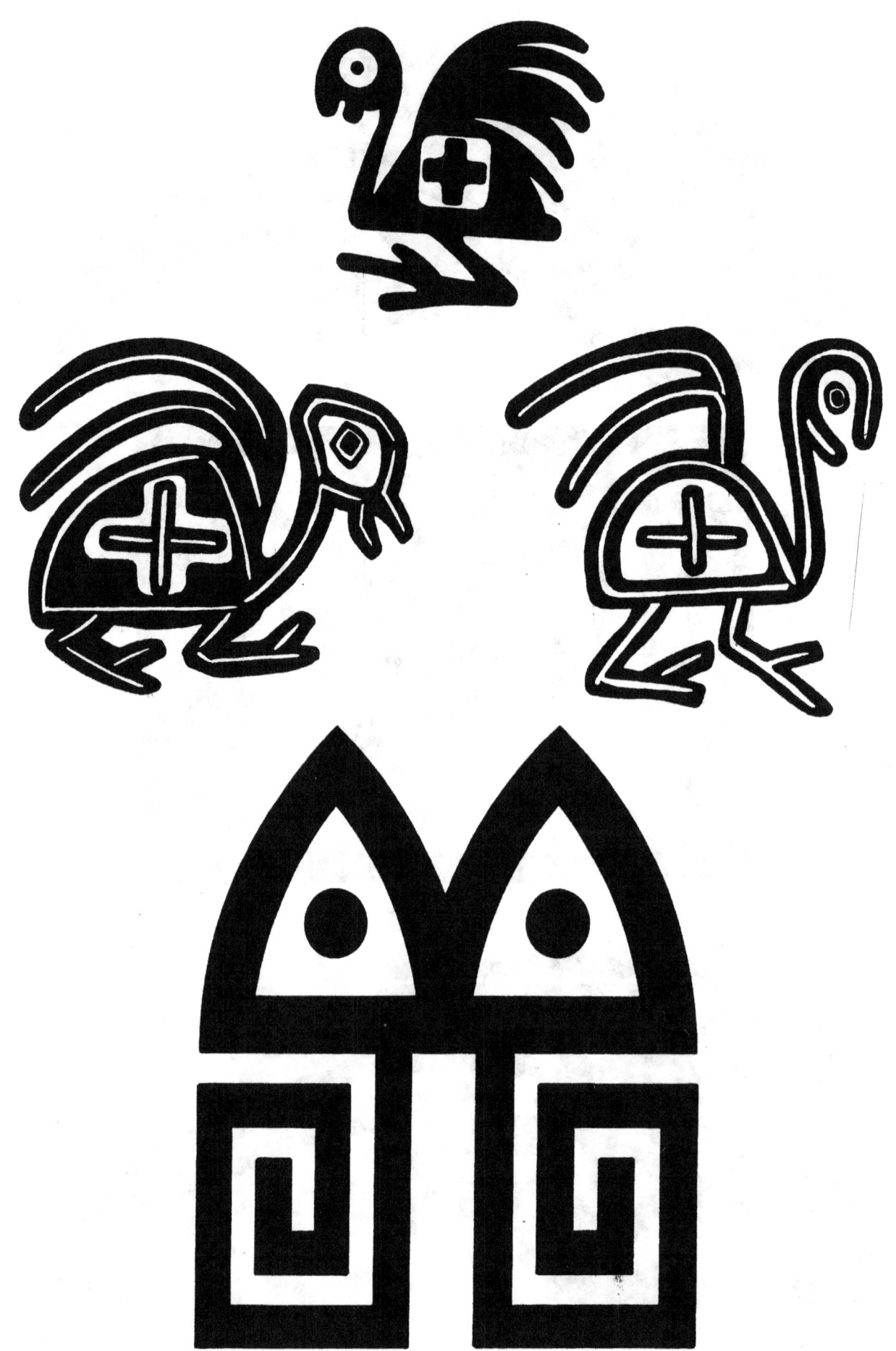

20   Belén Culture

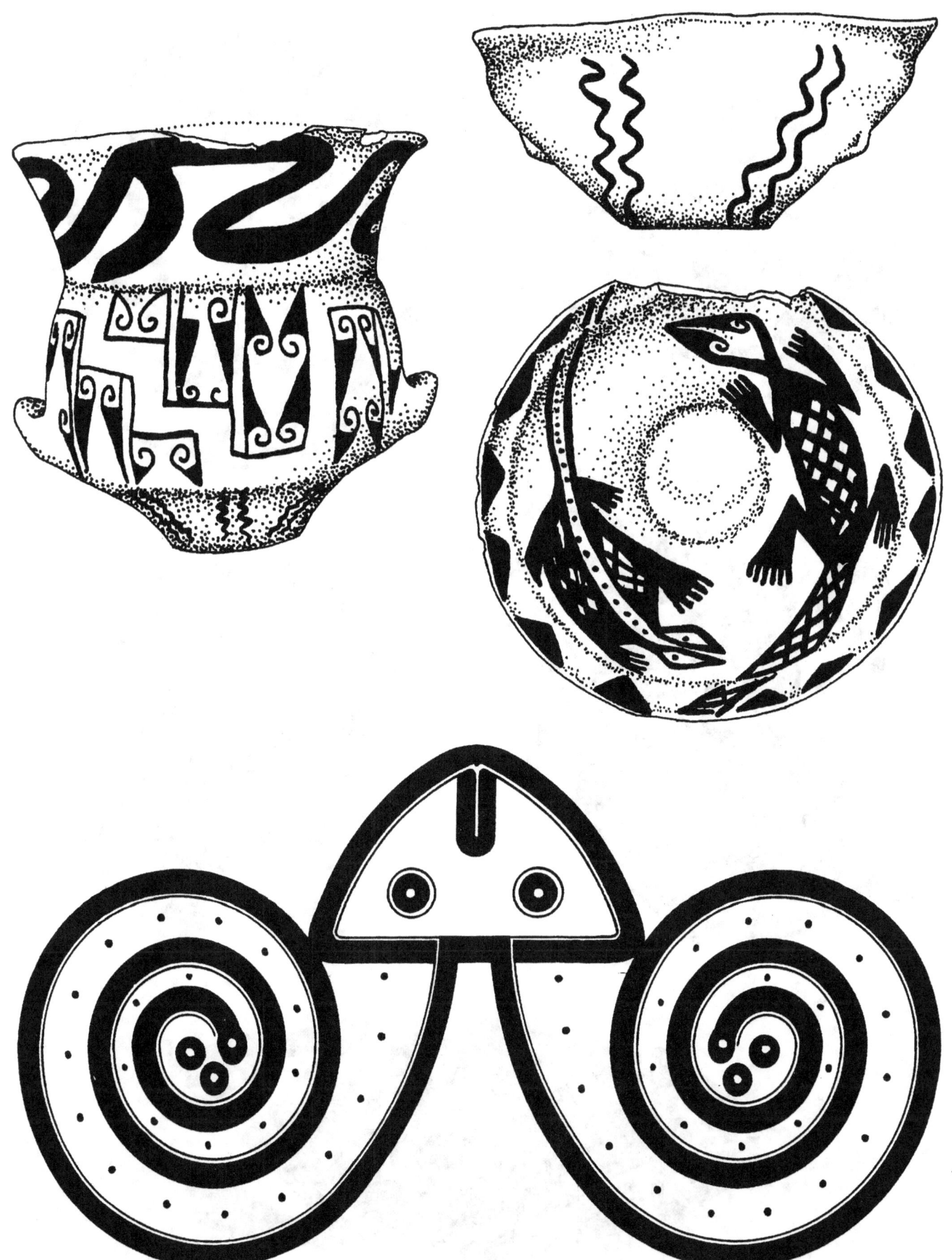

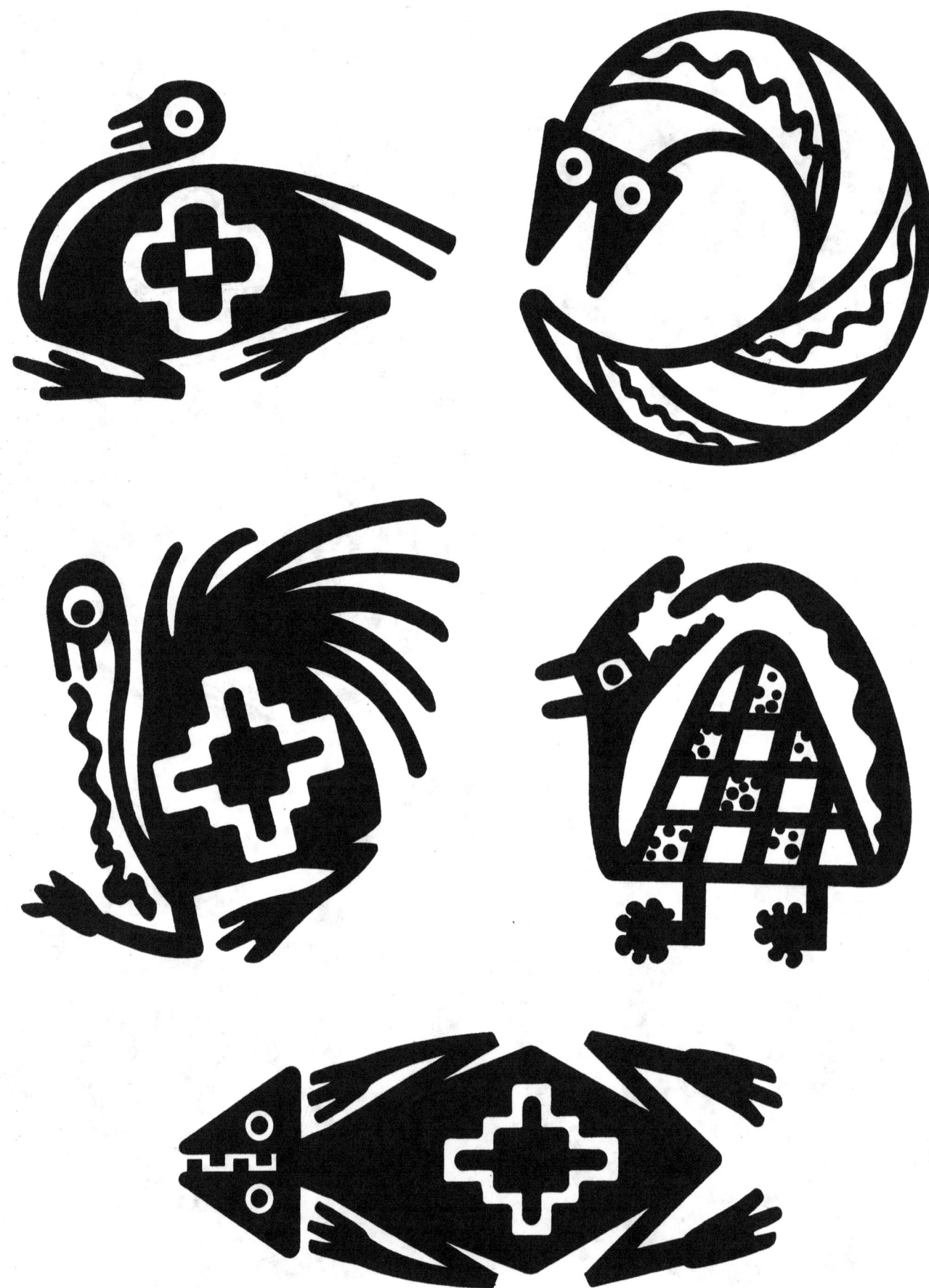

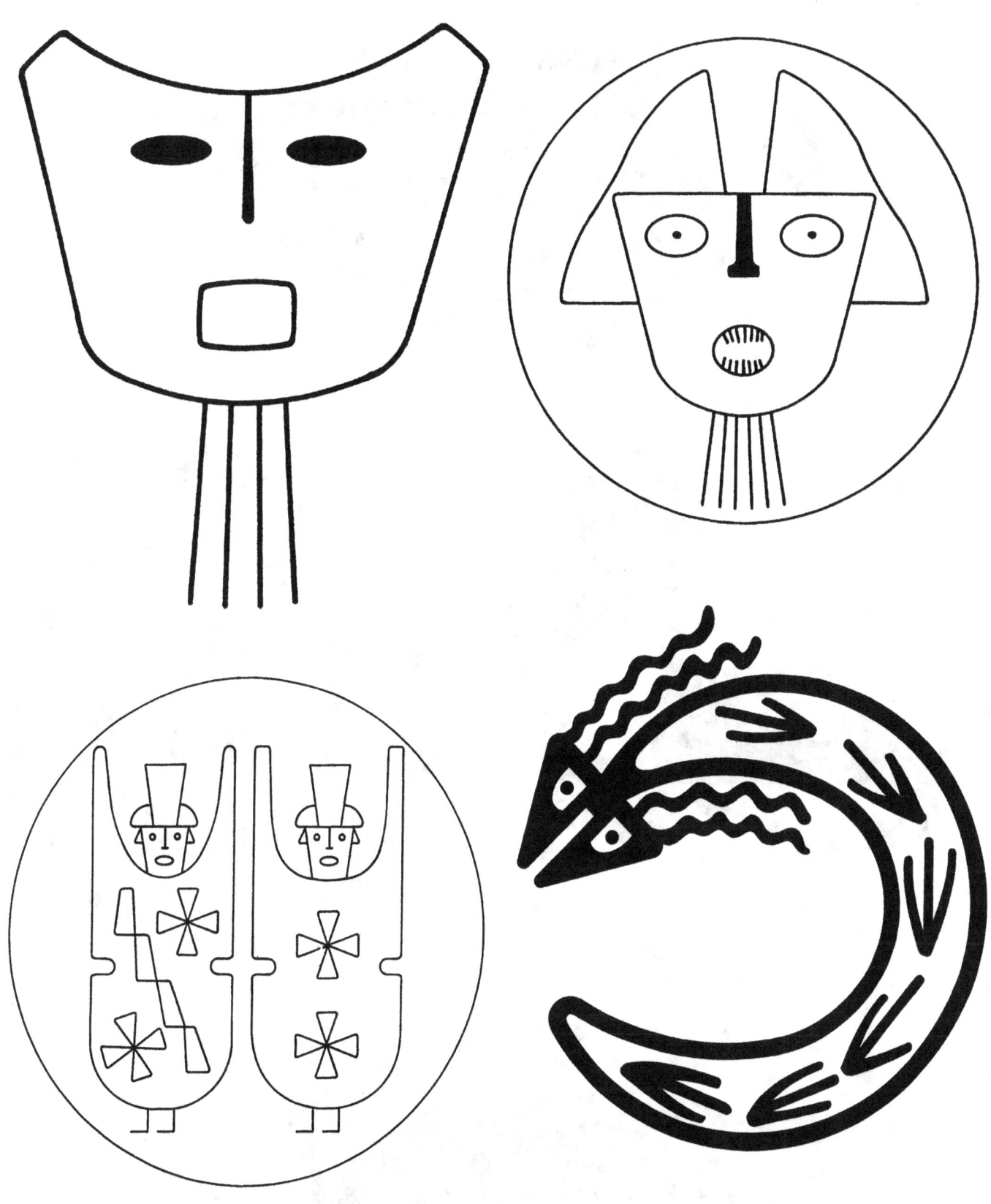

Santa María Culture   23

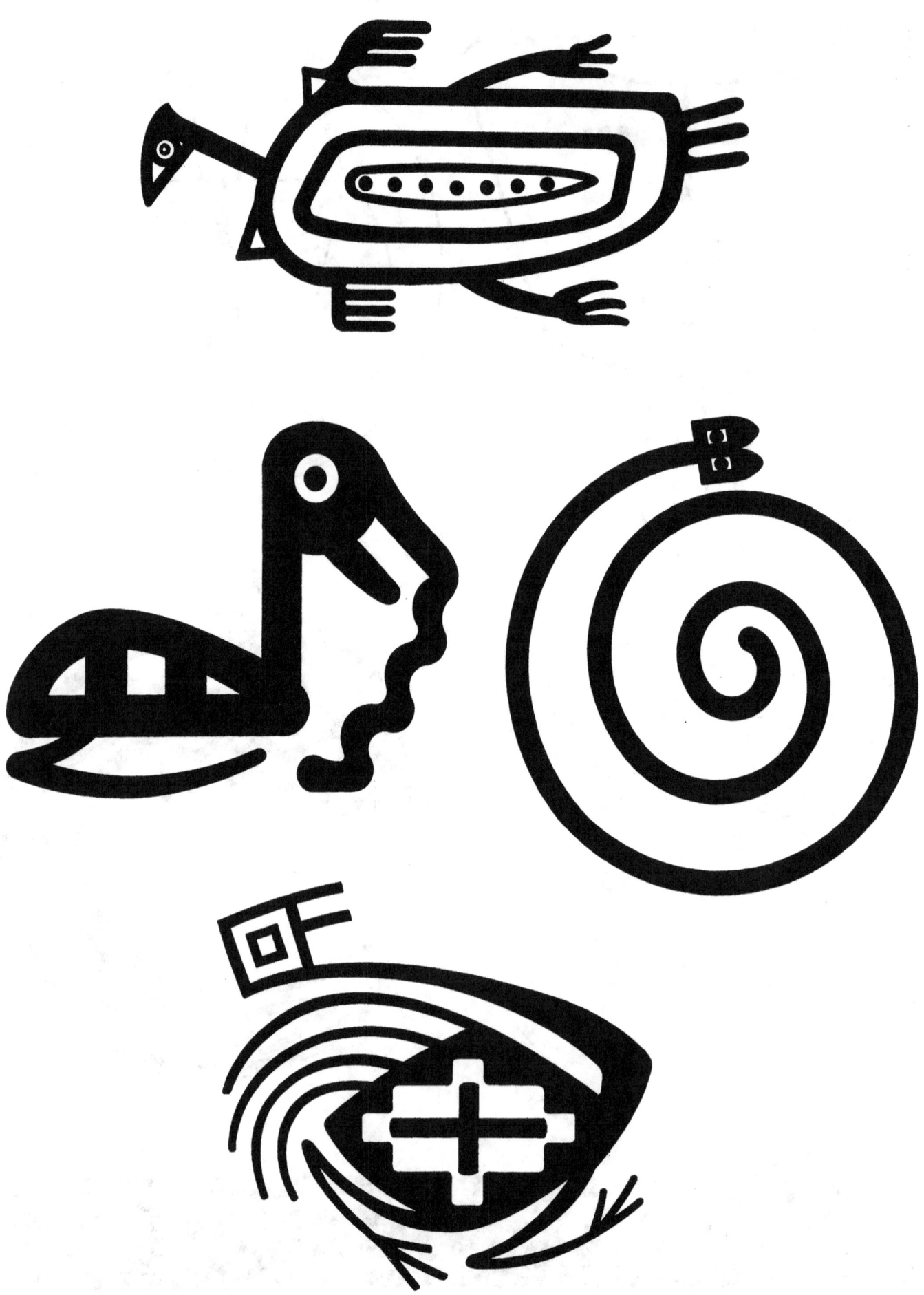

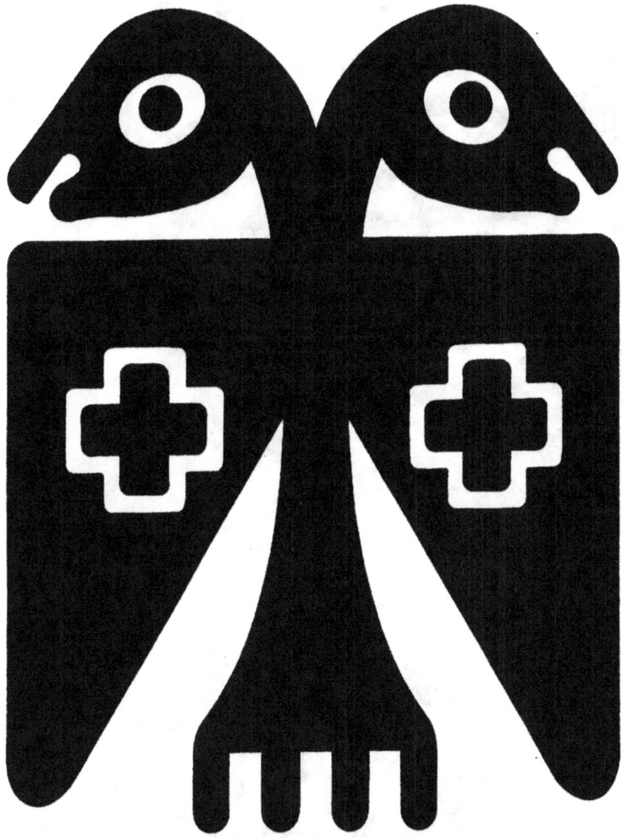

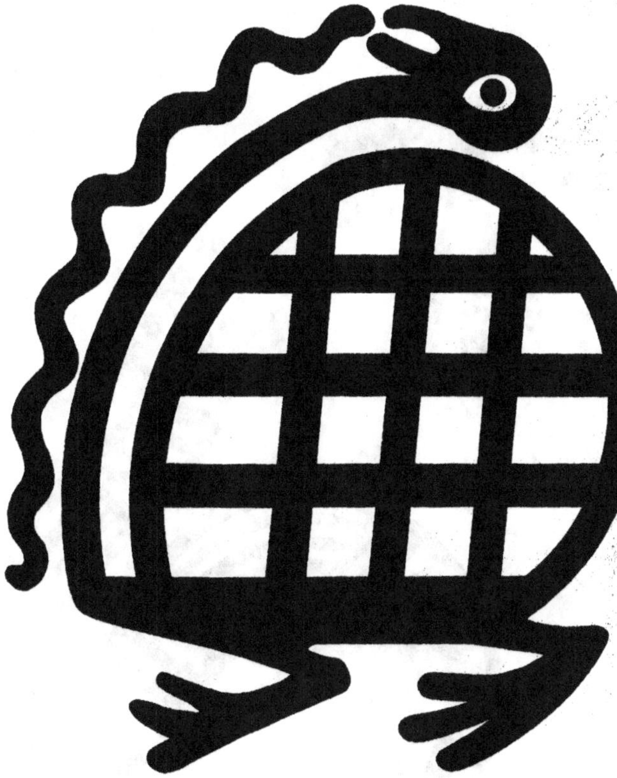

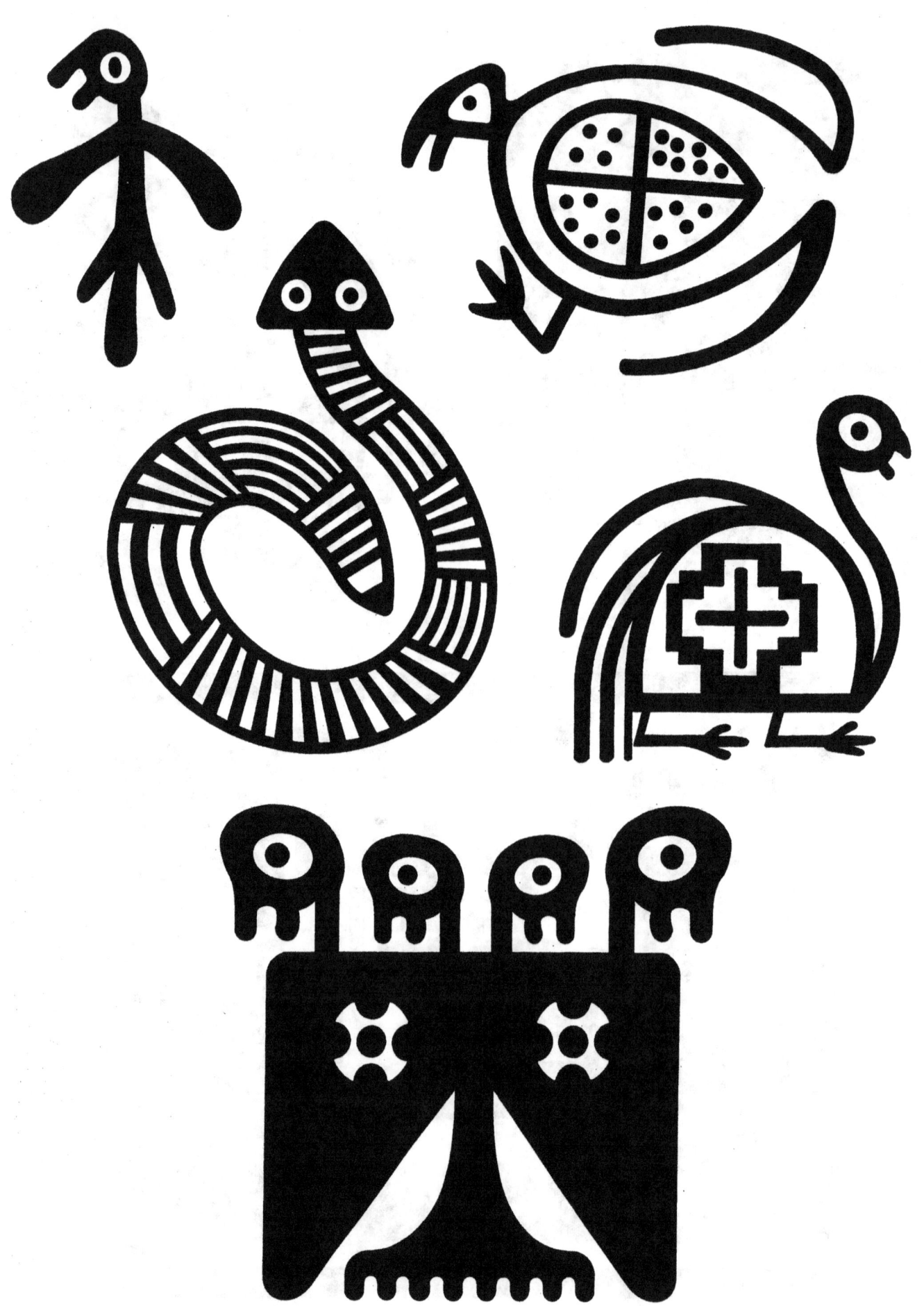

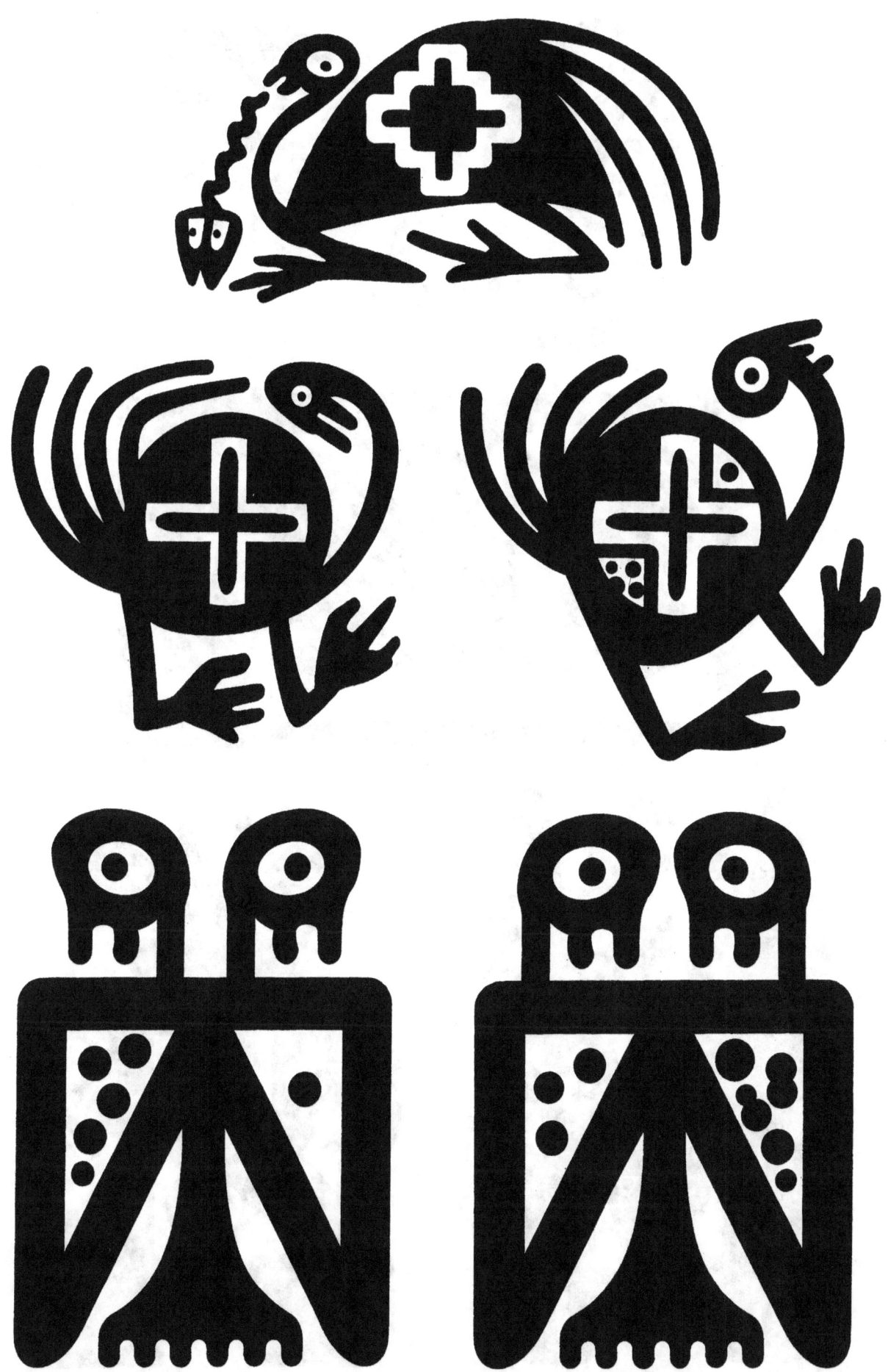

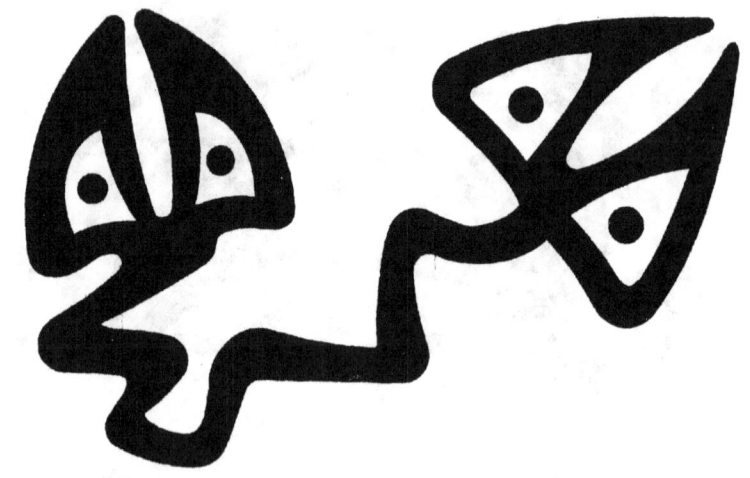

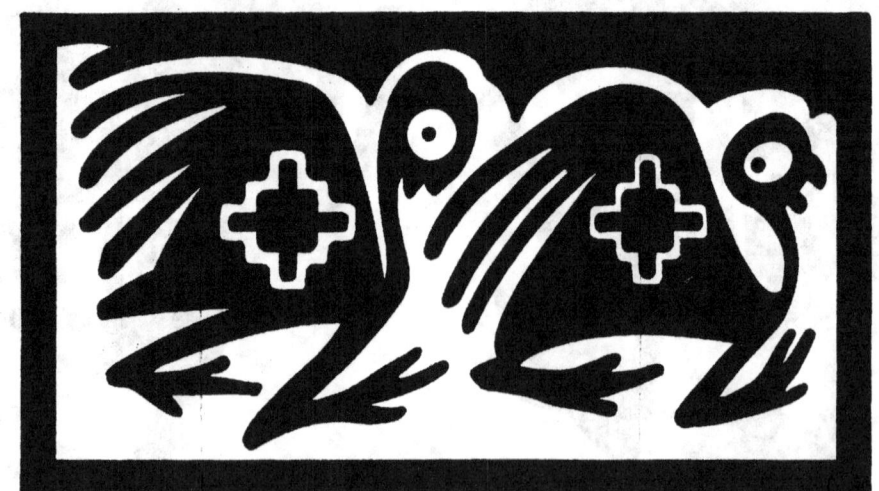

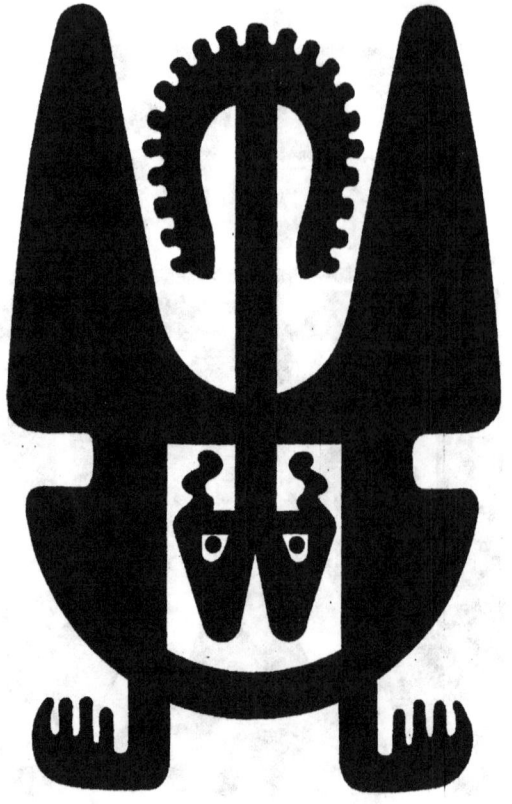

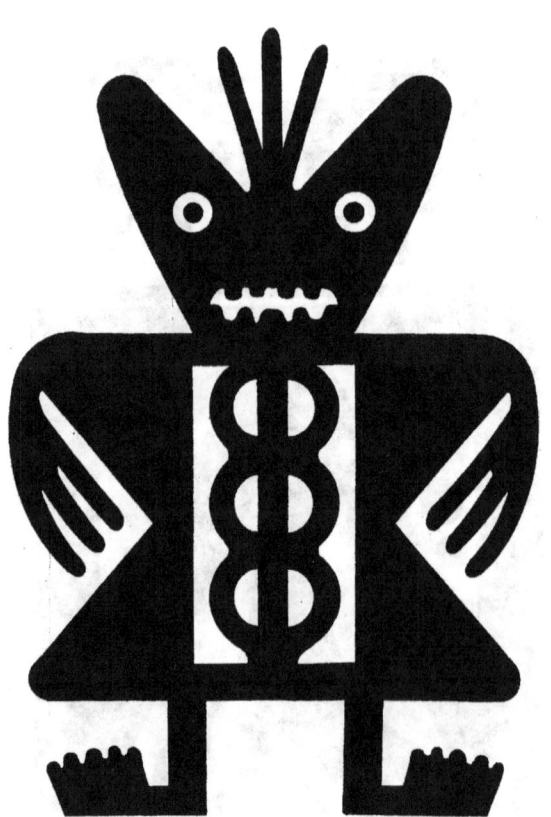

28   Santa María Culture

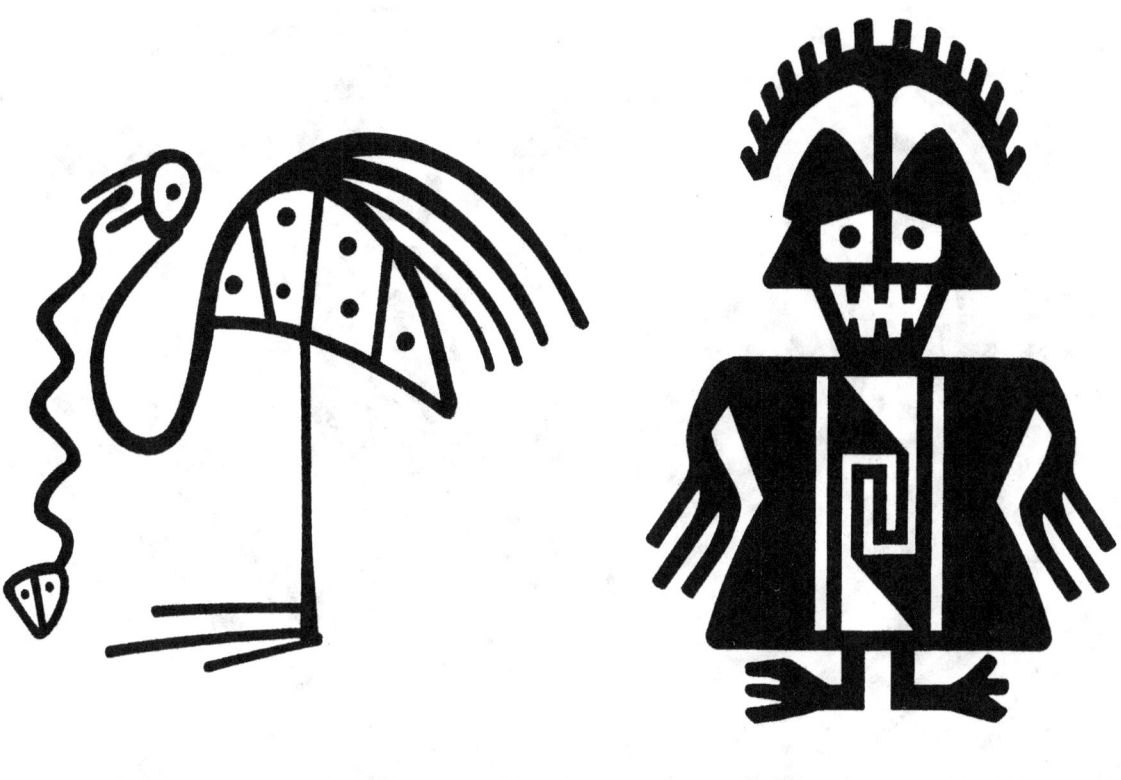

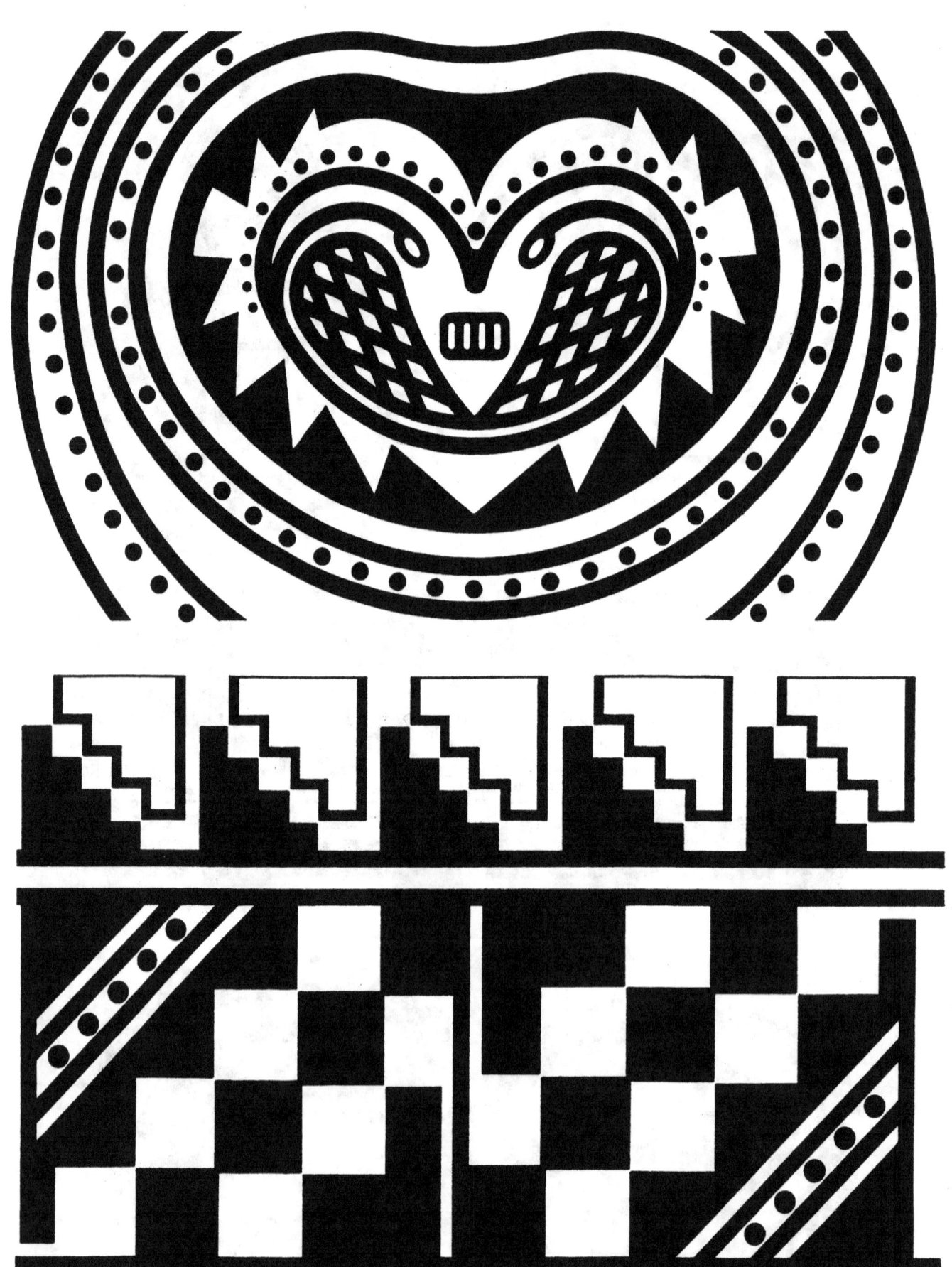

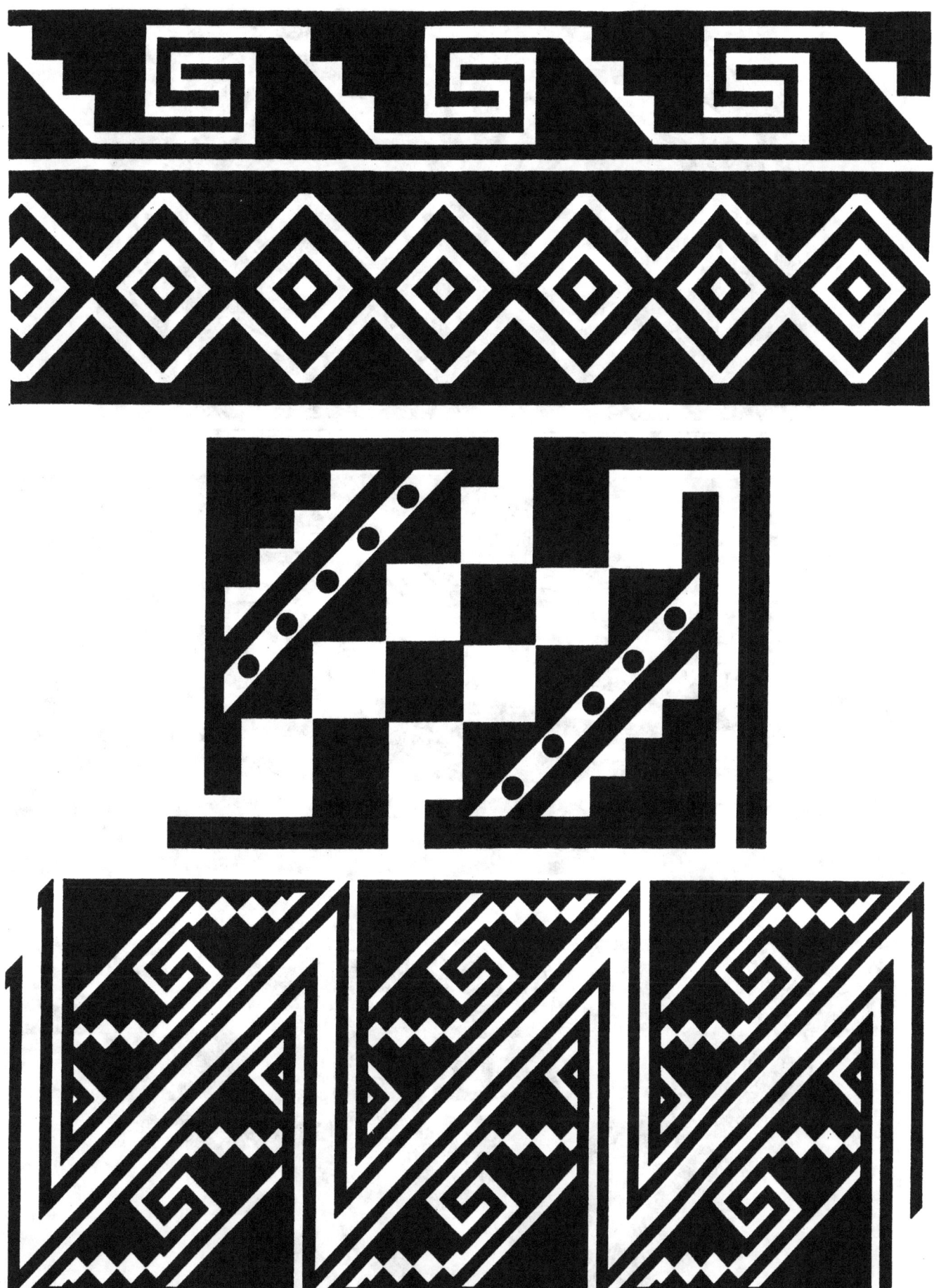

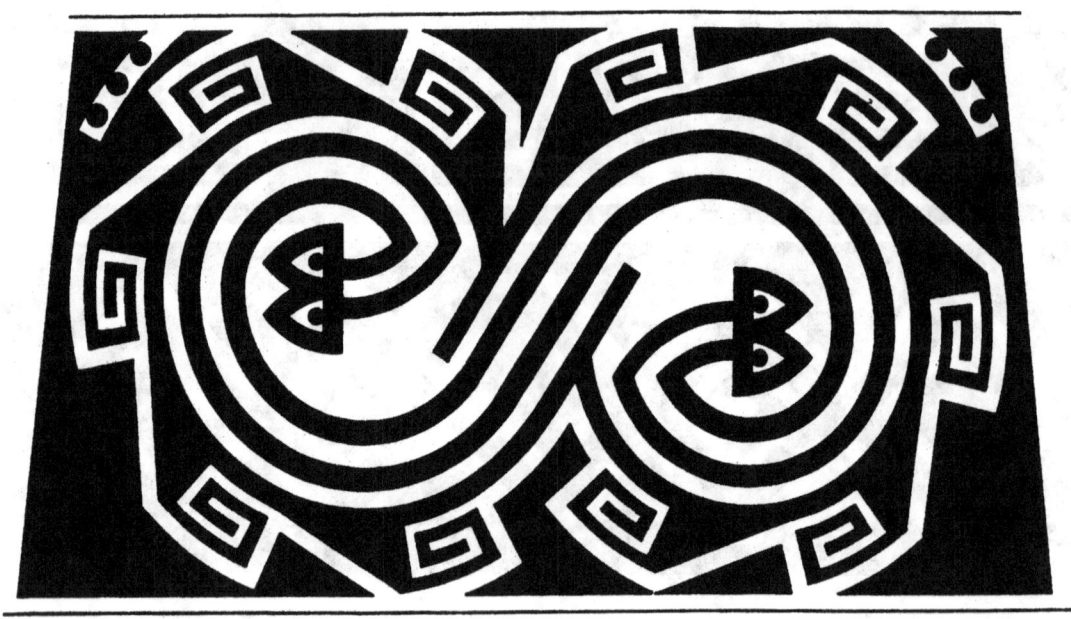

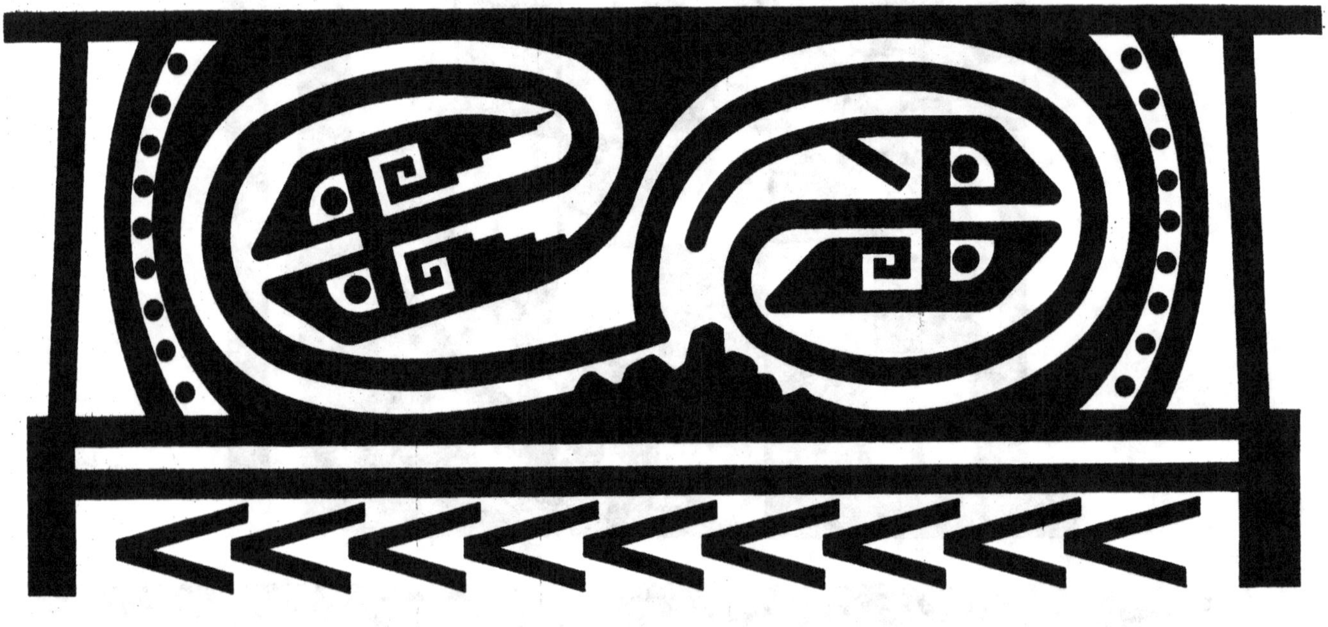

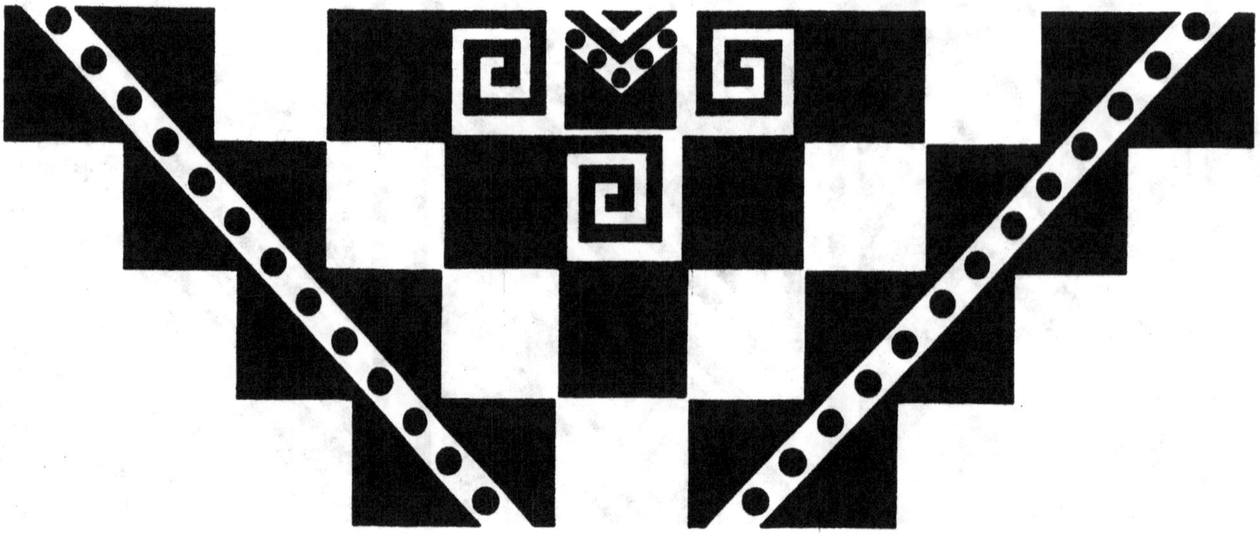

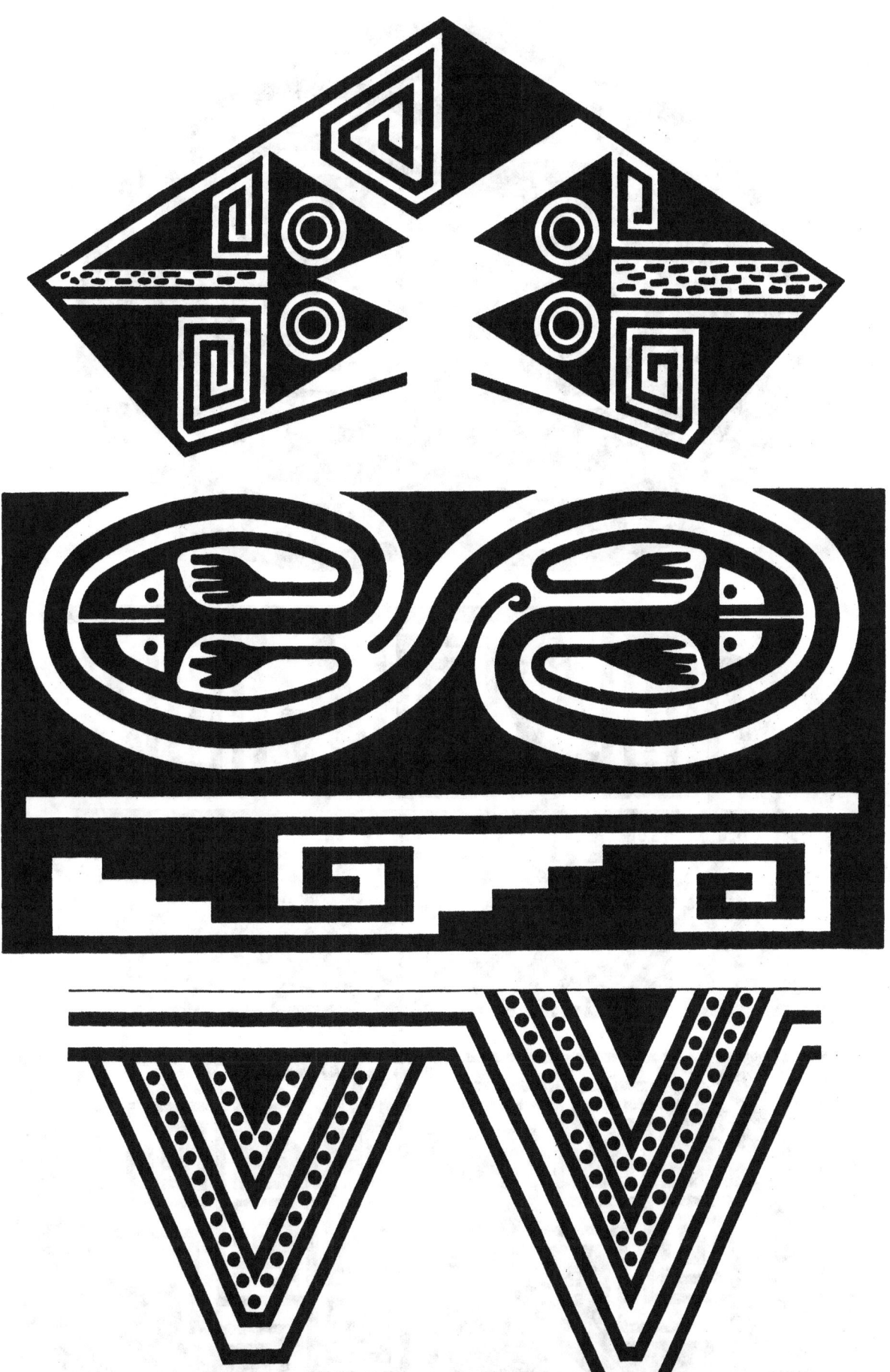

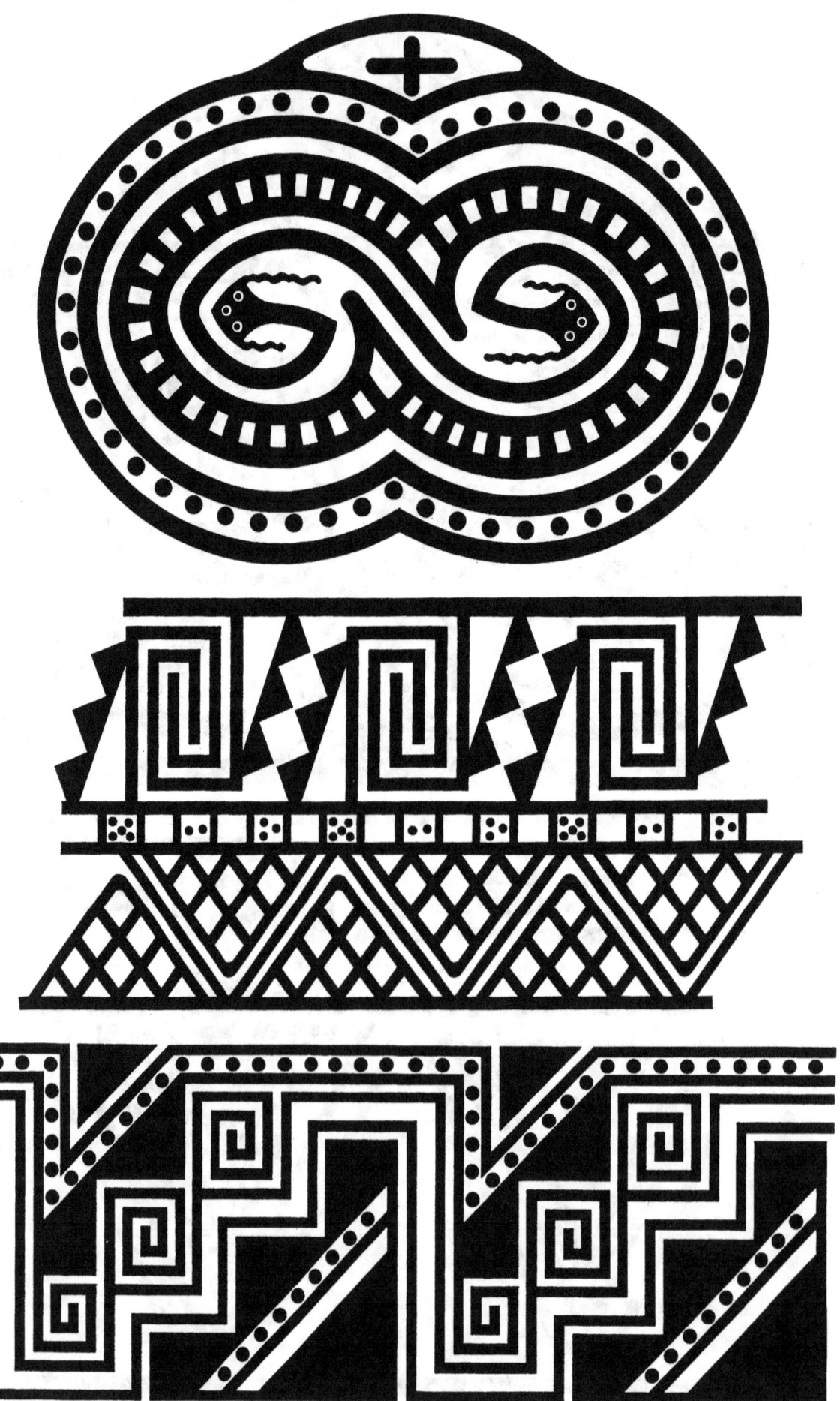

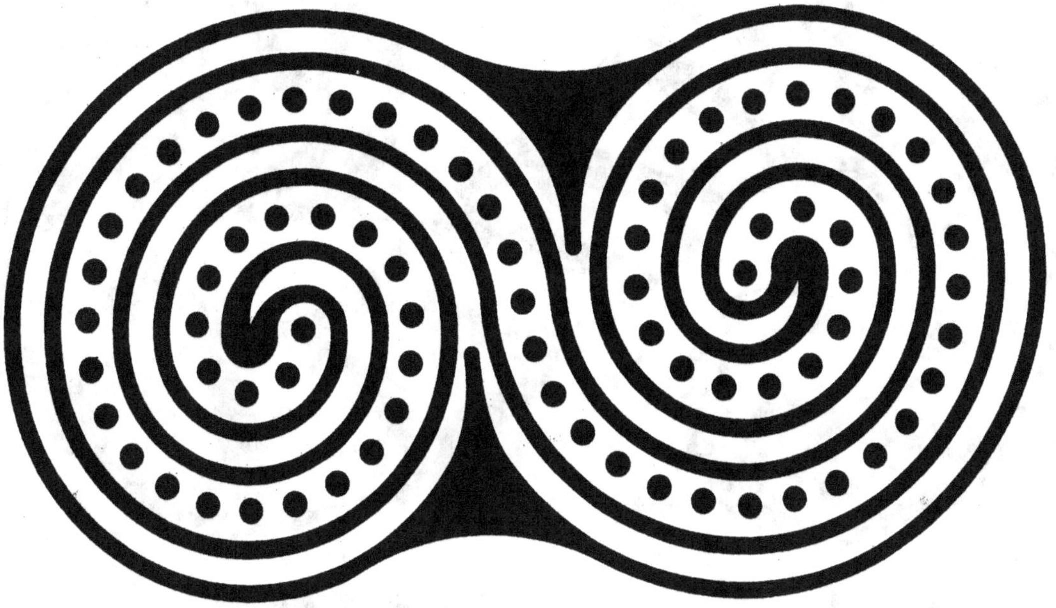

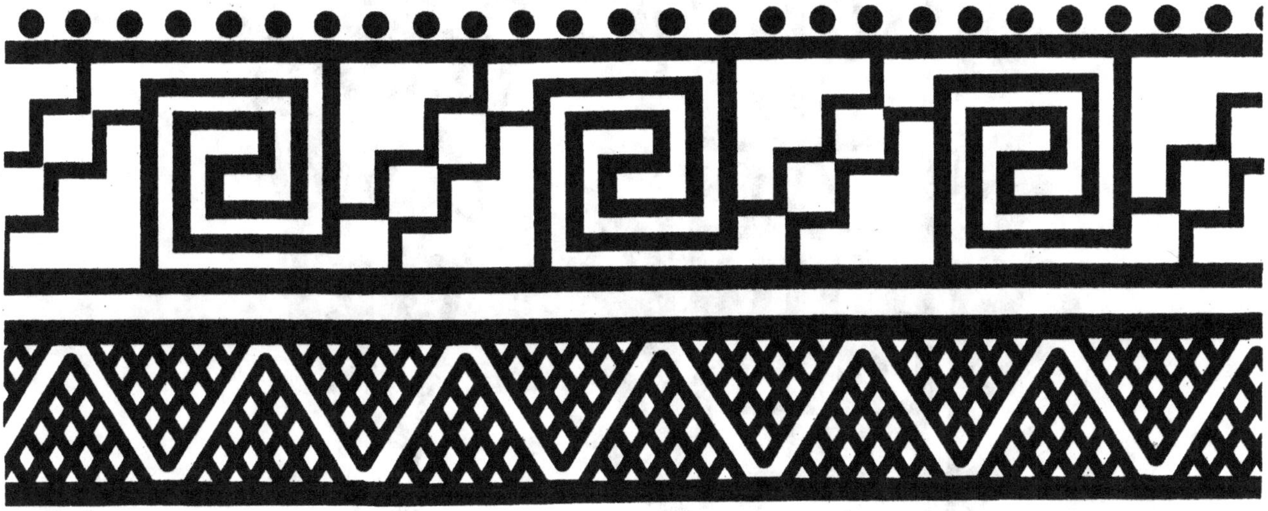

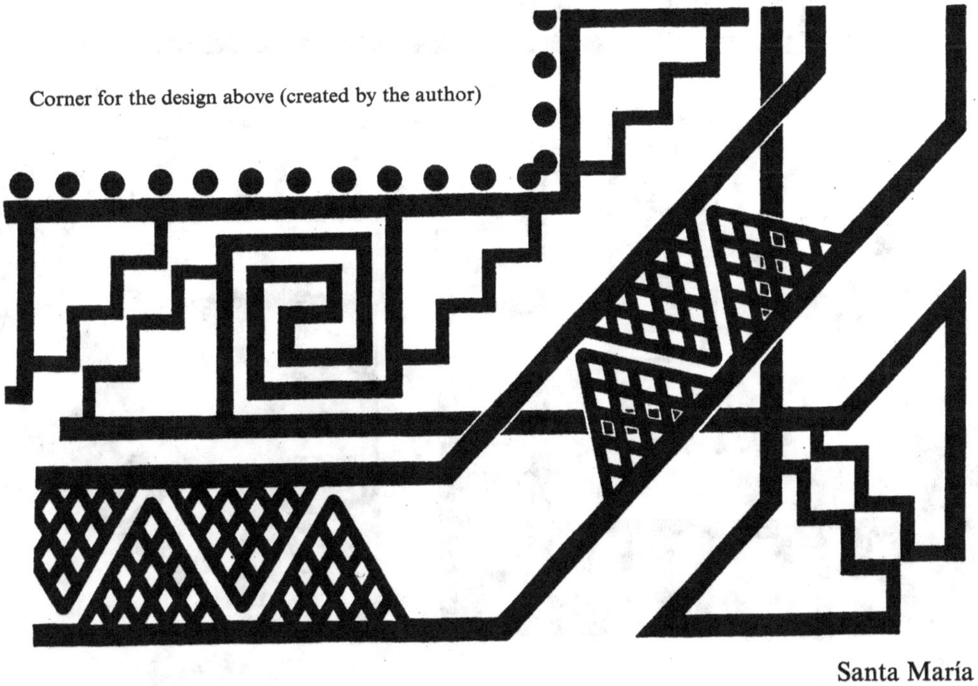

Corner for the design above (created by the author)

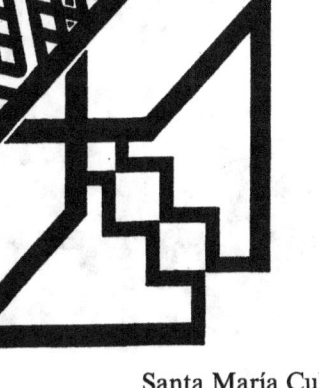

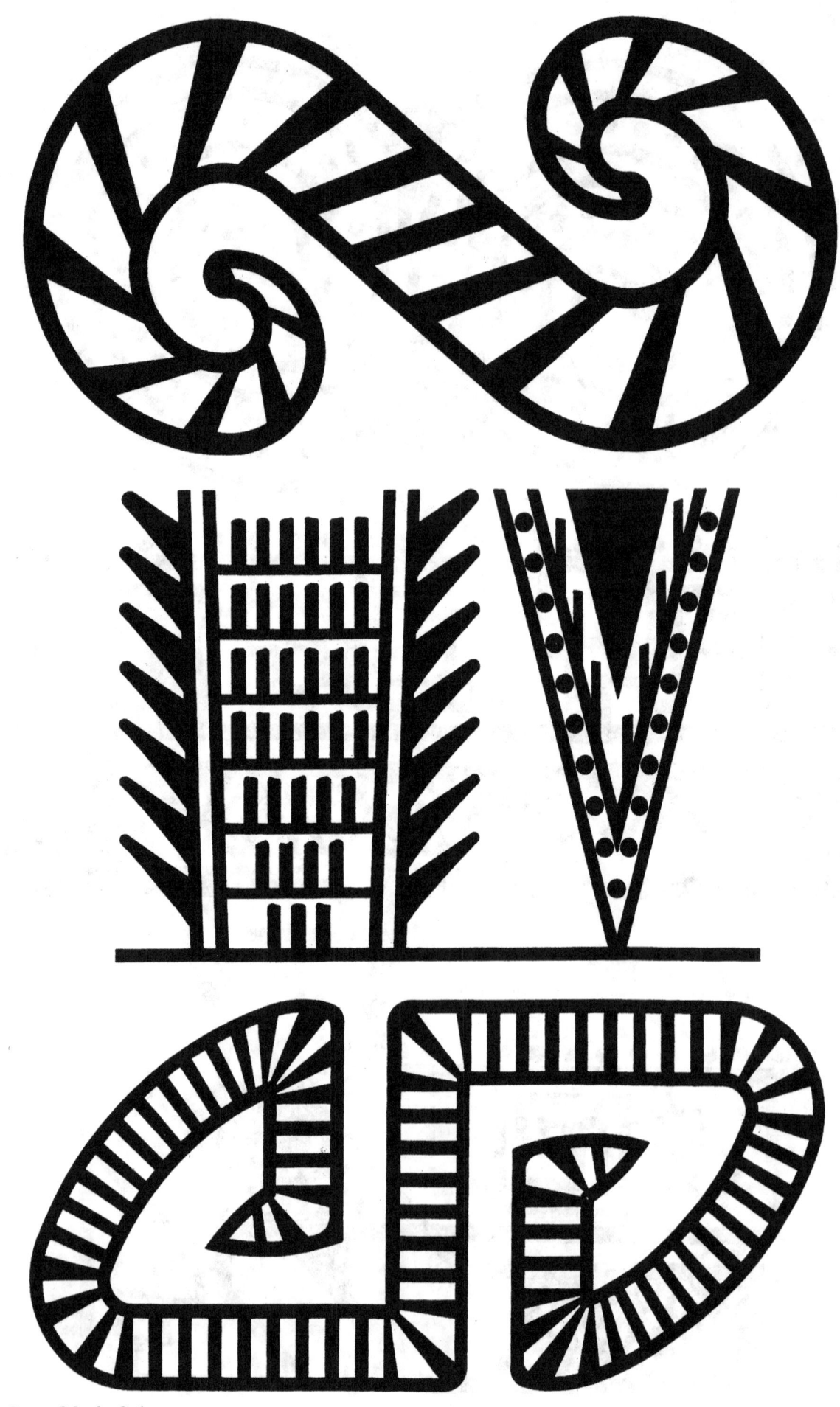

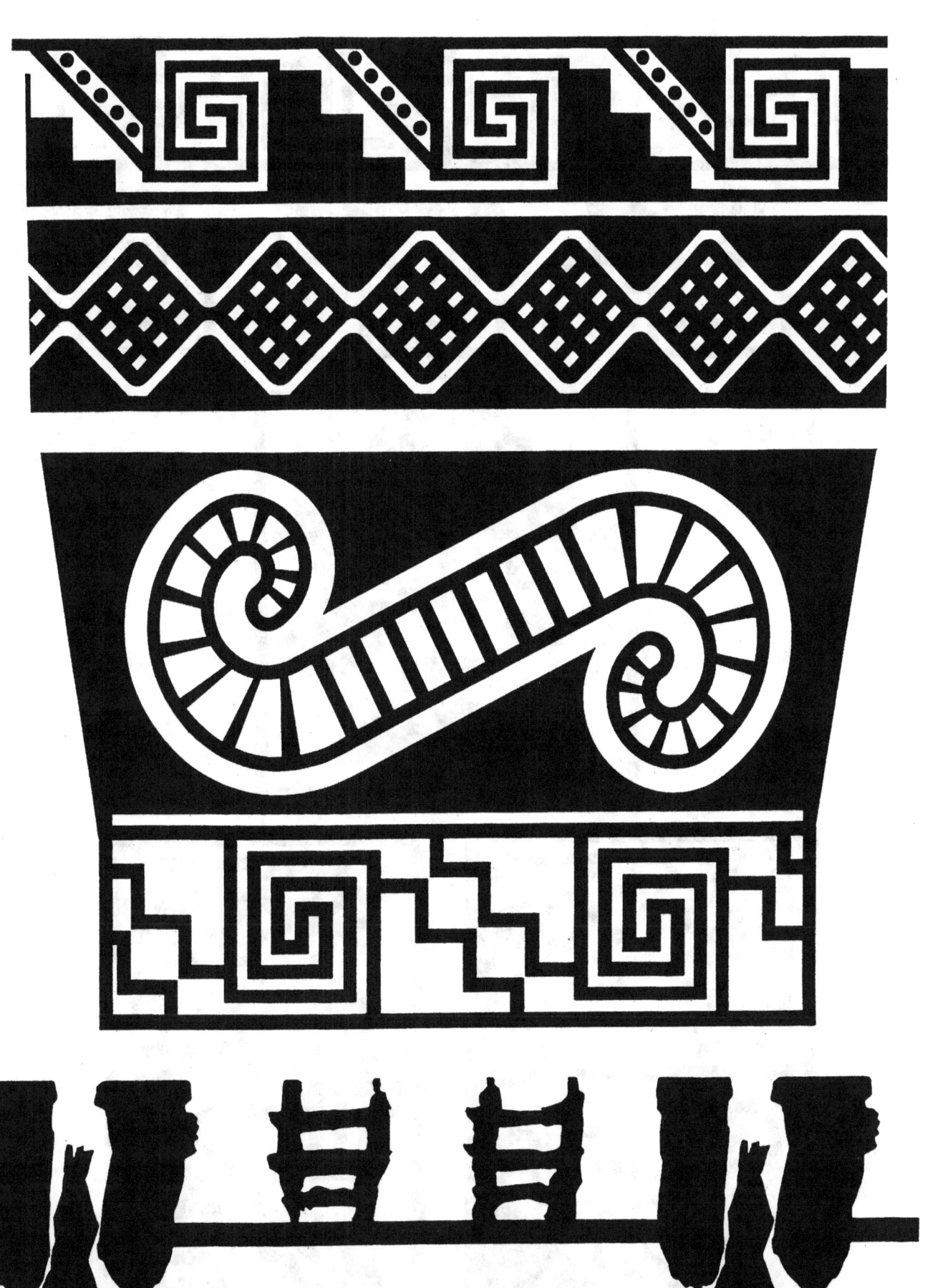

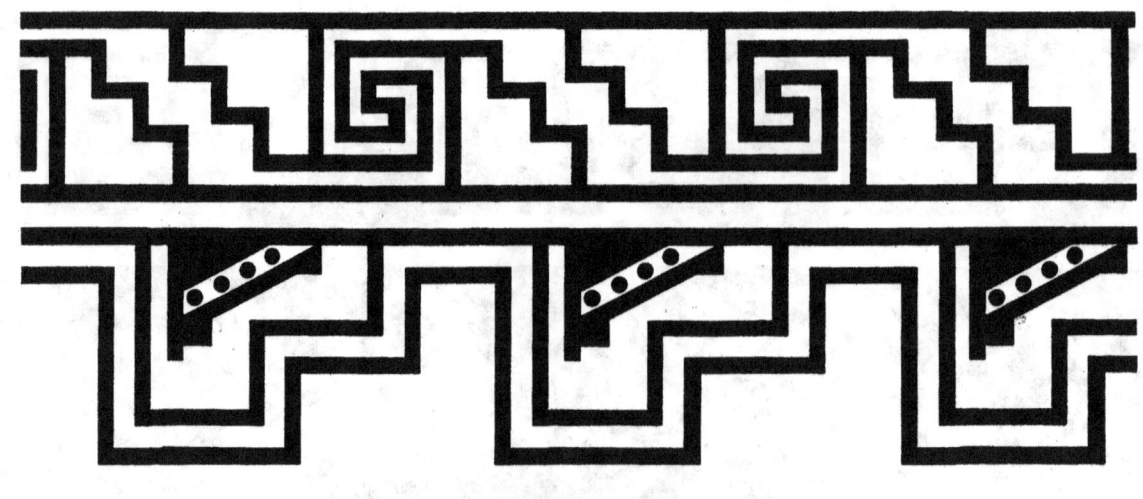

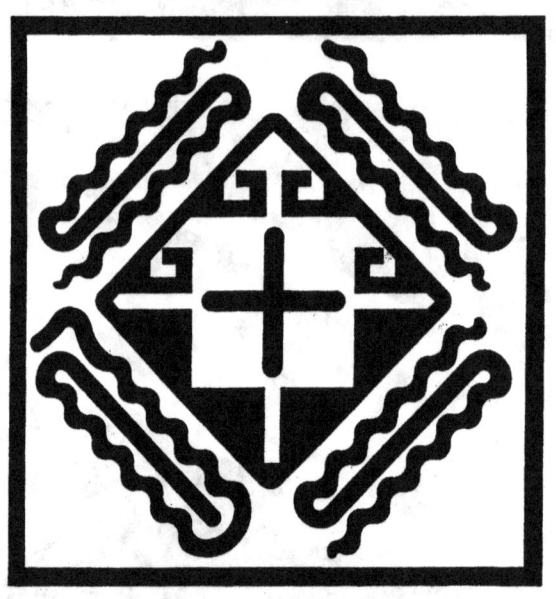

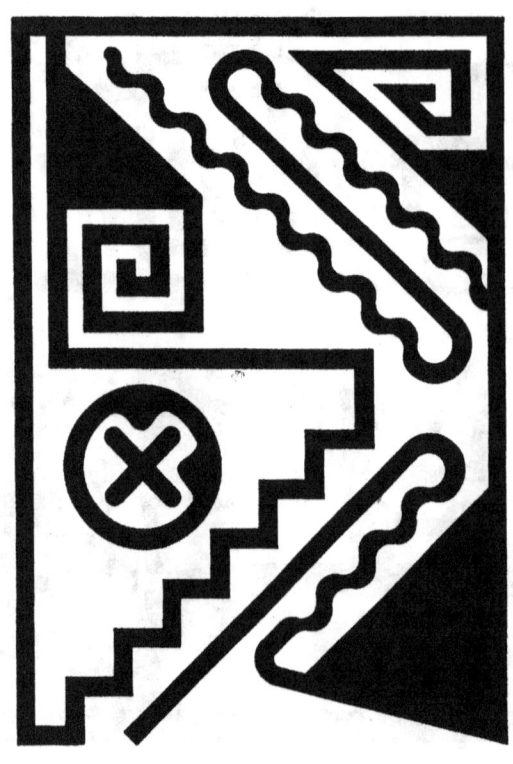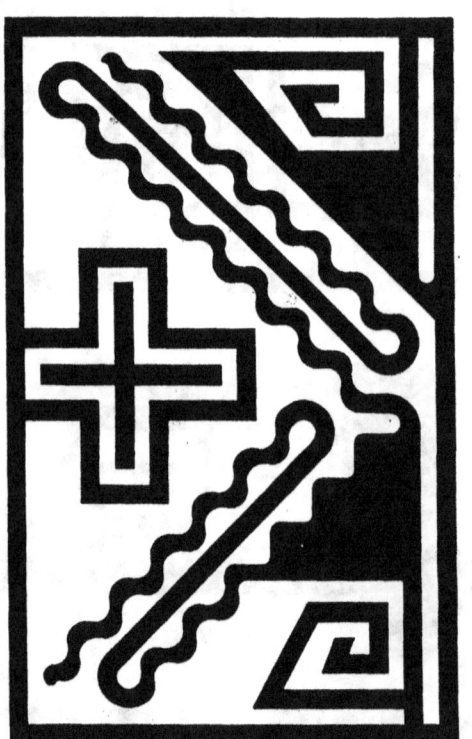

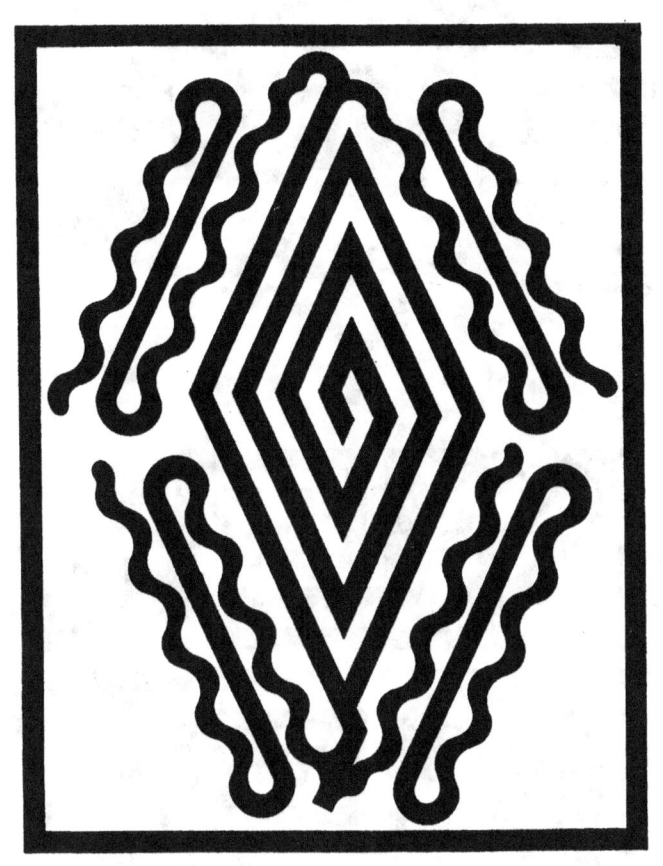

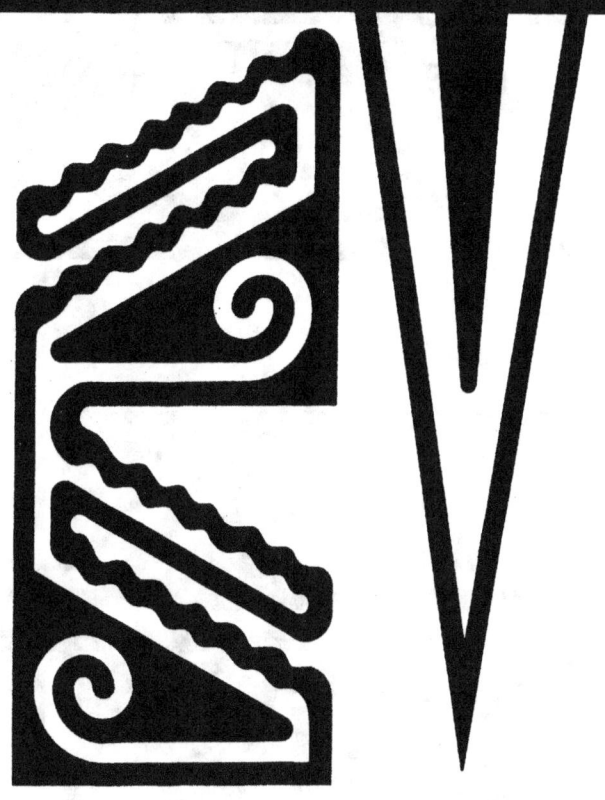

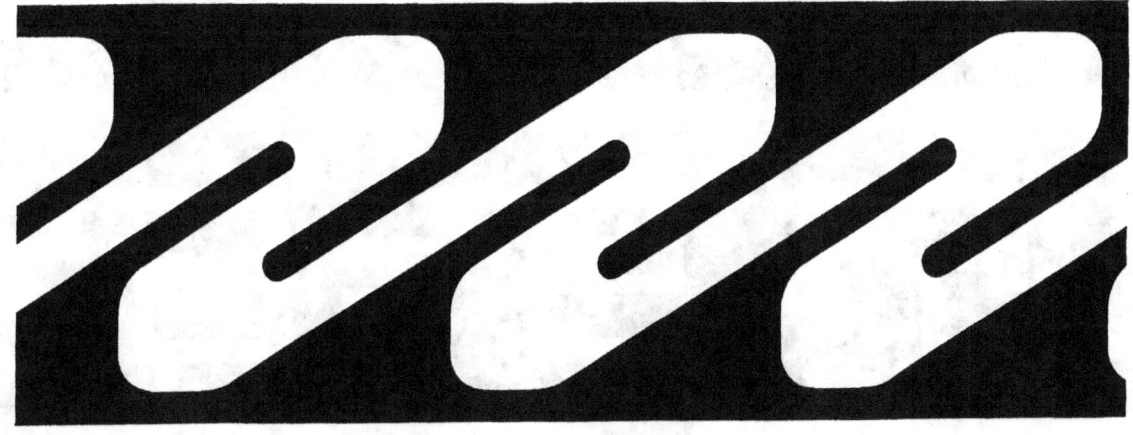

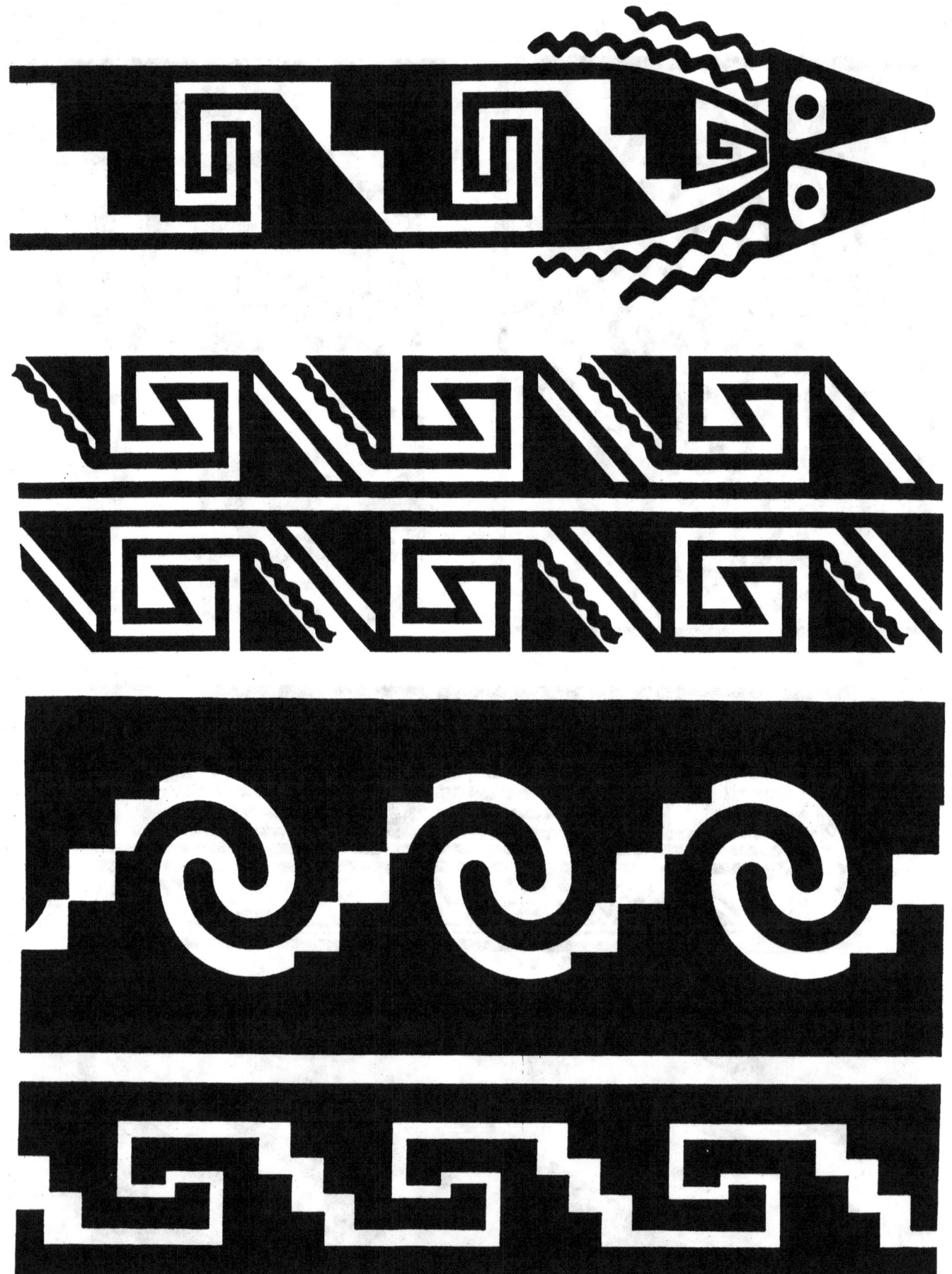

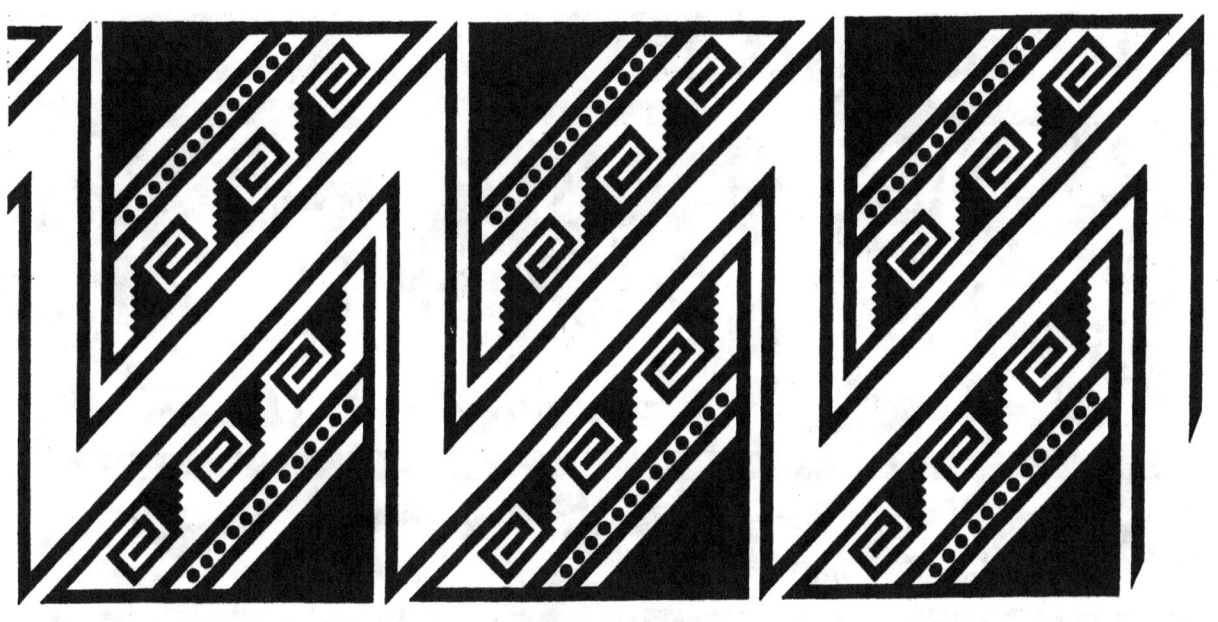

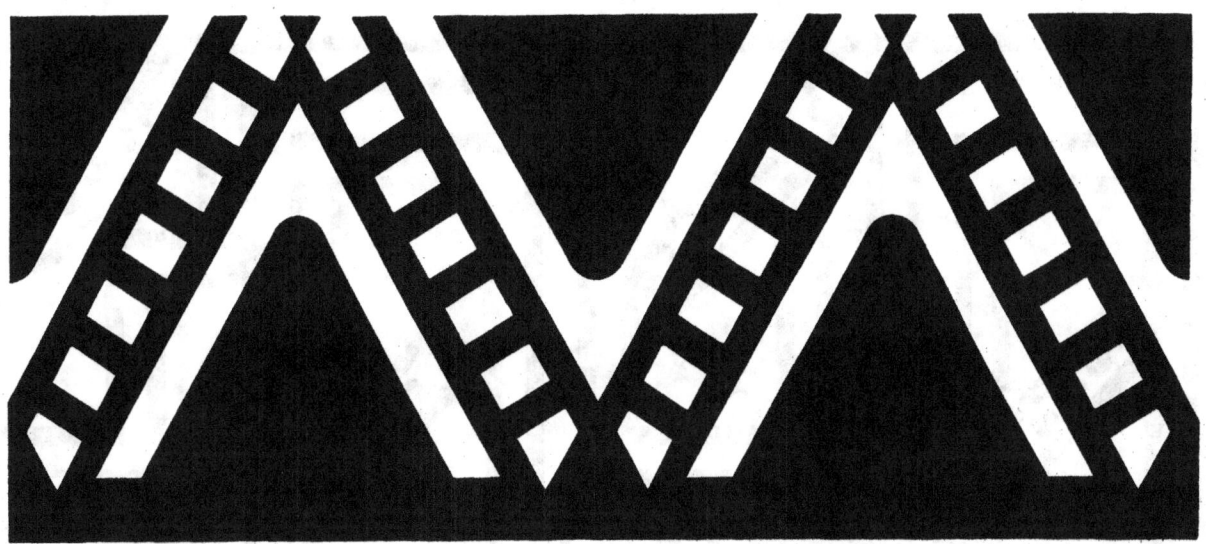

Corner for the design above (created by the author)

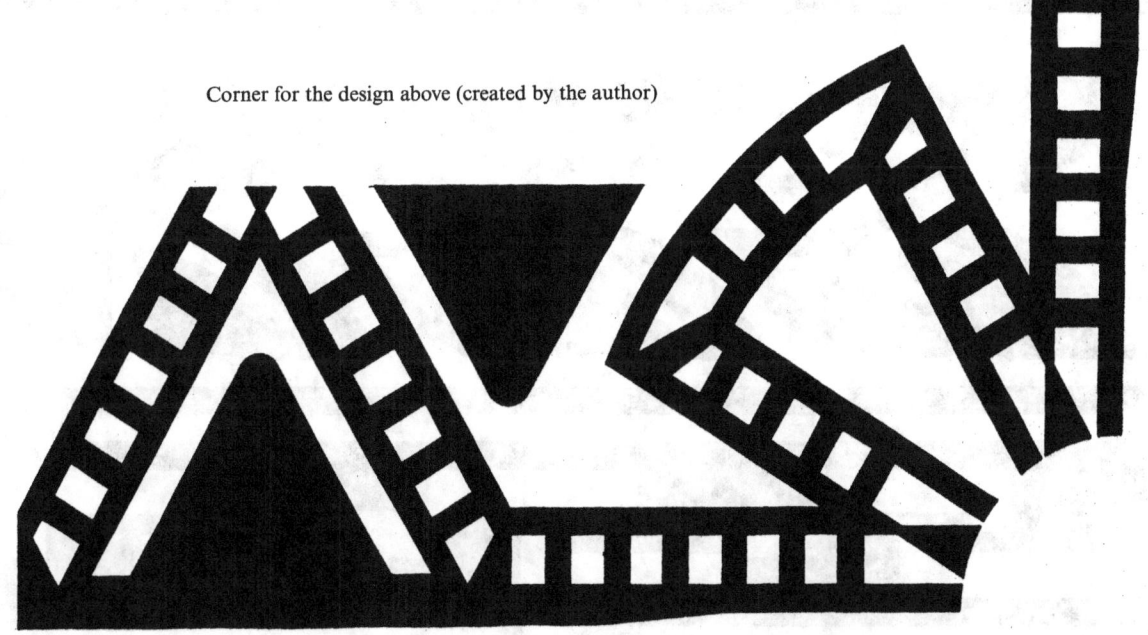

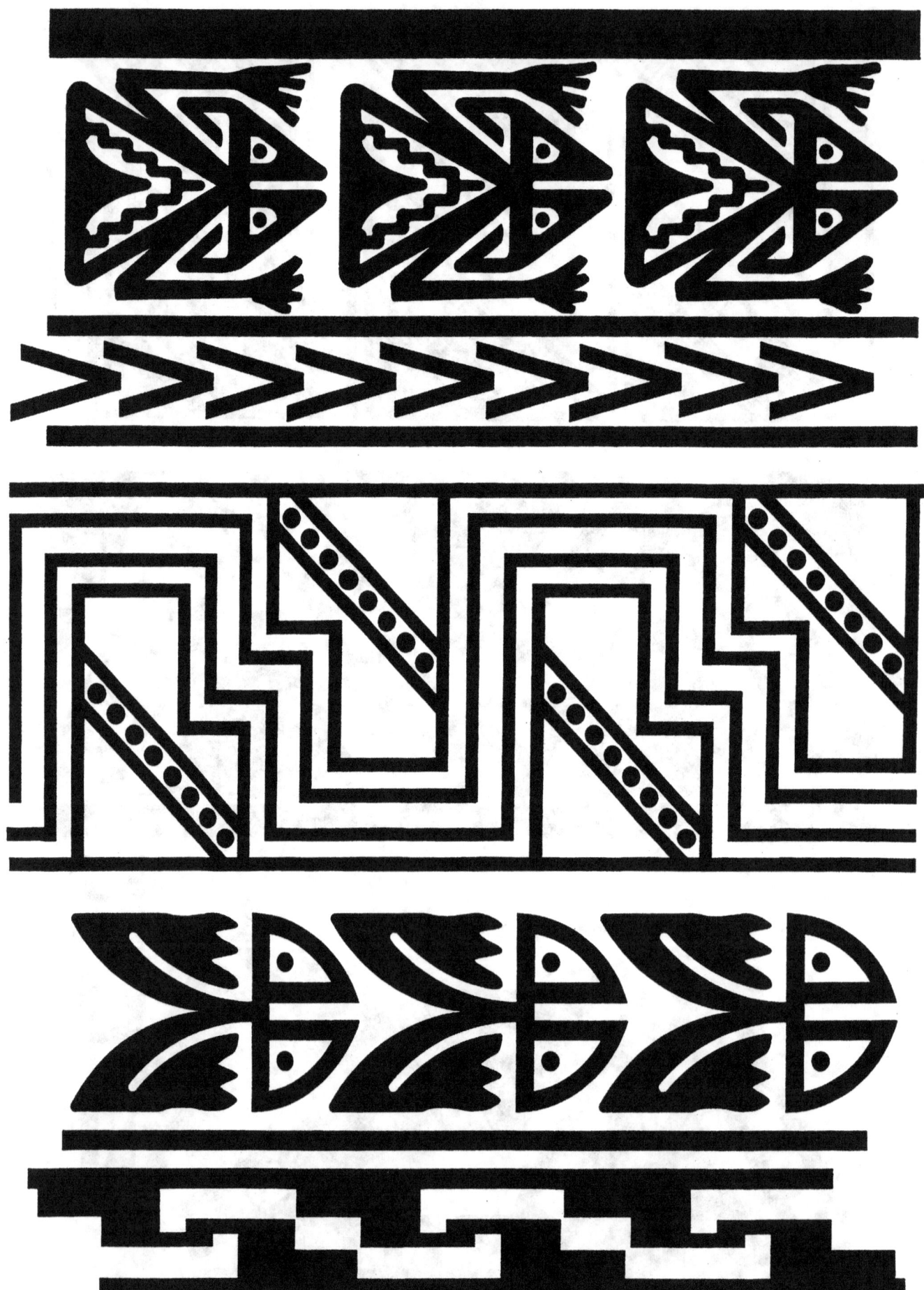

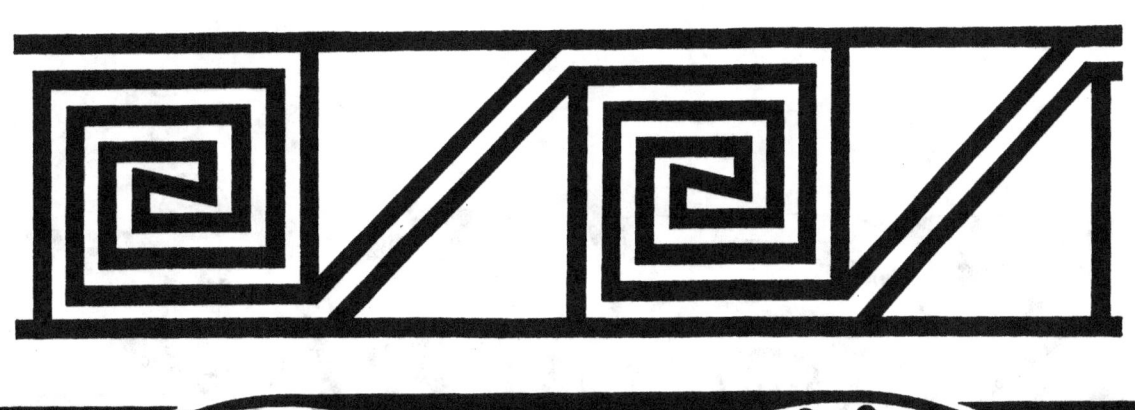

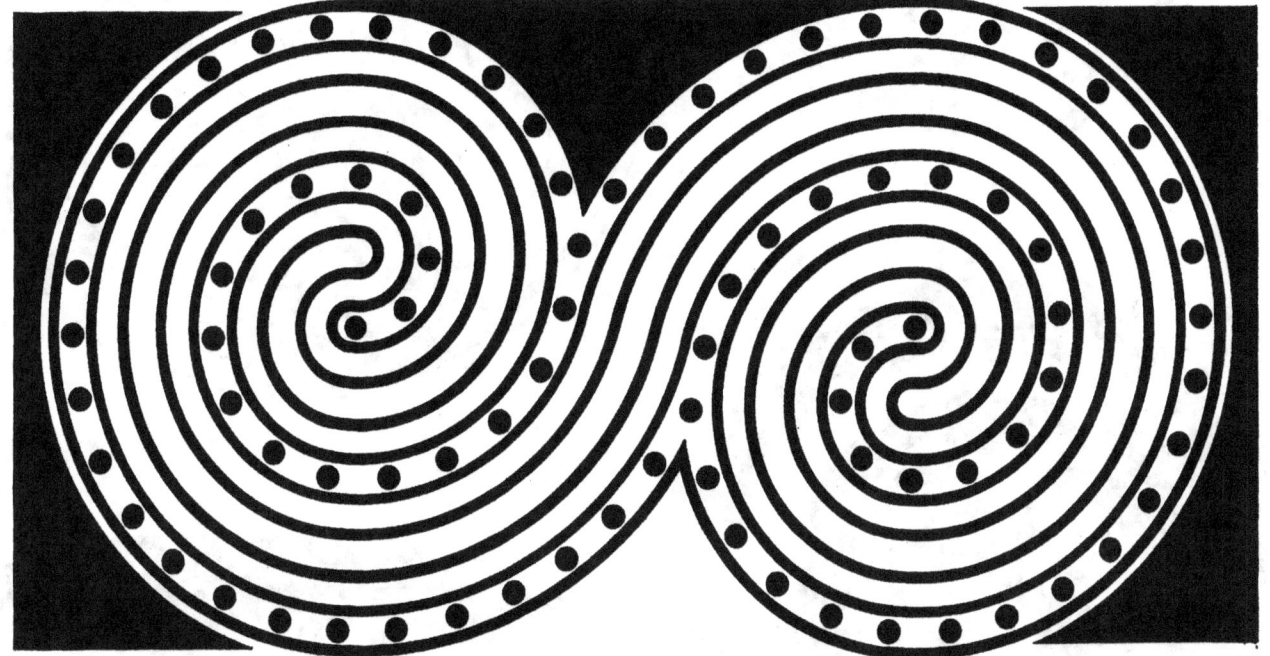

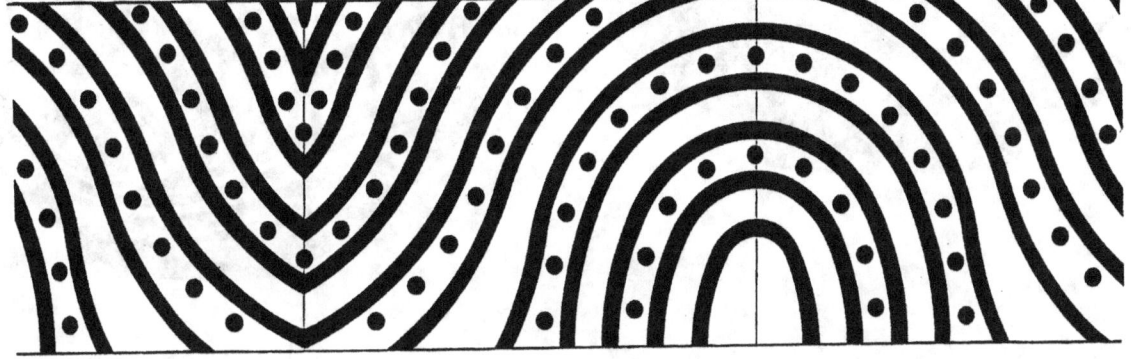

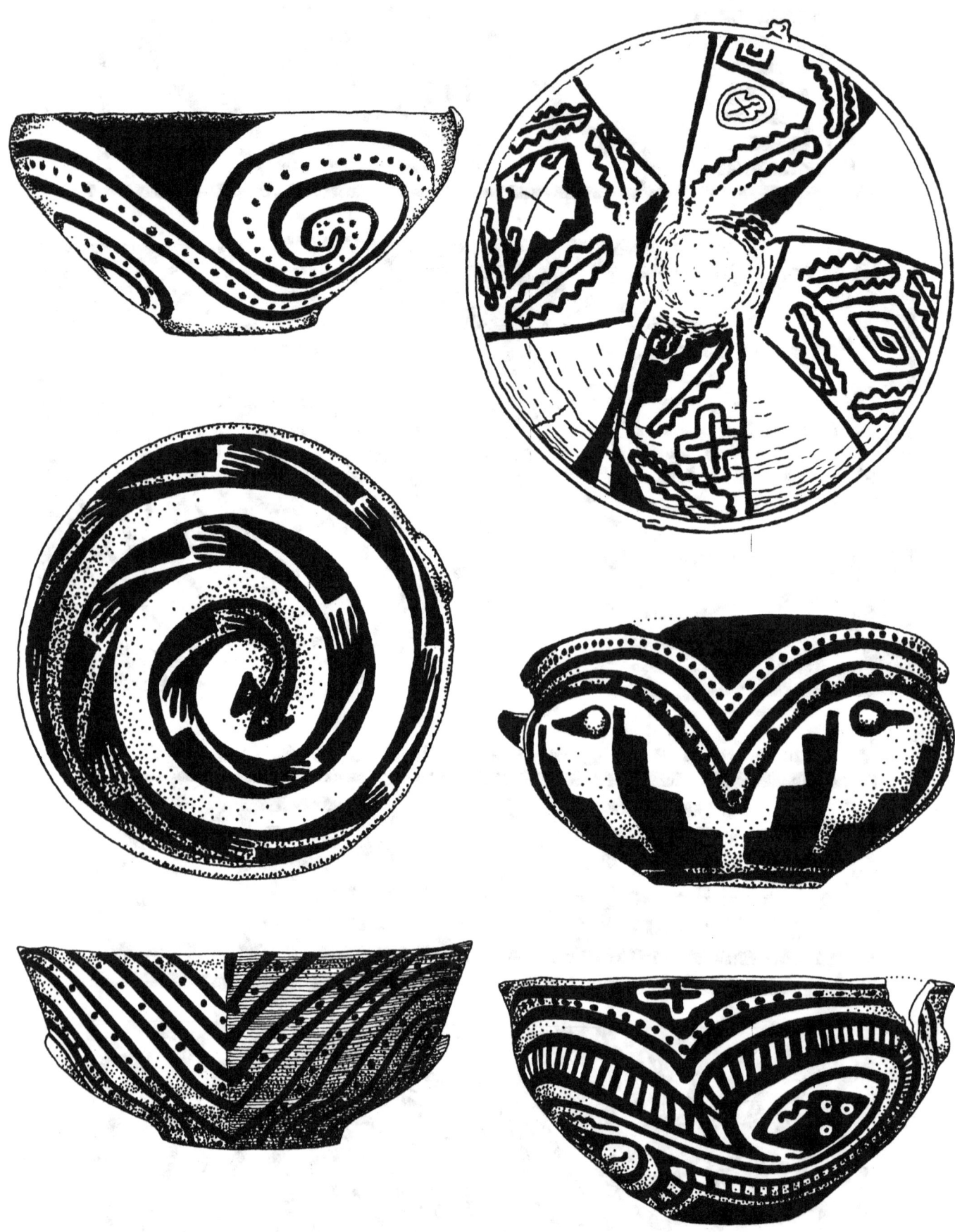

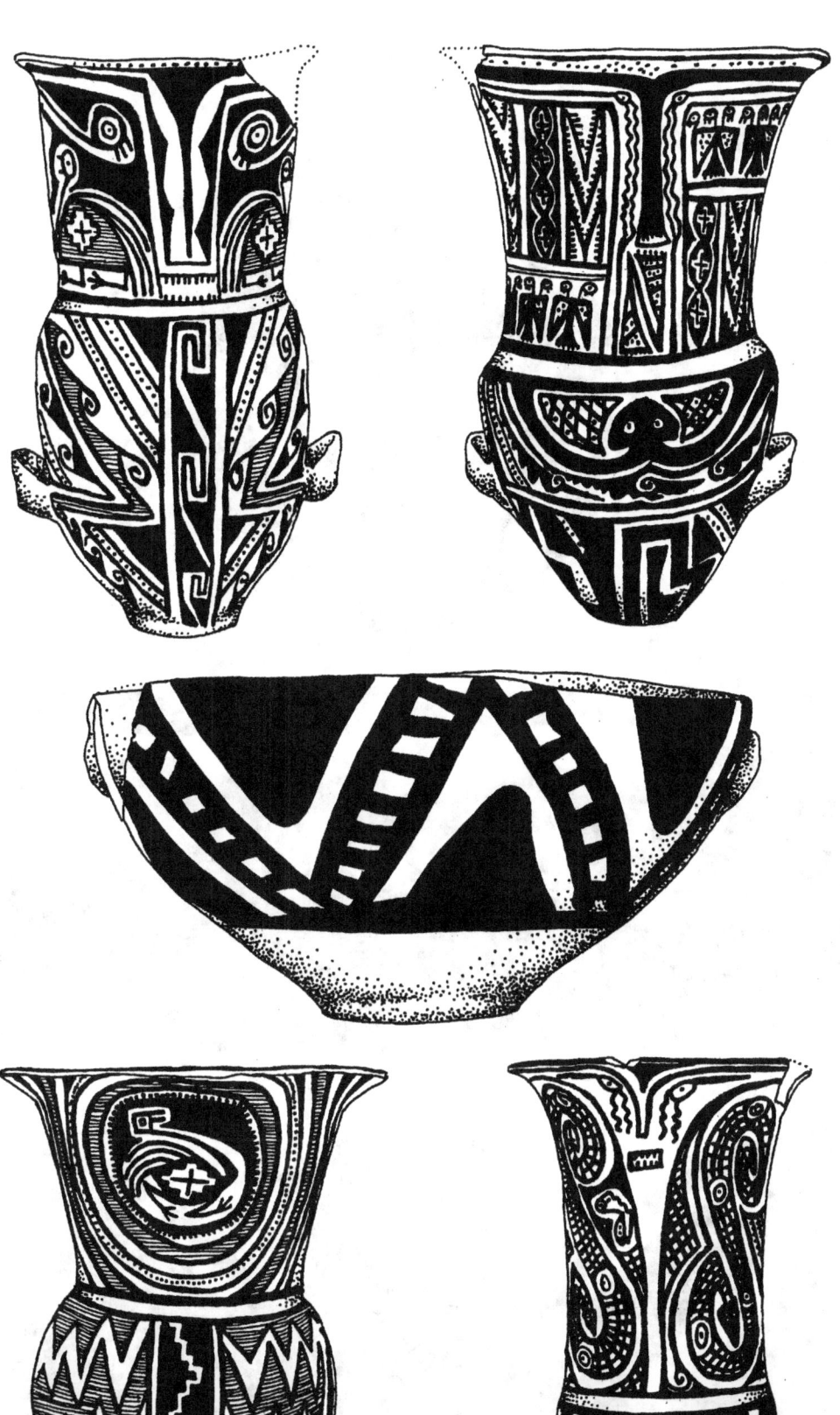

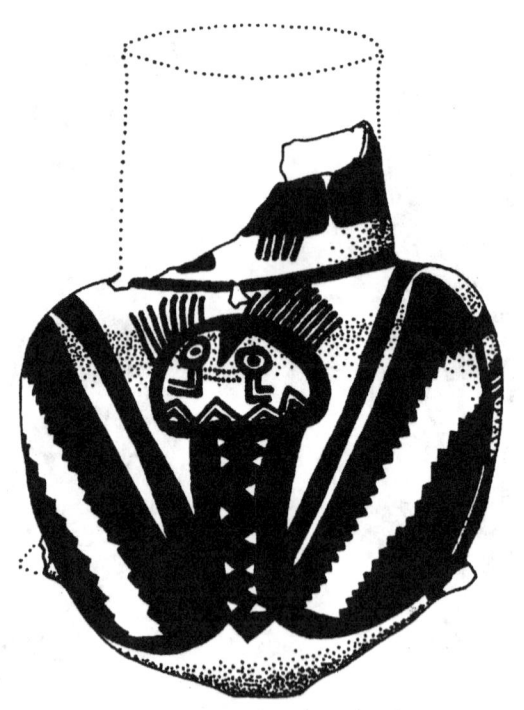

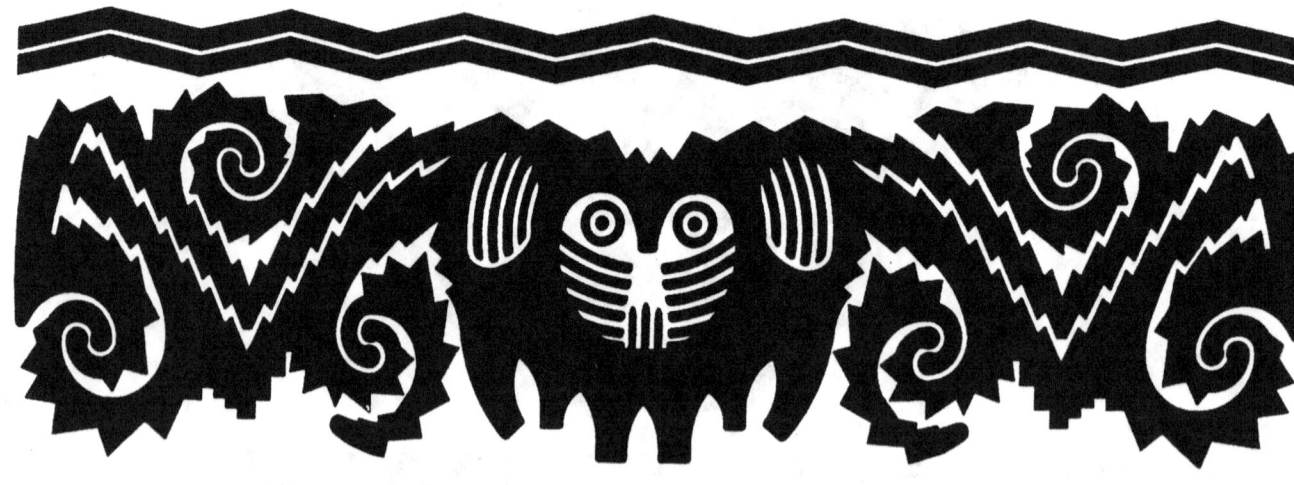

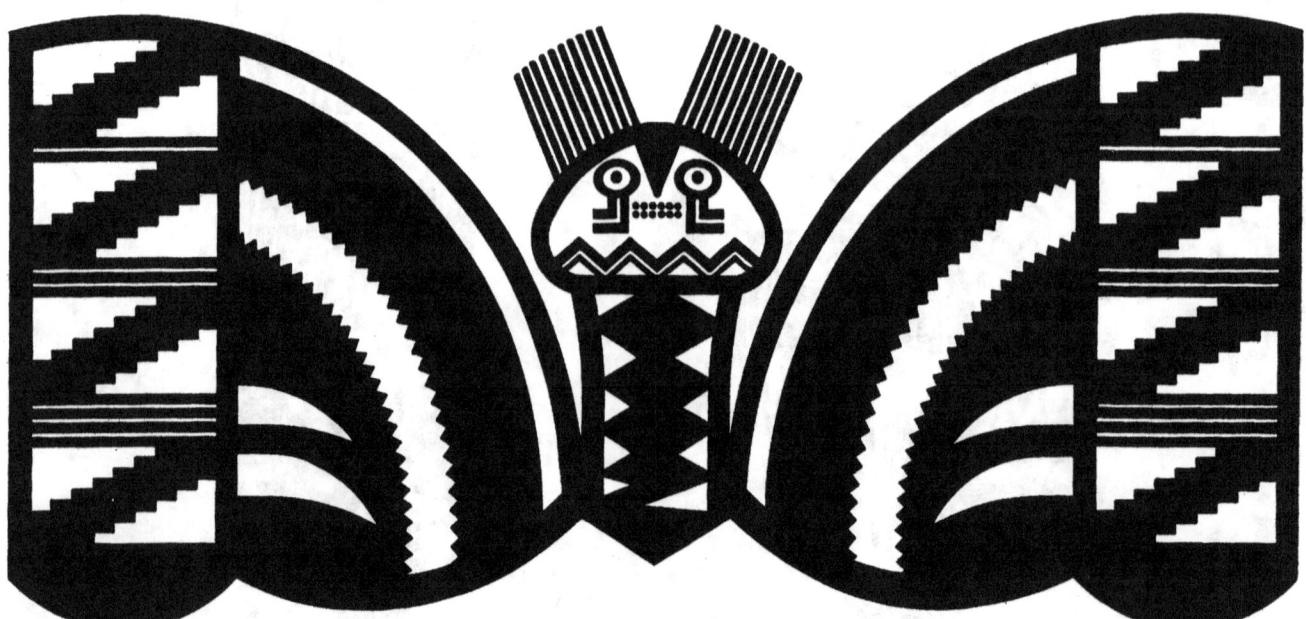

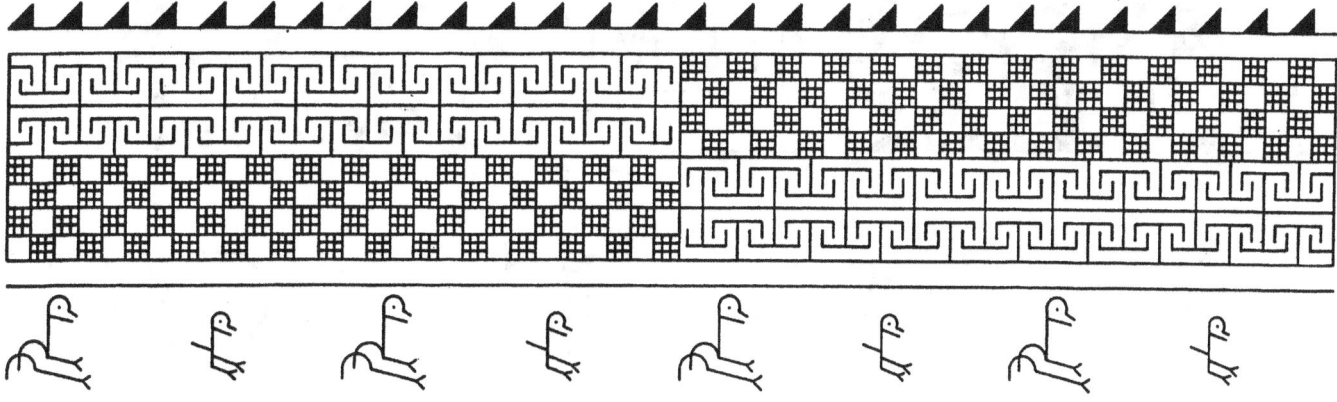

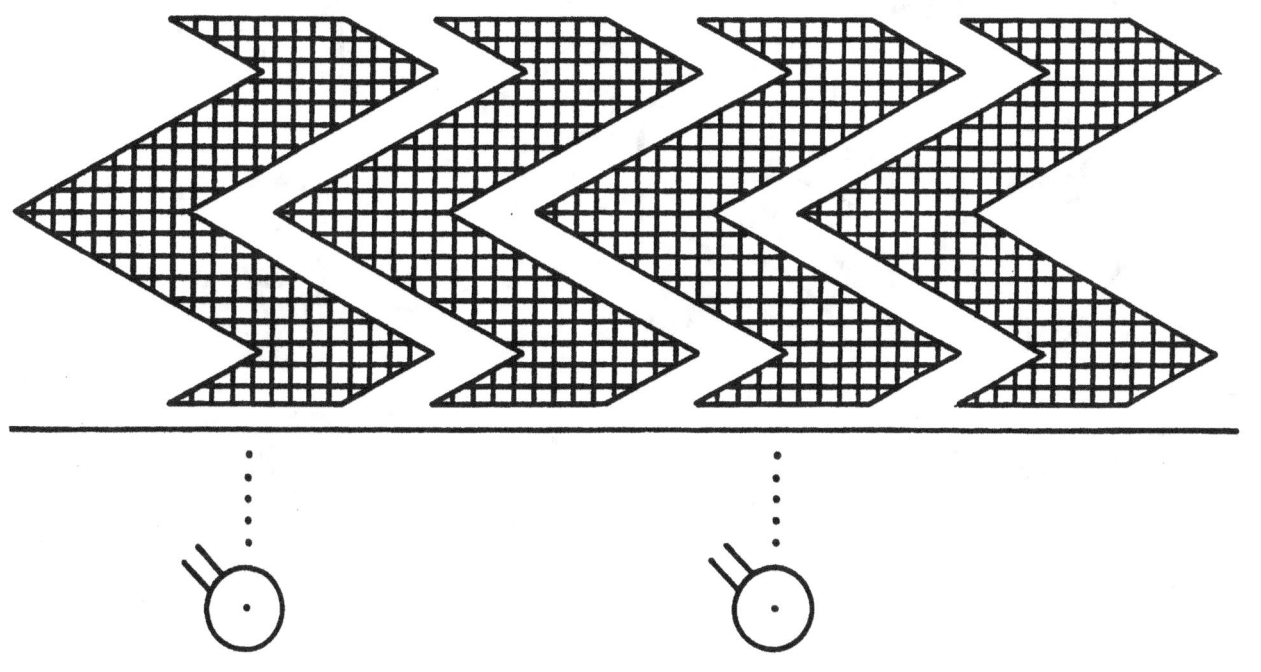

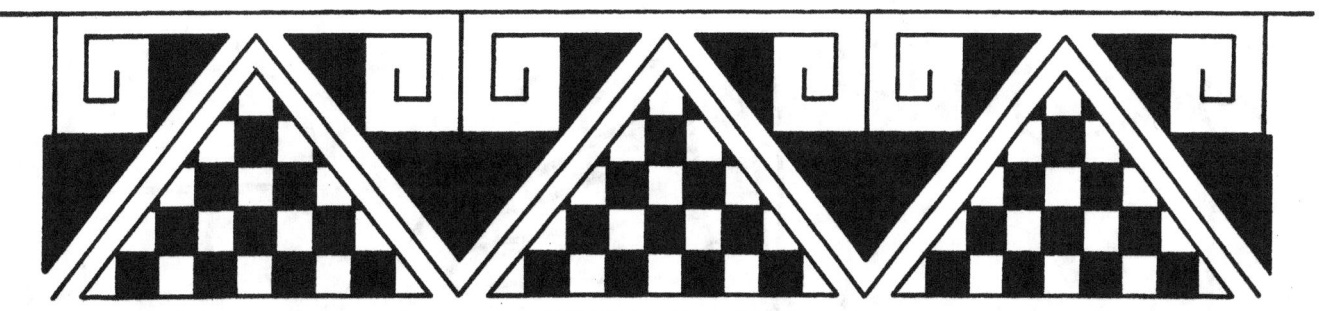

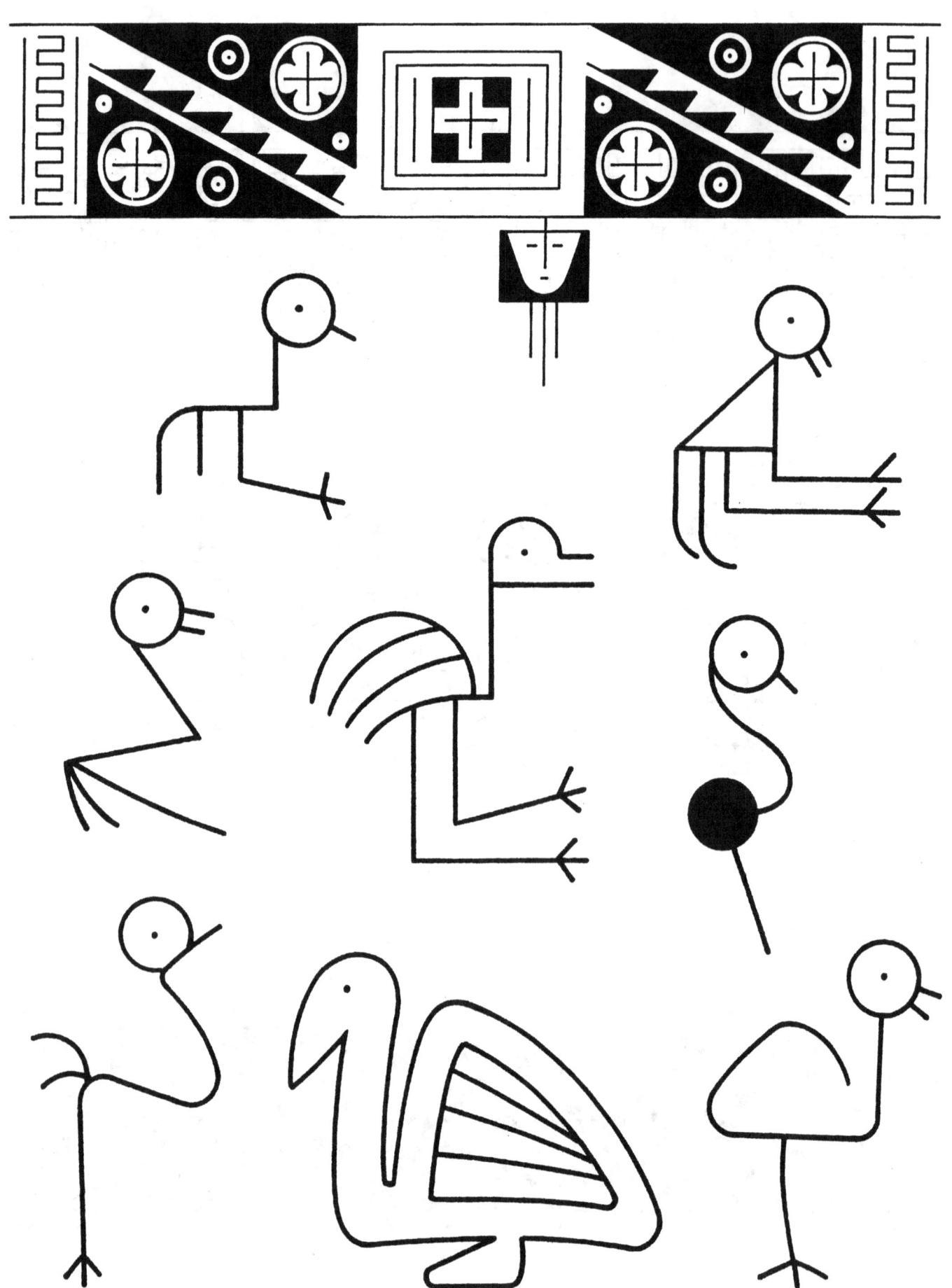

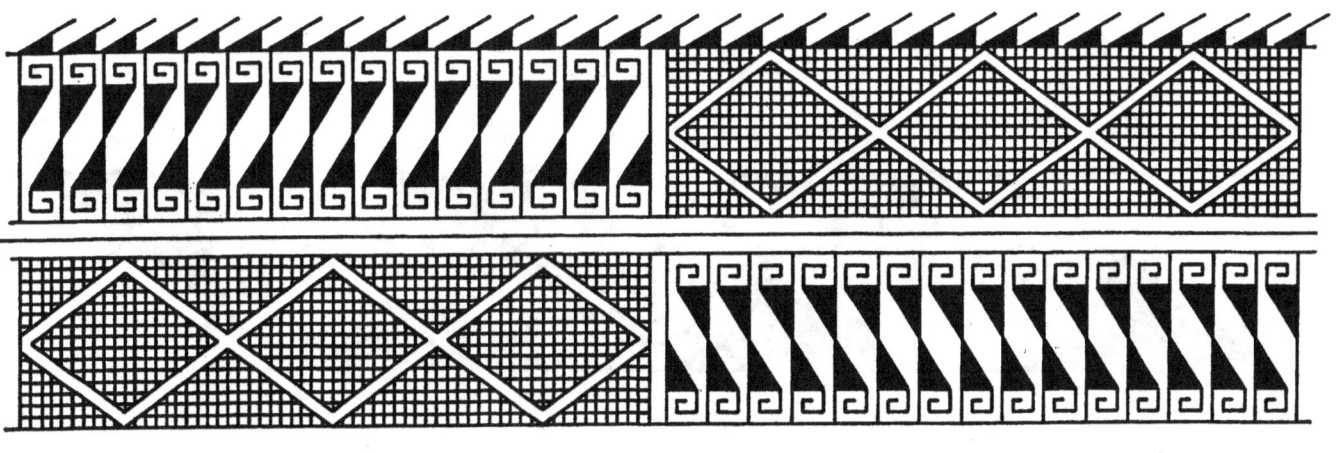

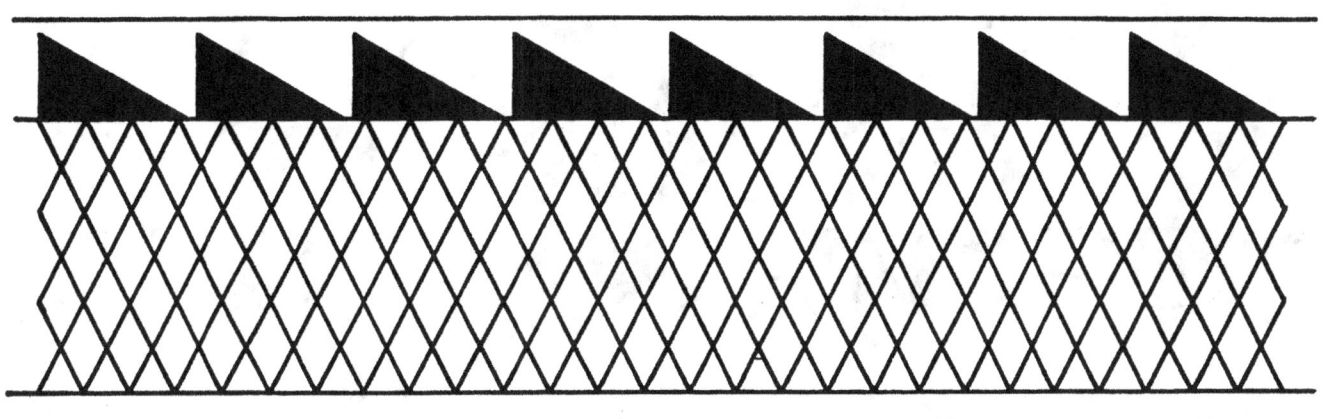

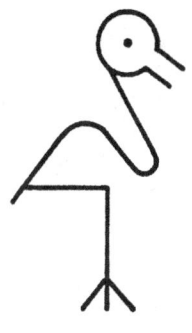

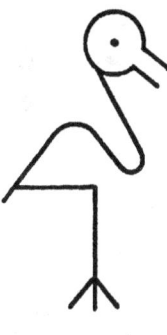

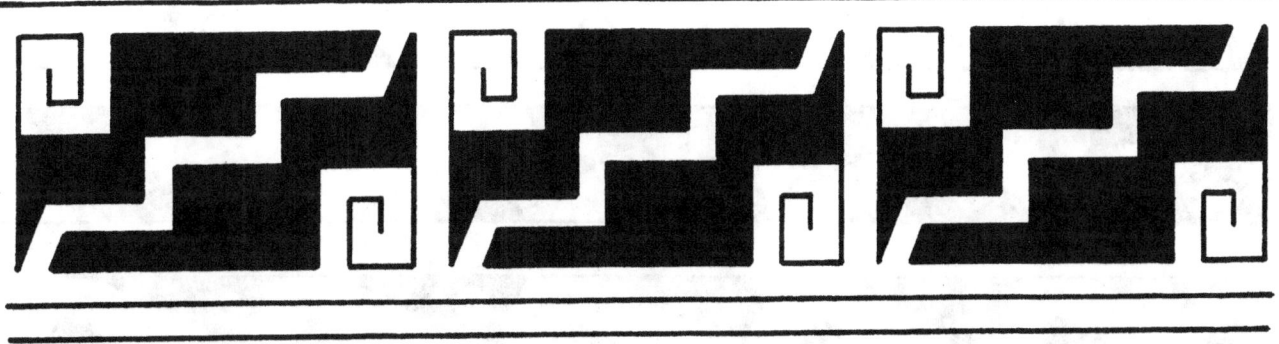

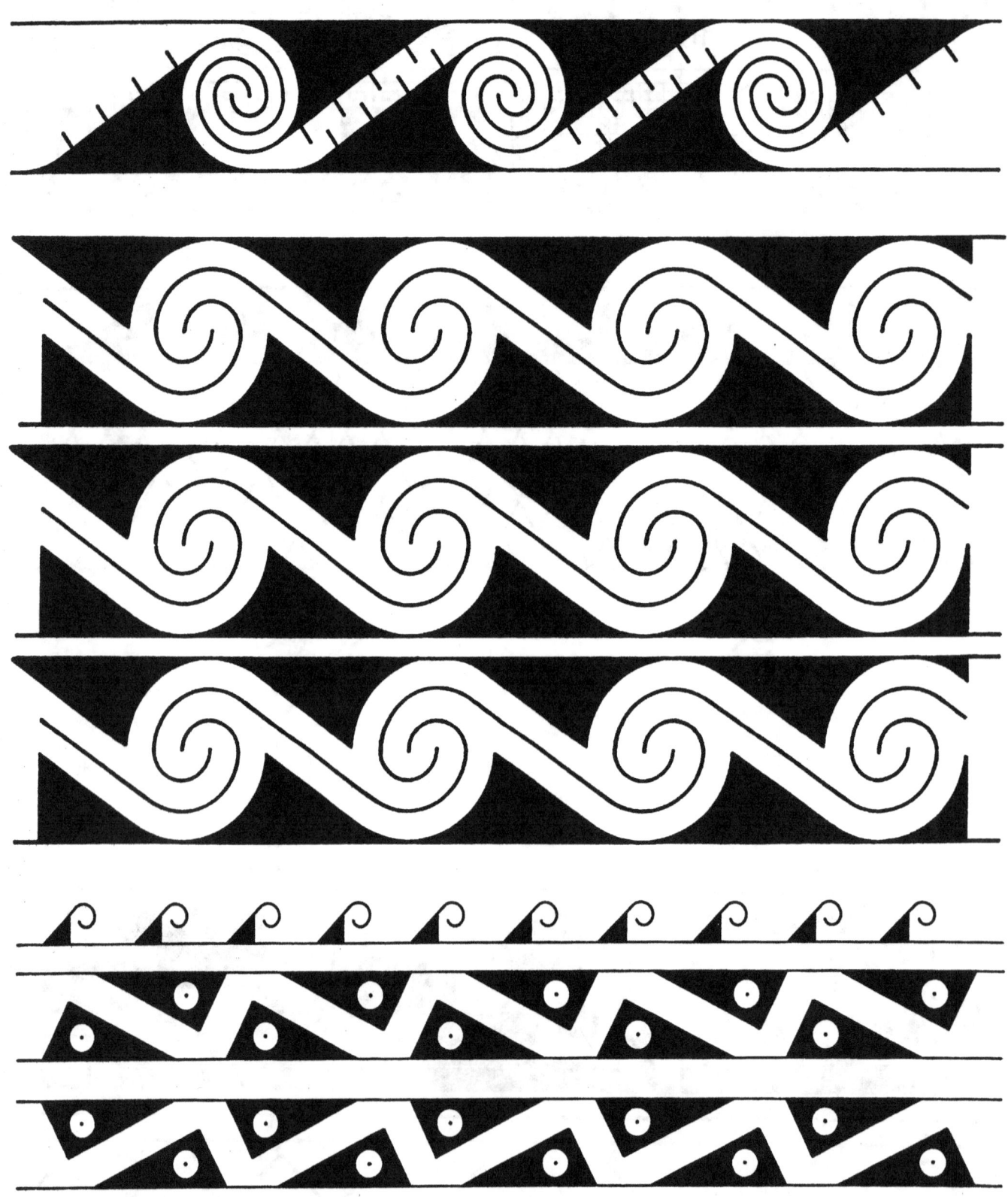

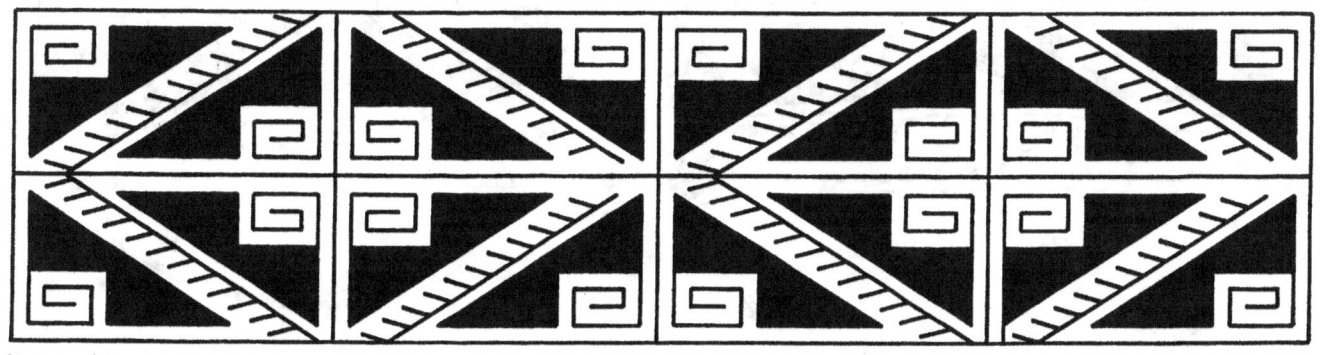

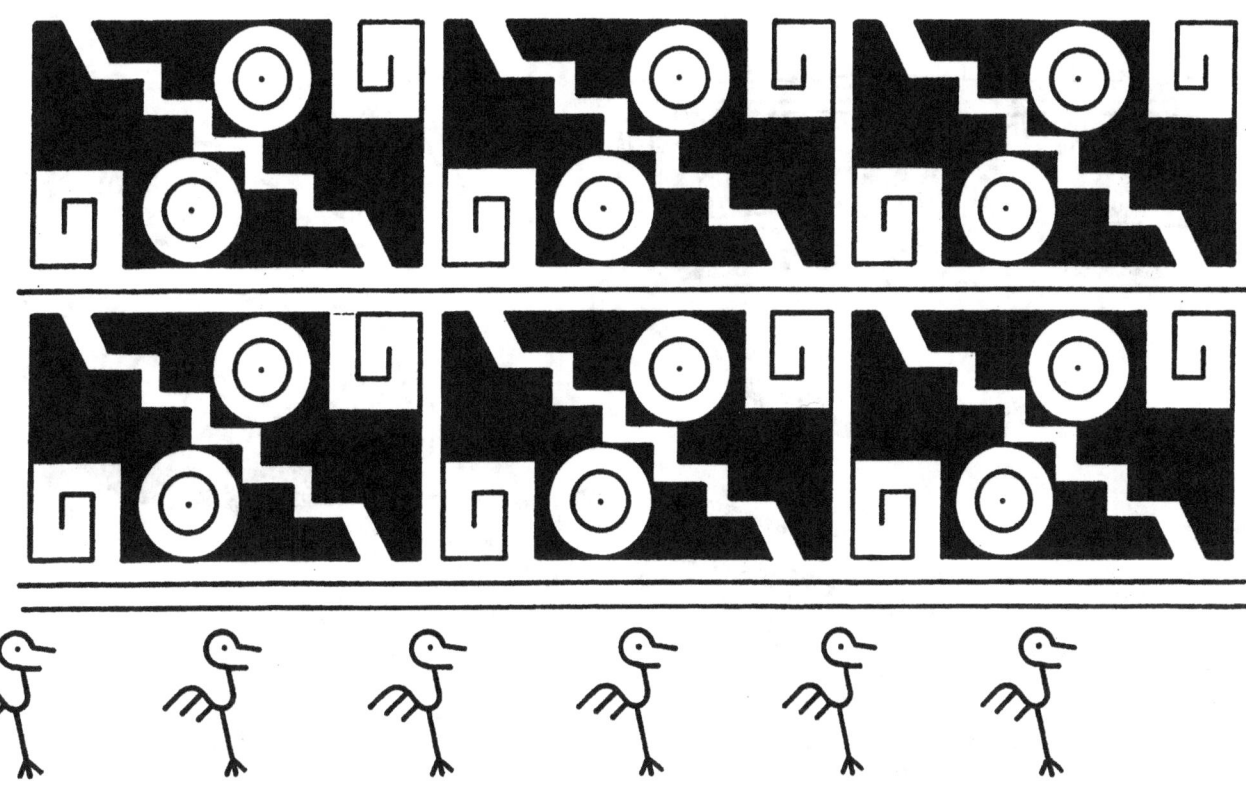

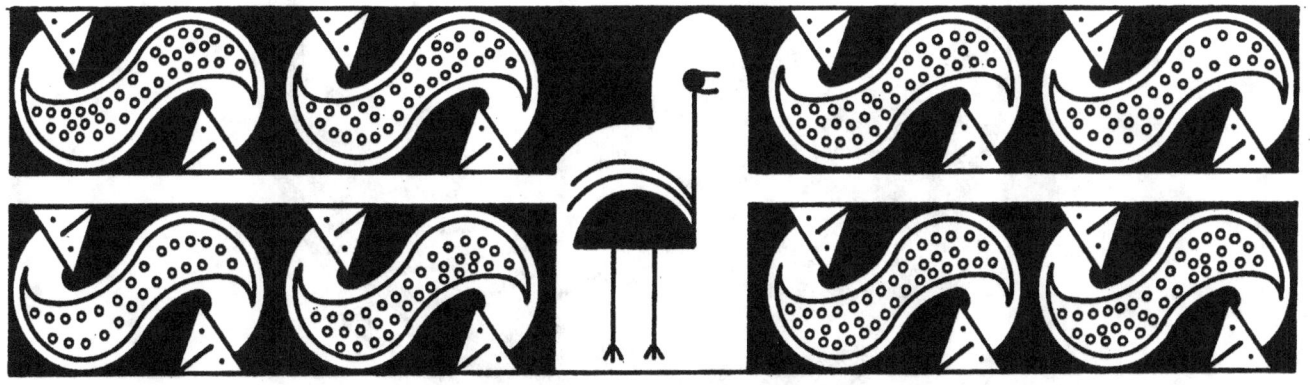

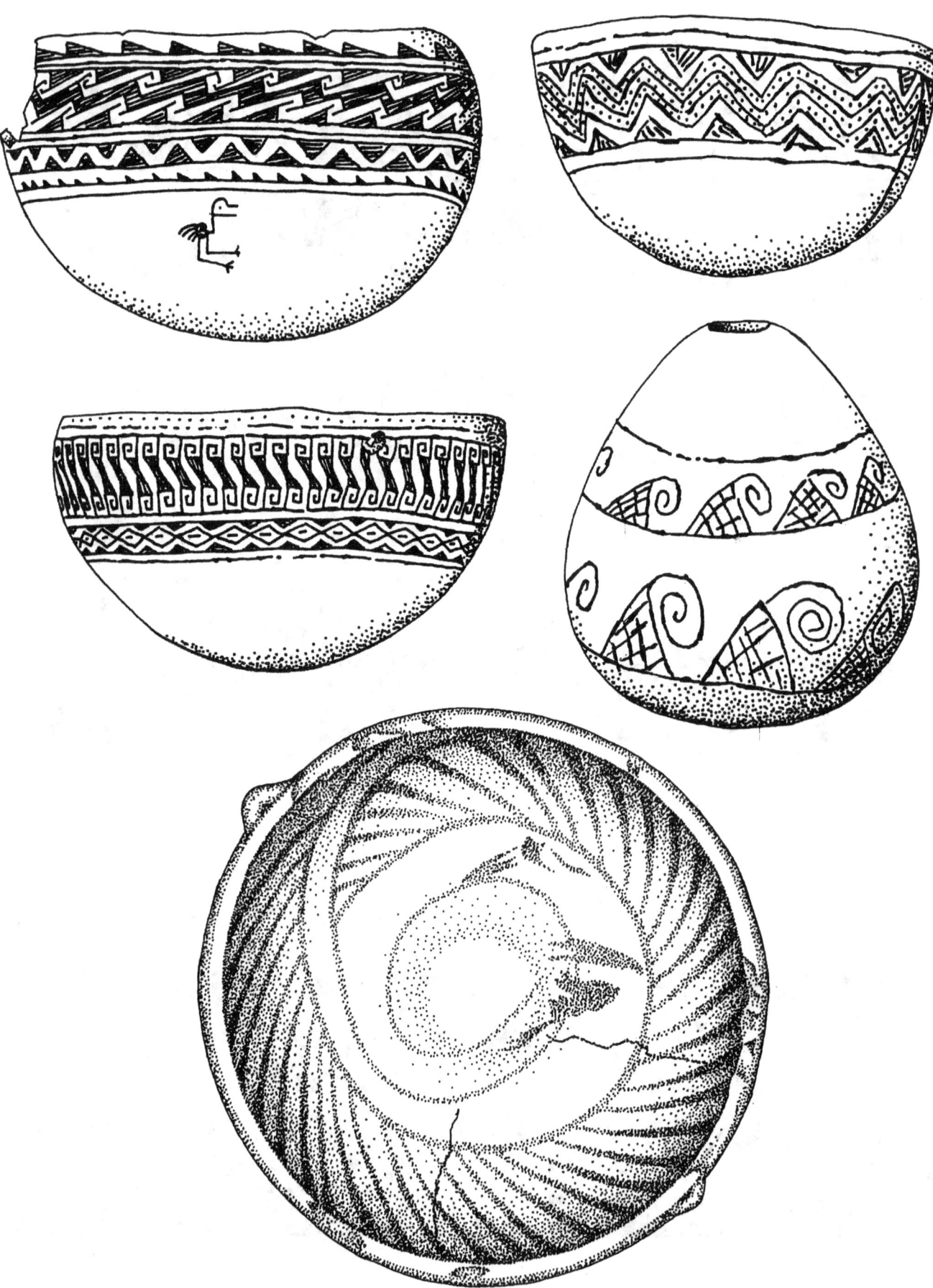

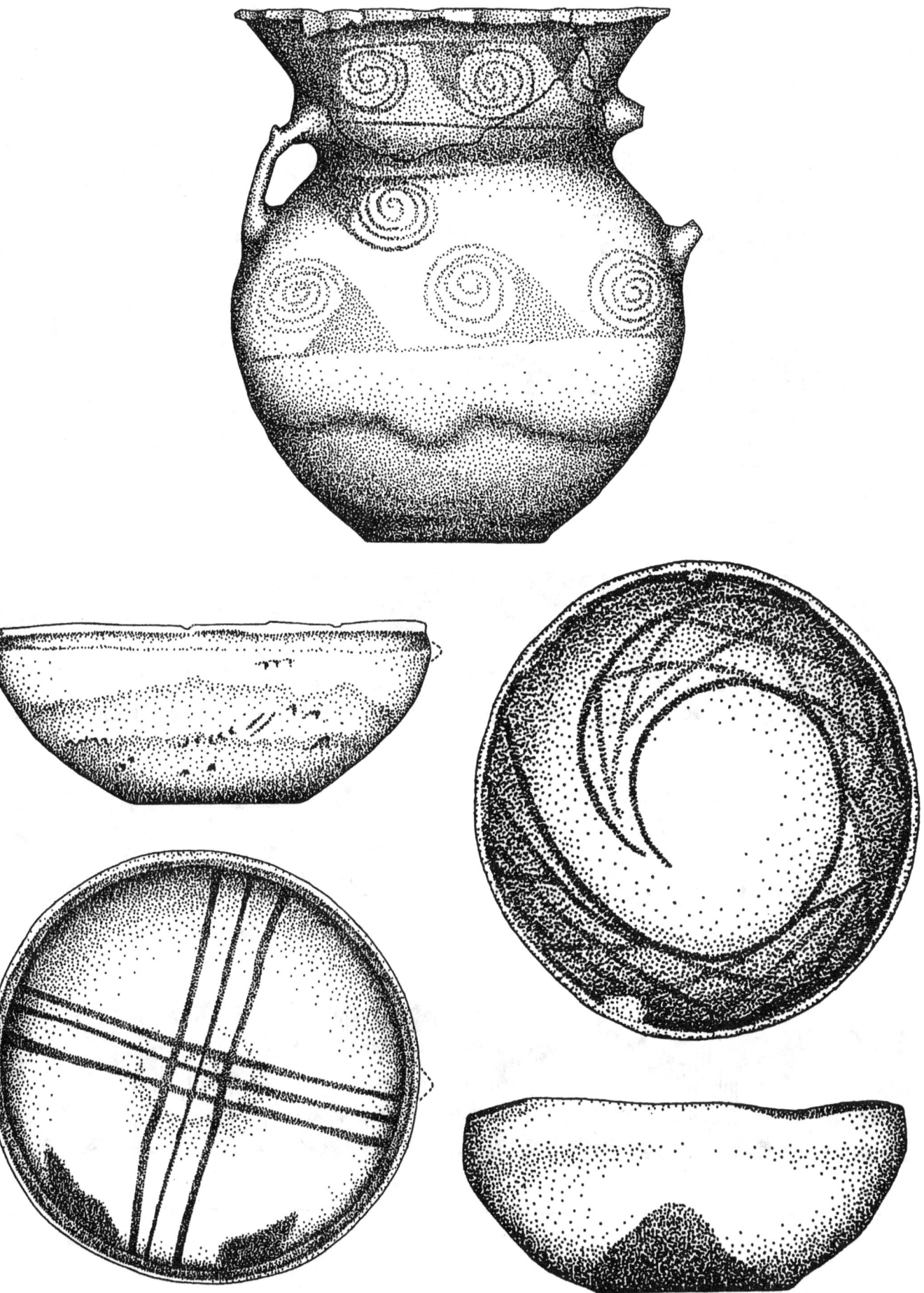

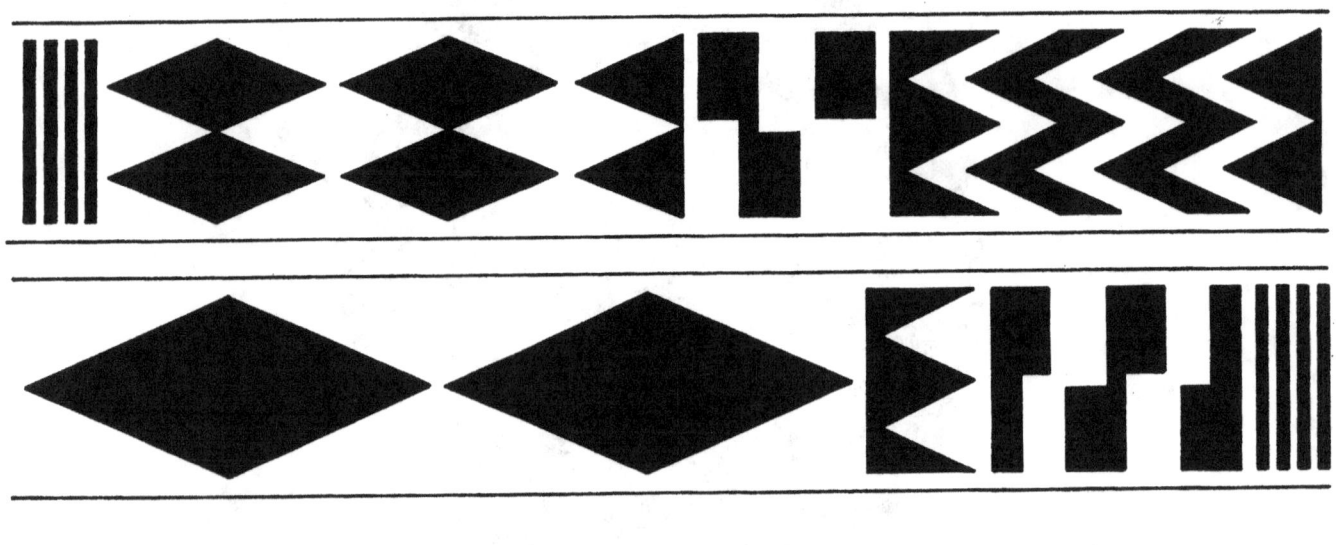

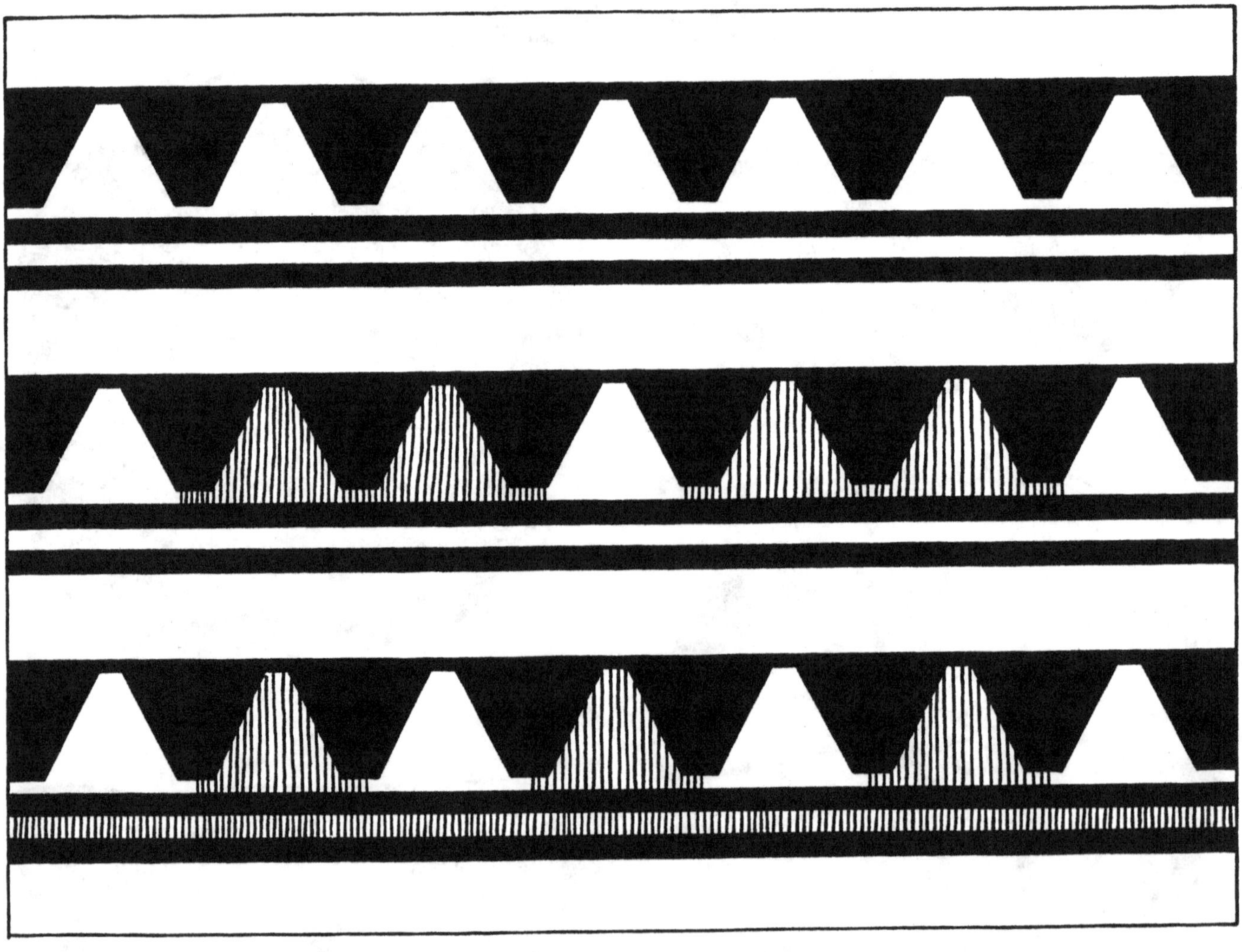

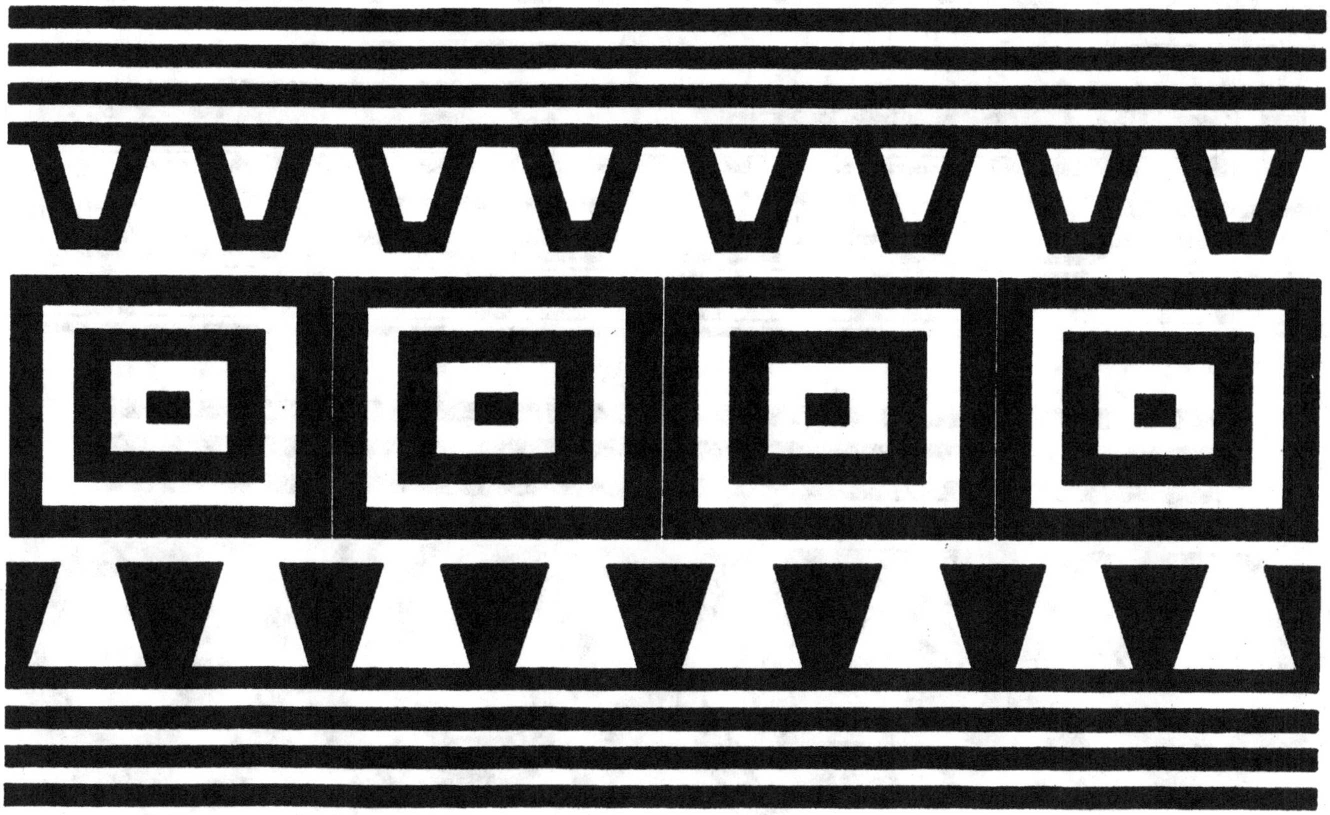

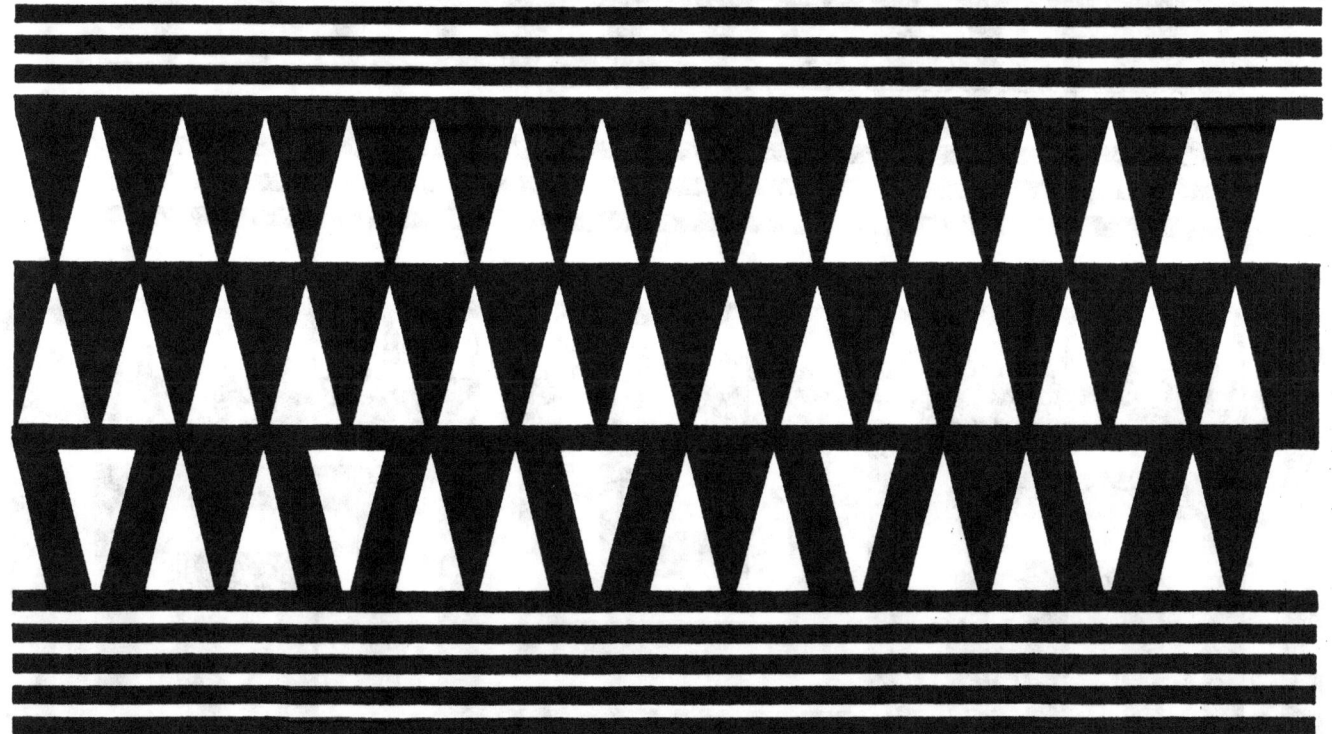

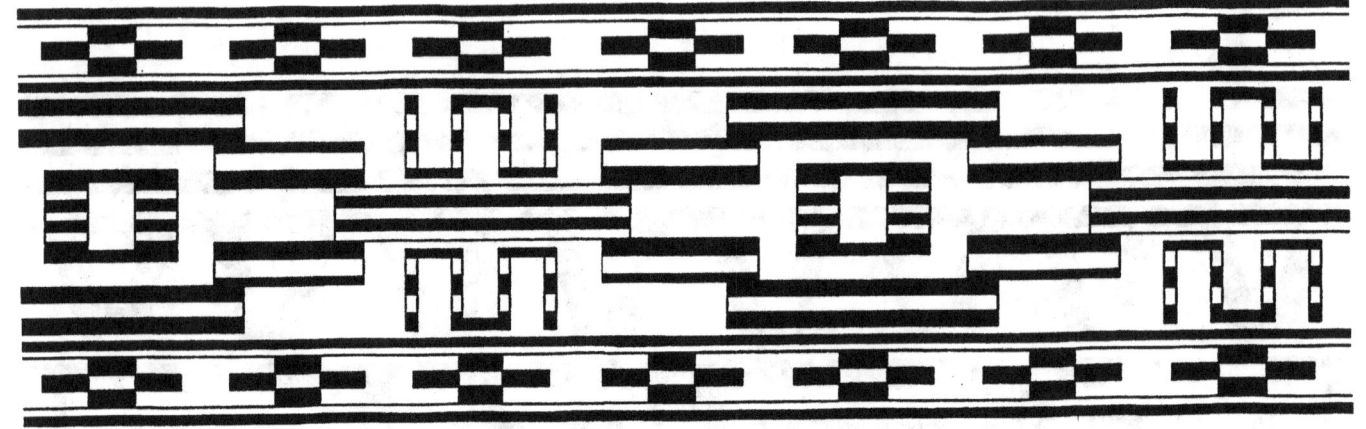

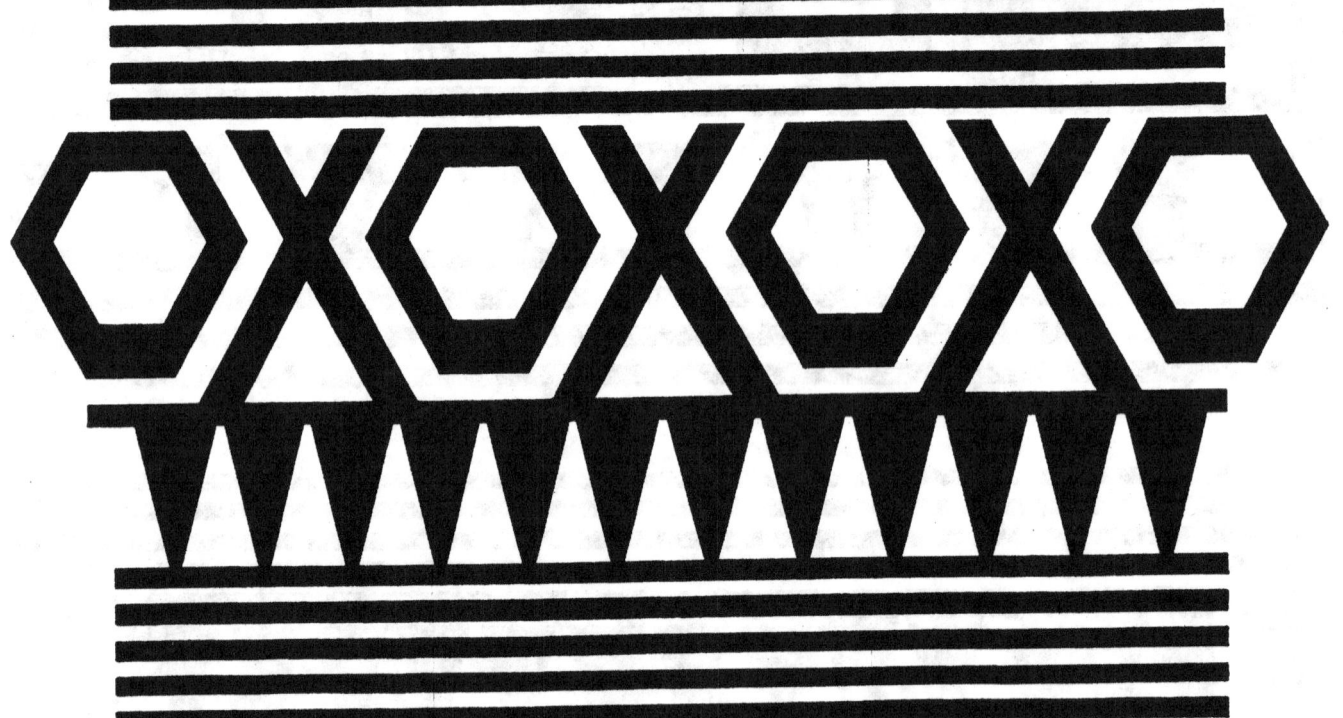

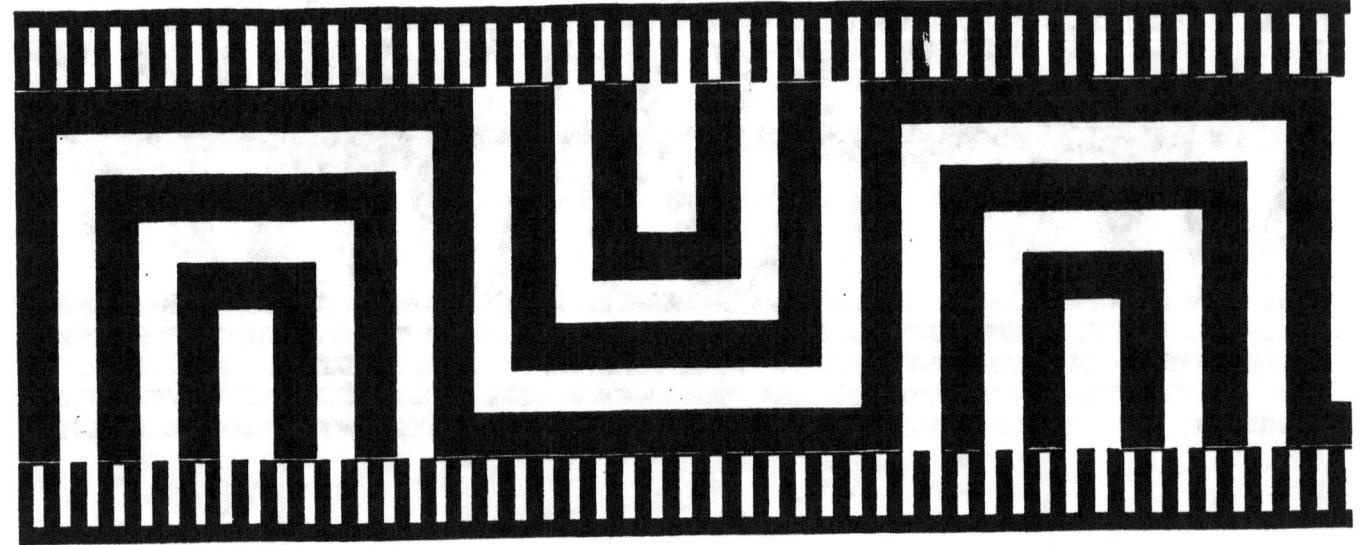

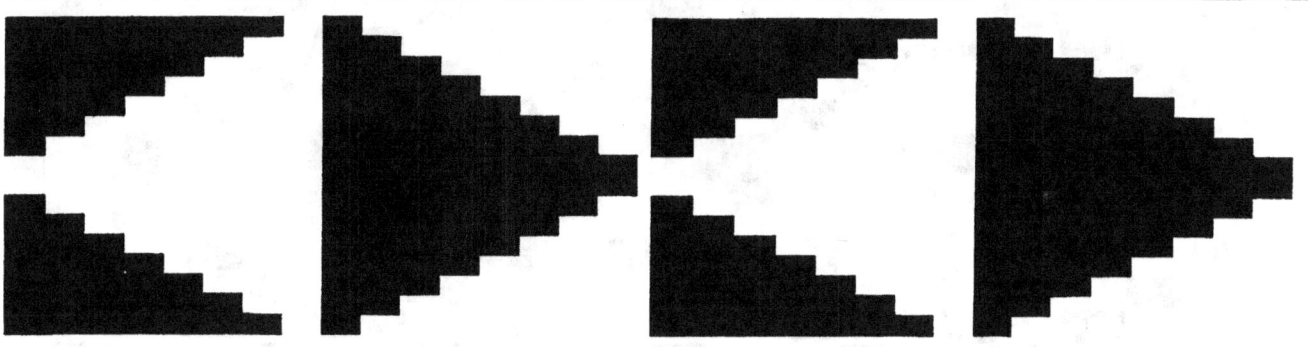

Corner for the design above (created by the author)

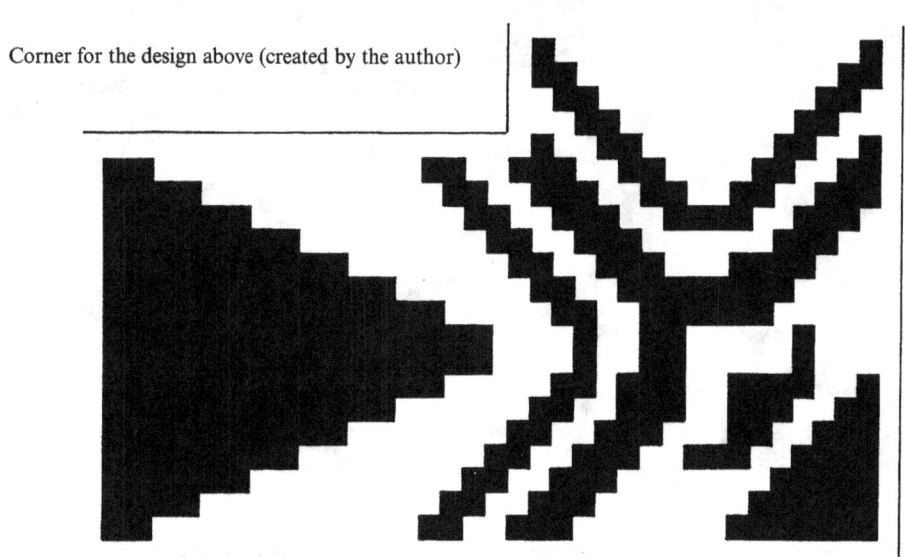

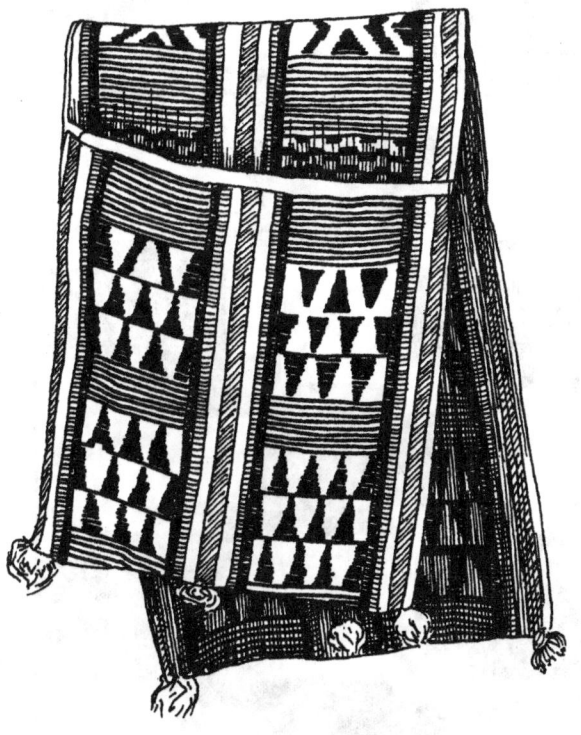

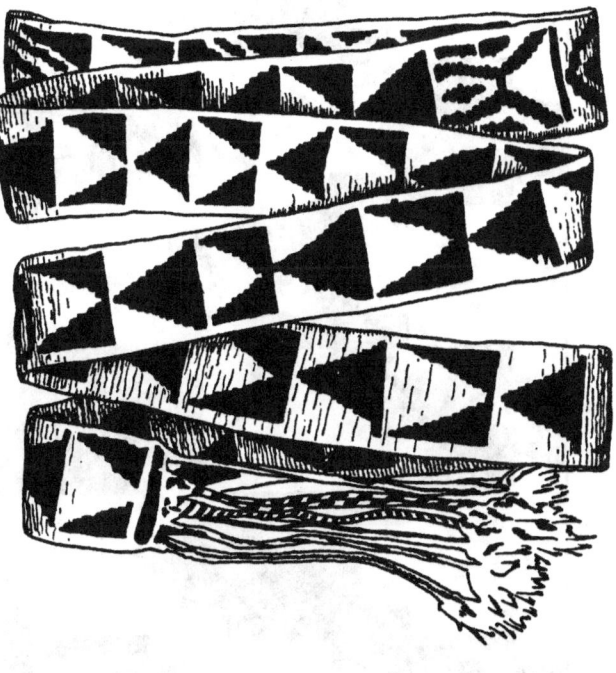

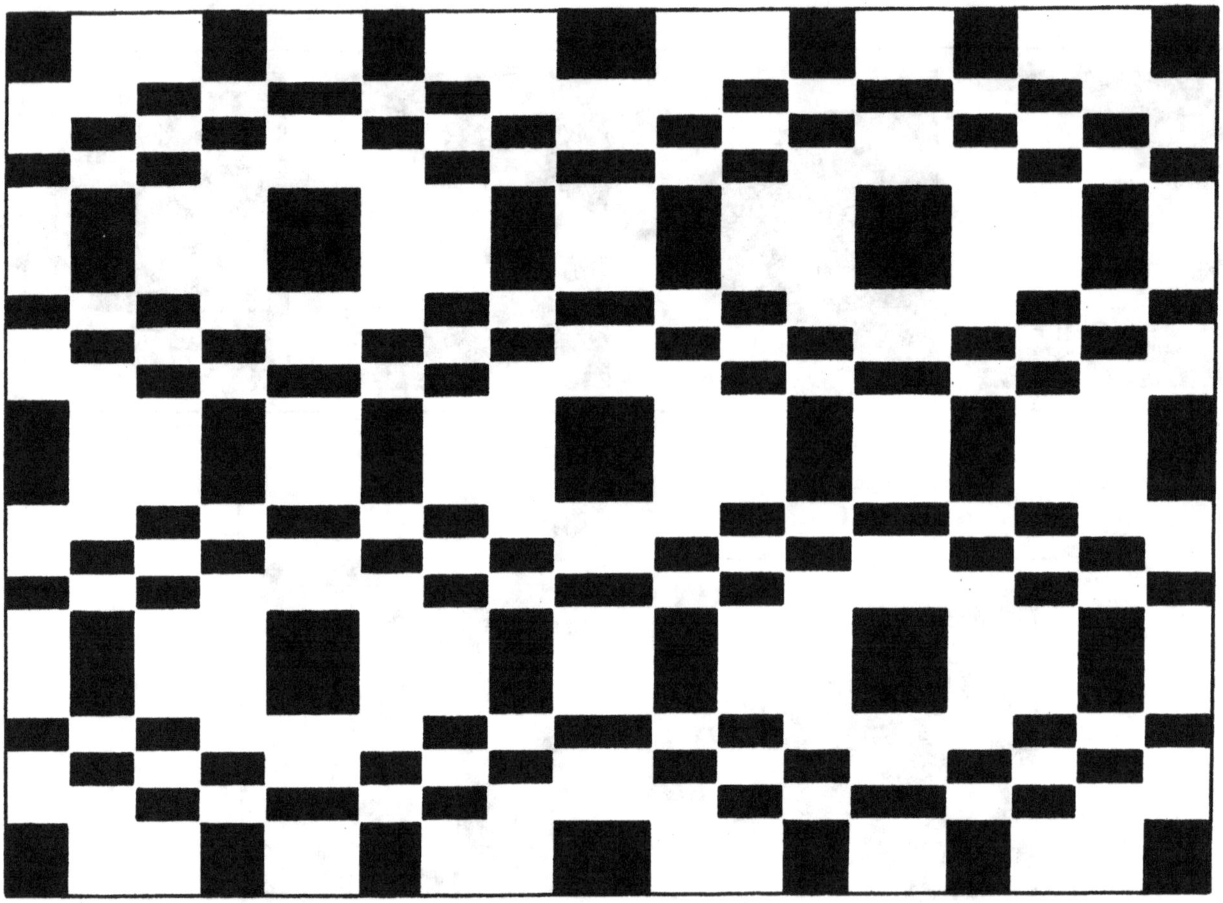

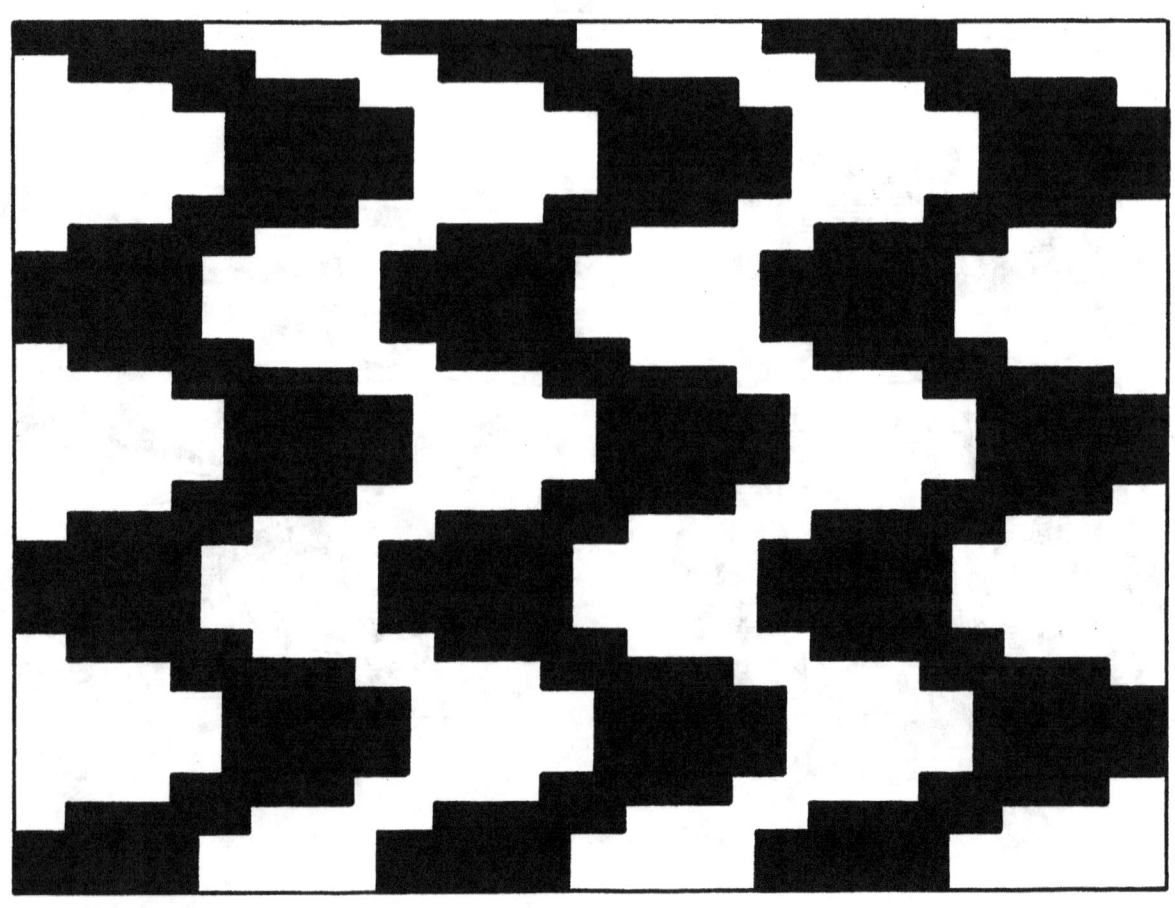

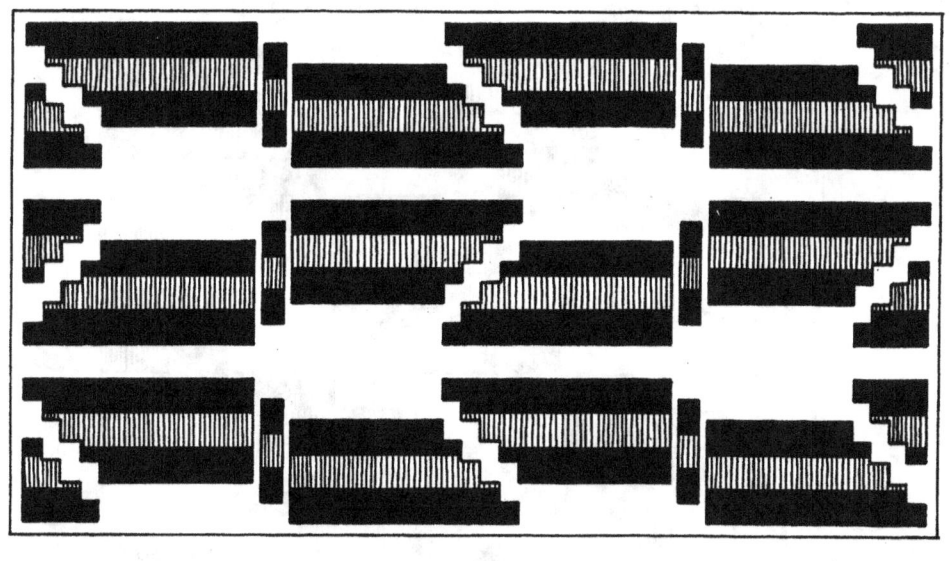

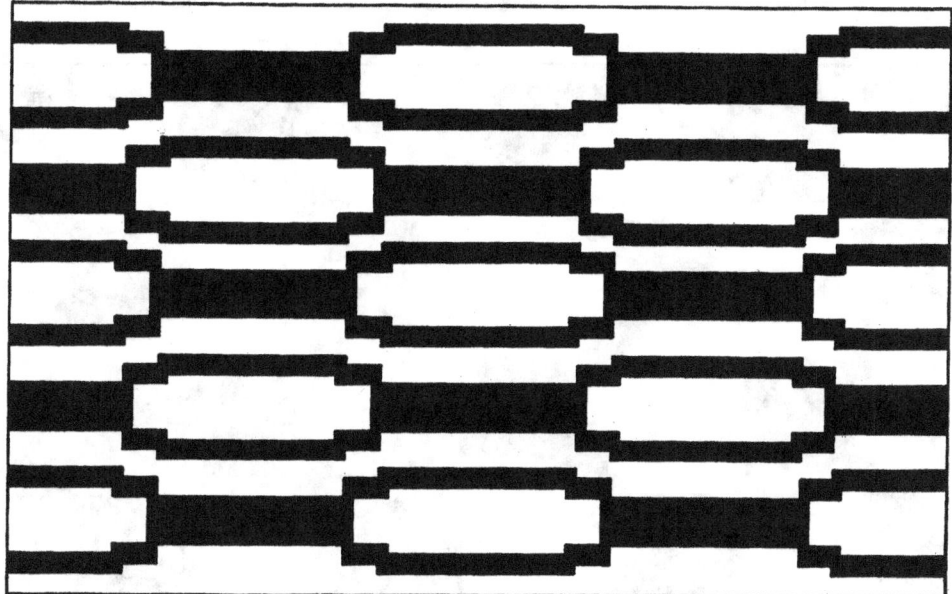

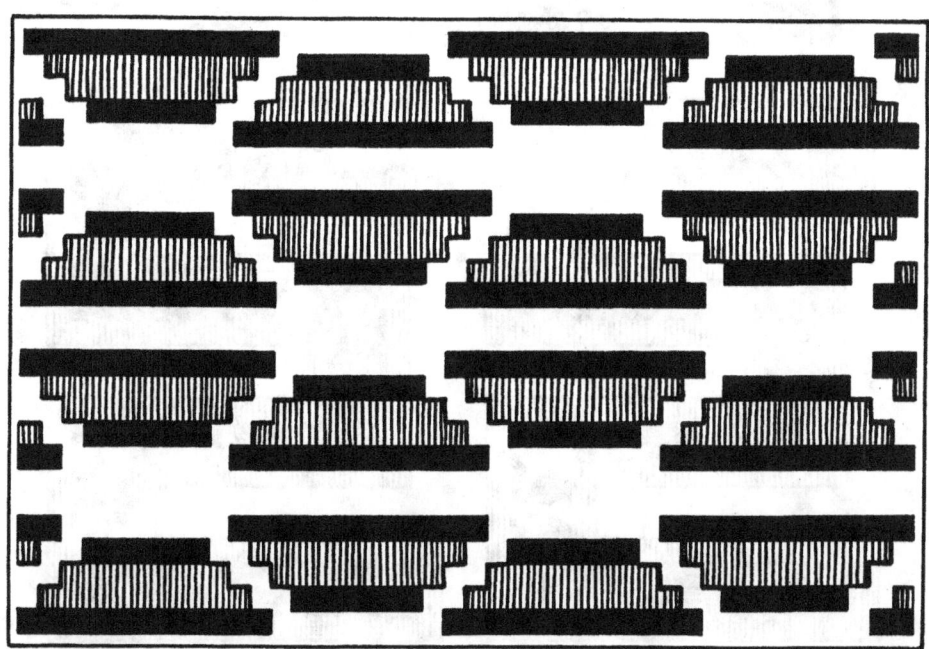

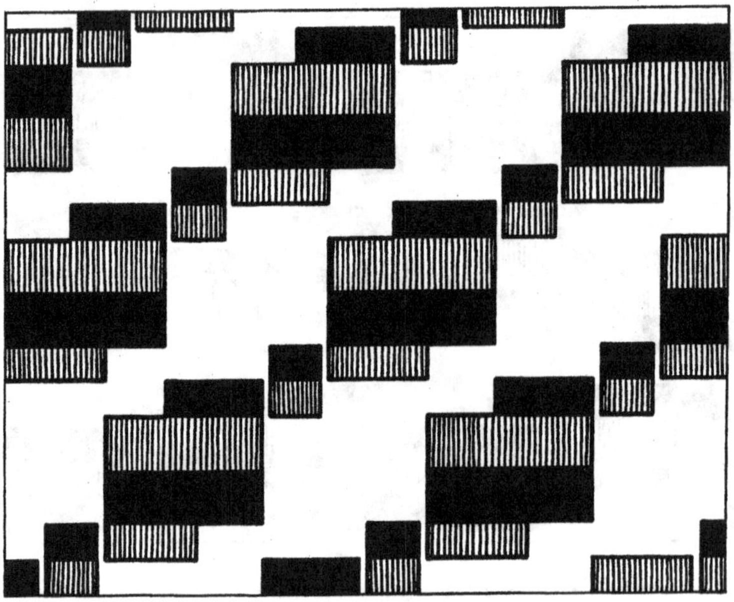

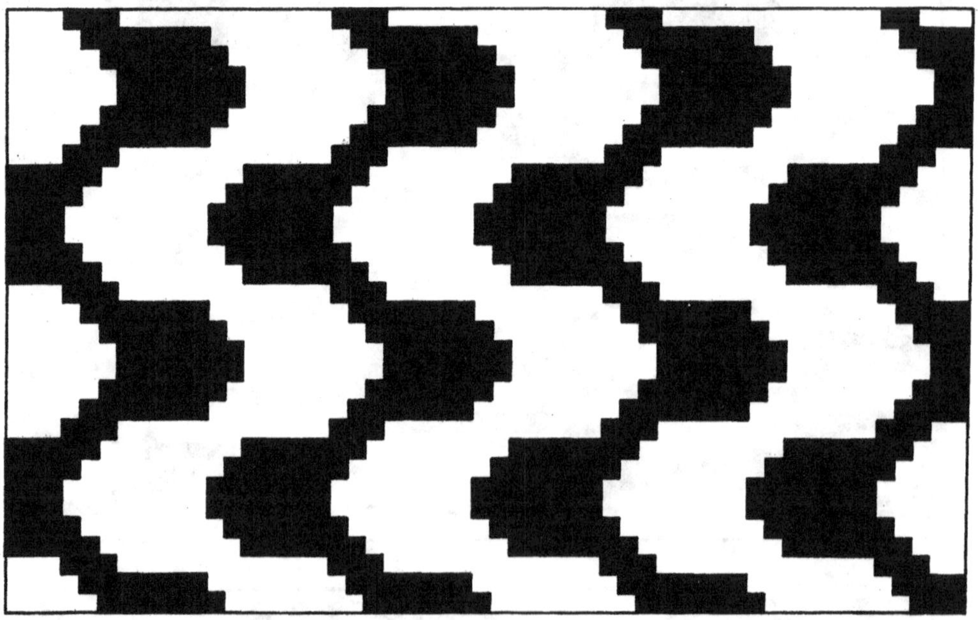

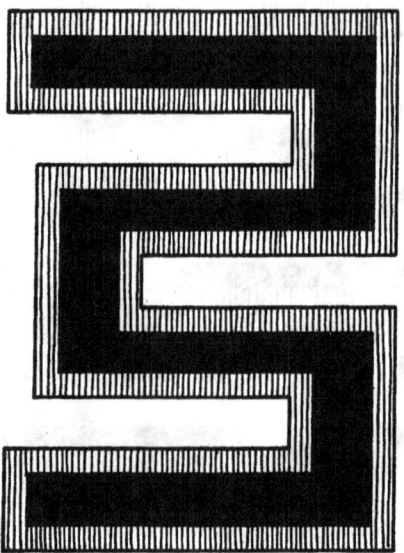
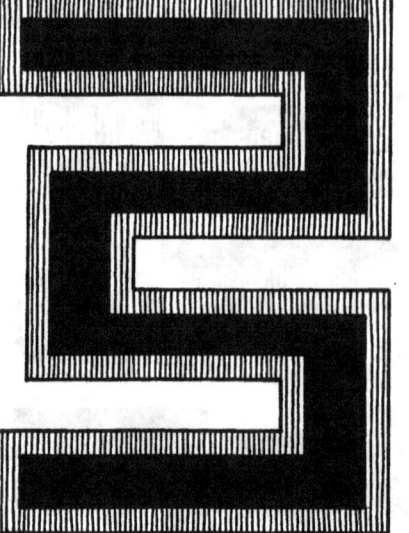

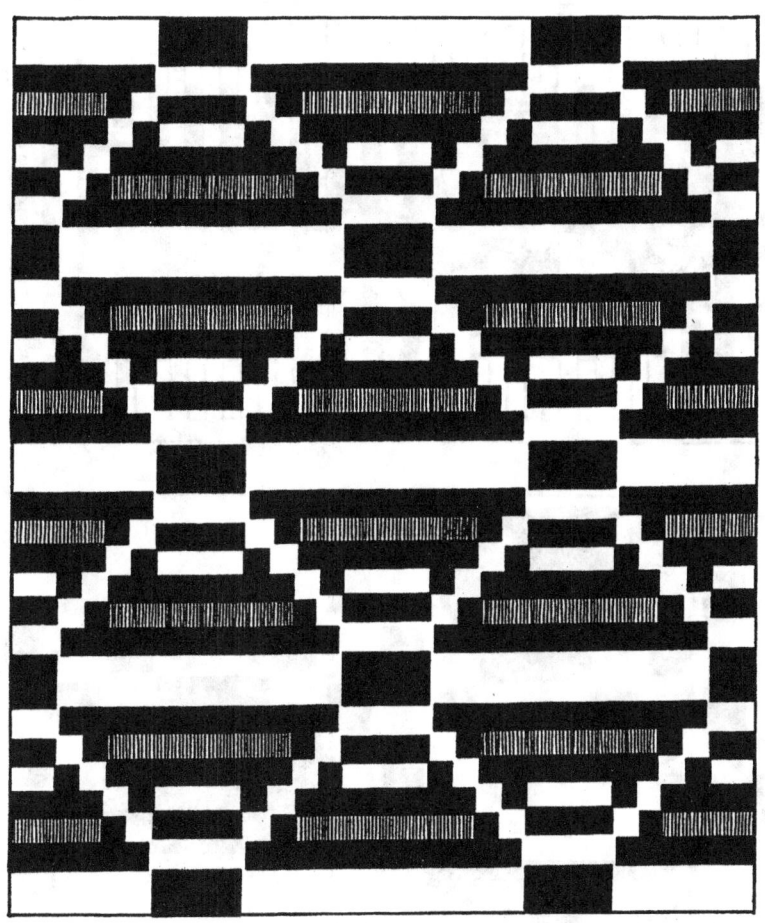

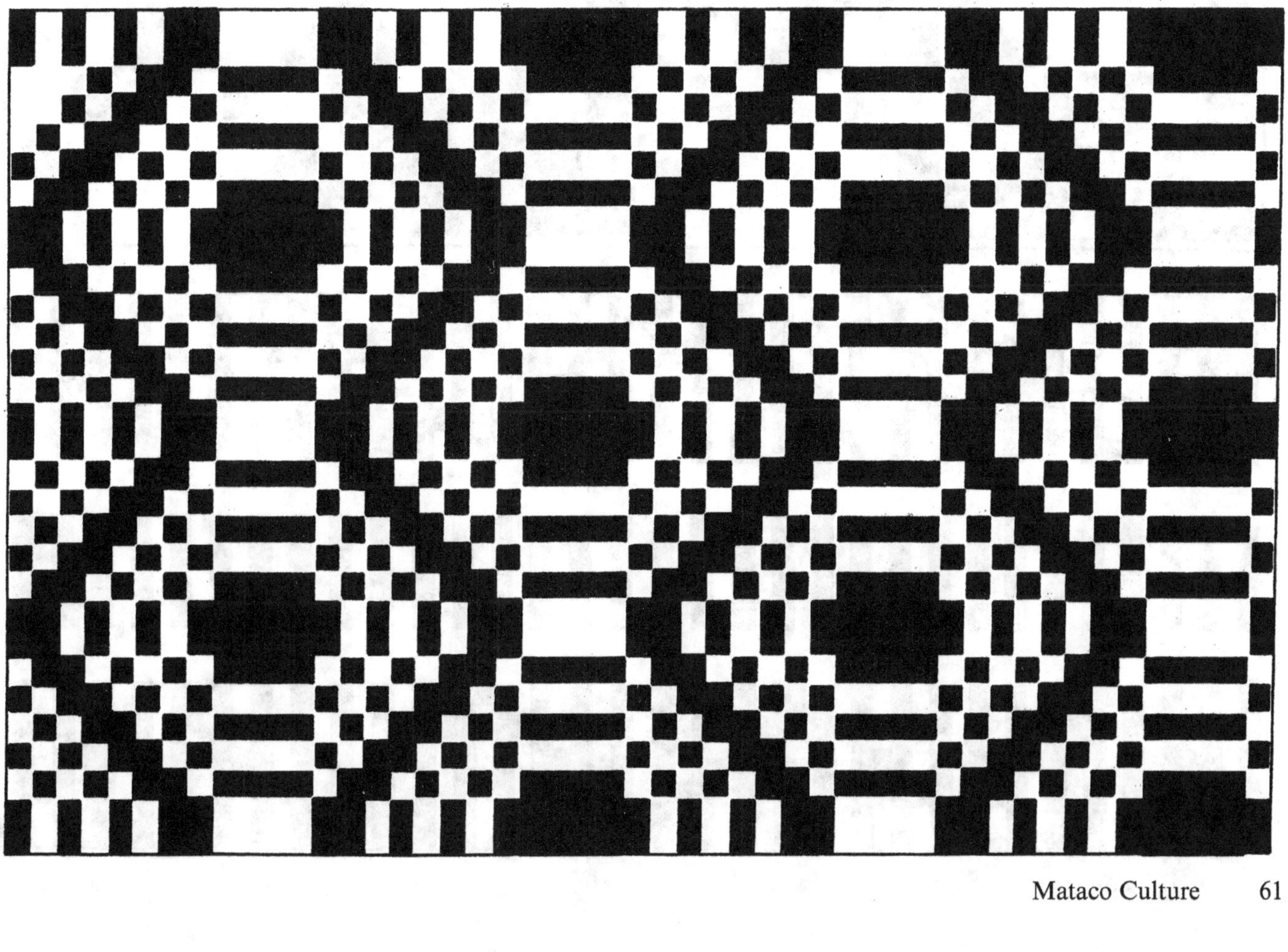

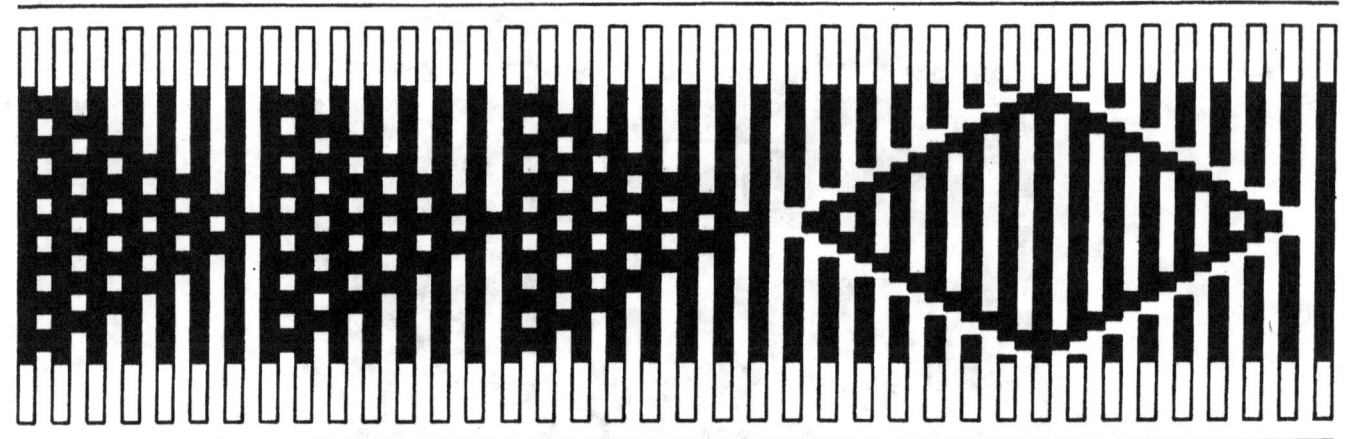

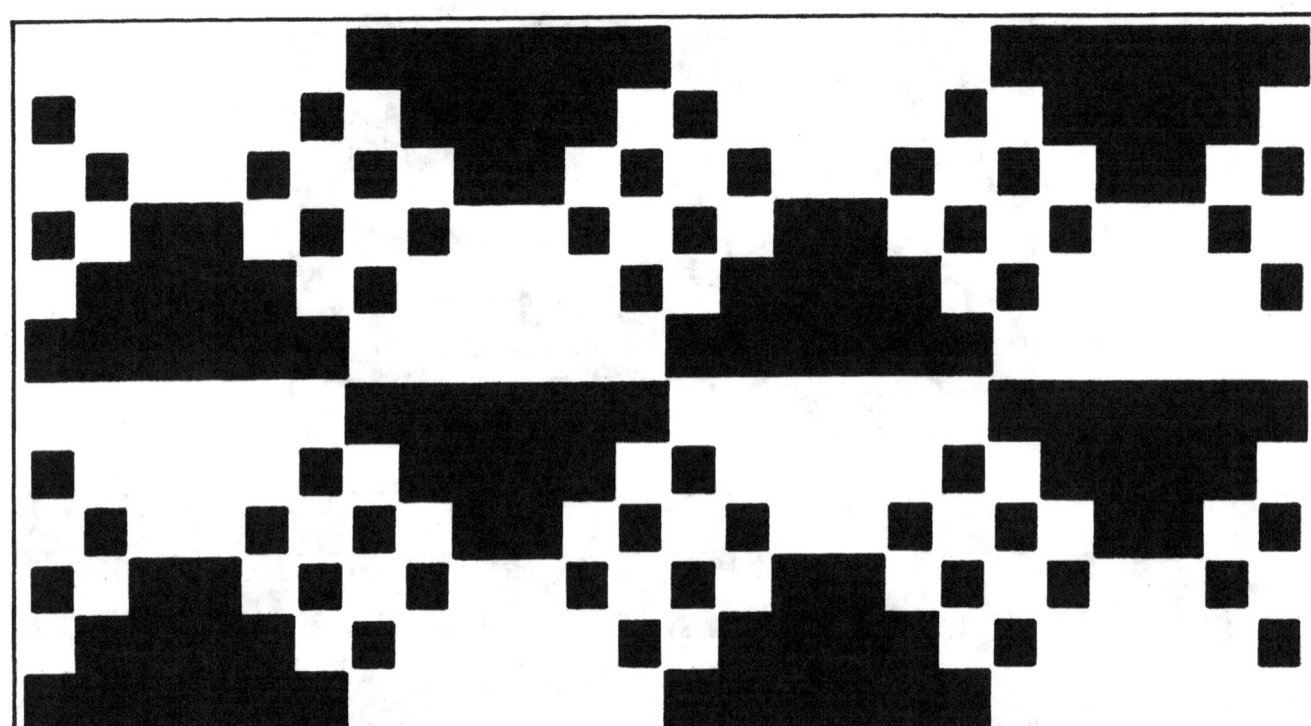

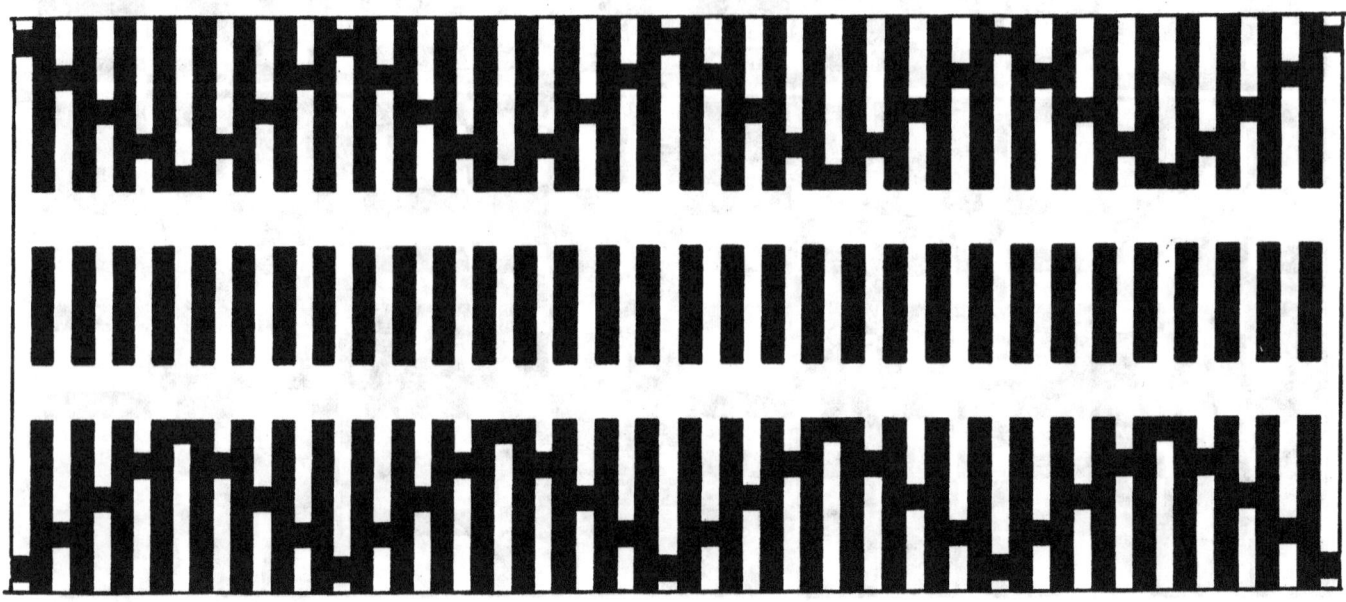

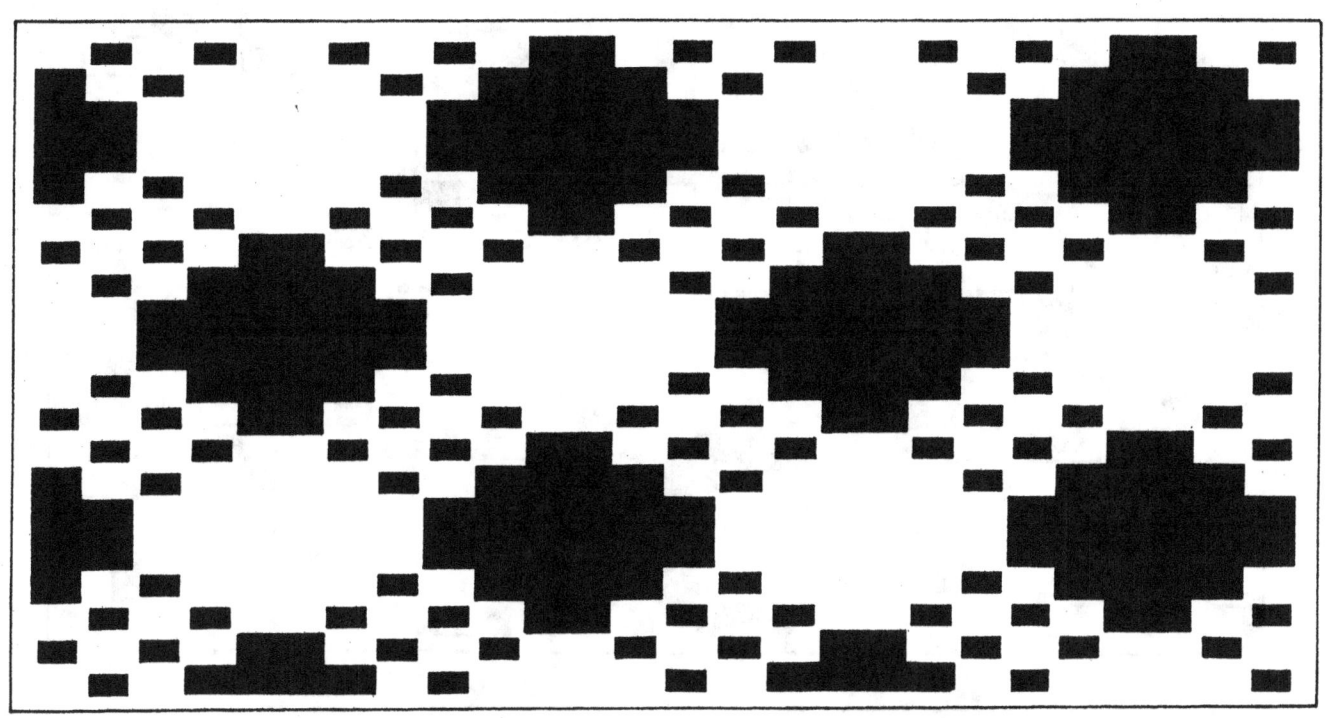

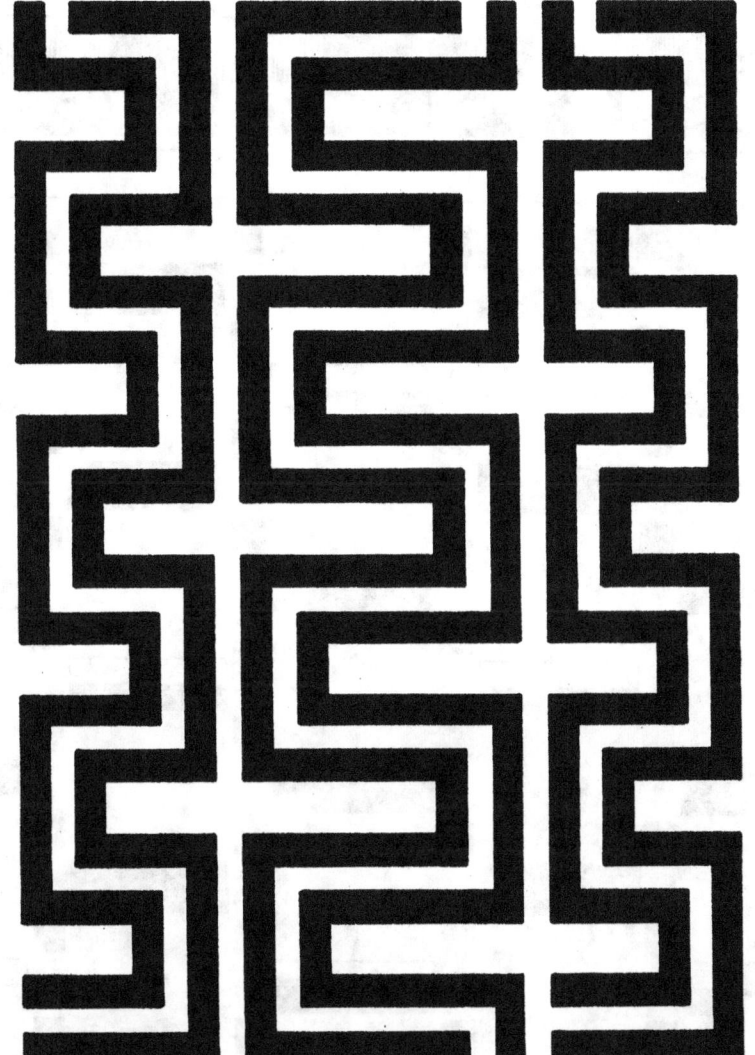

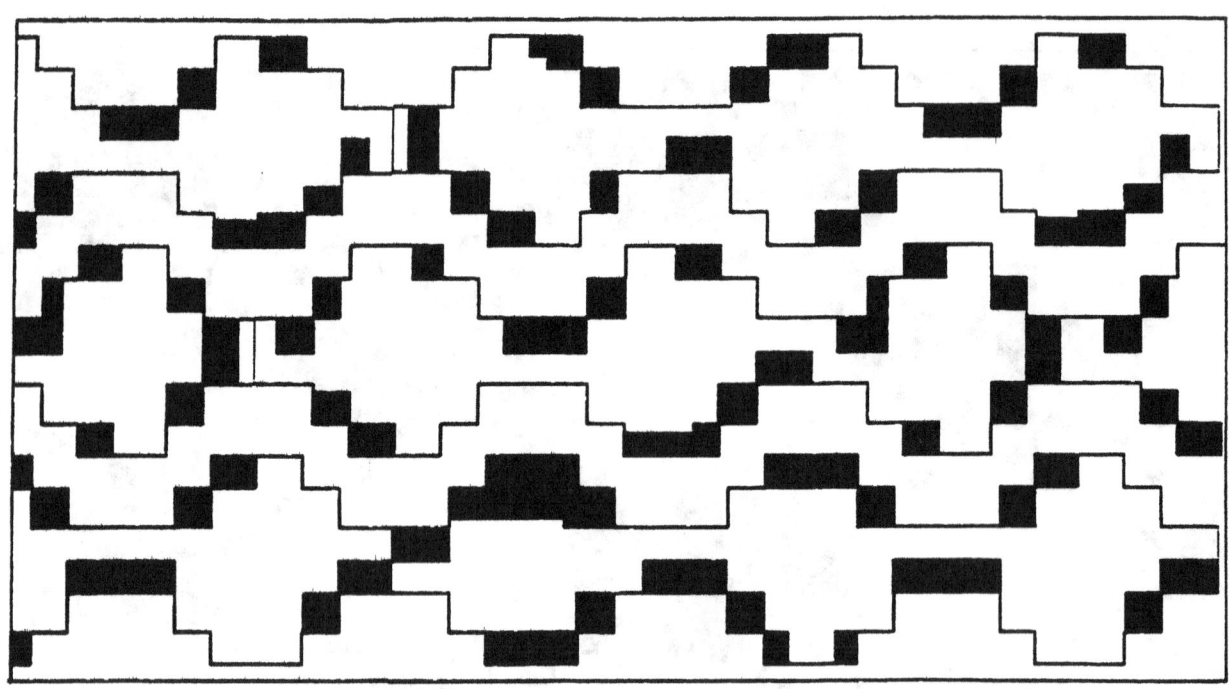

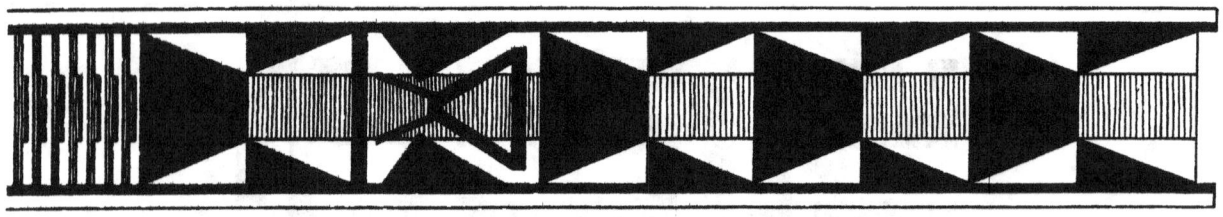

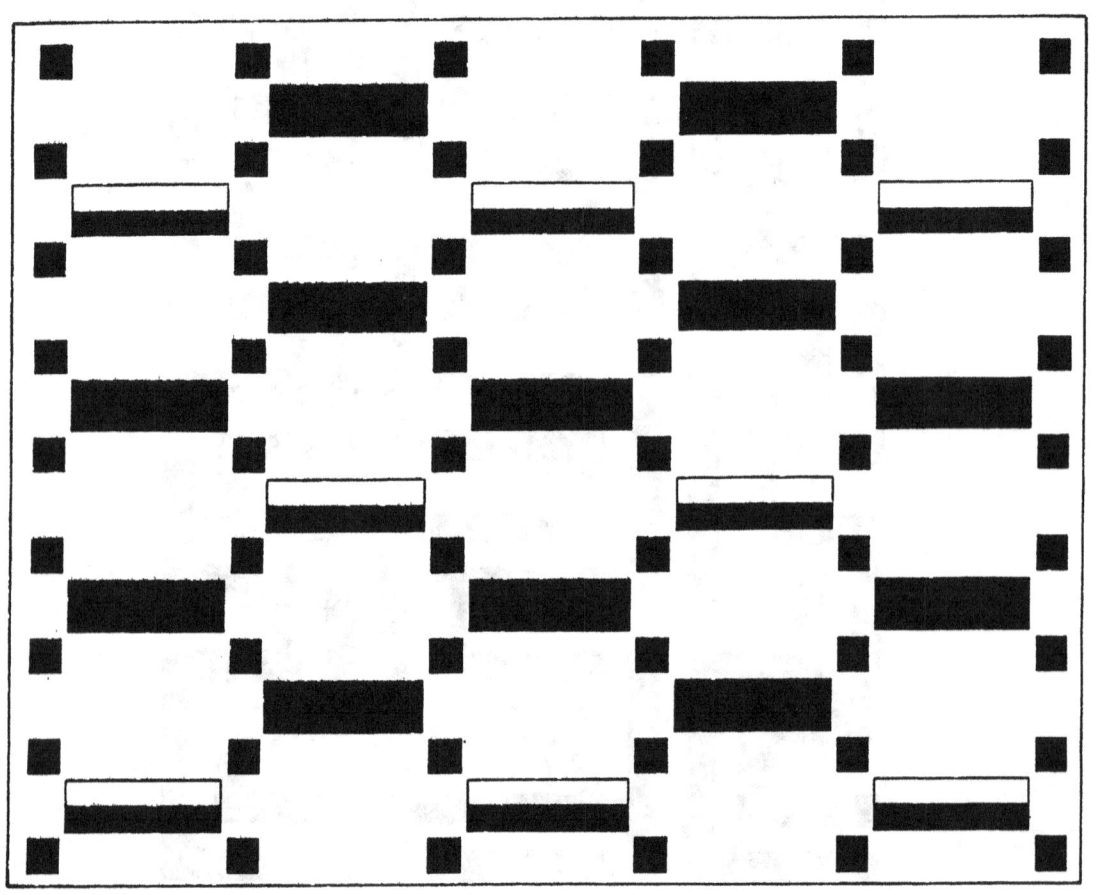

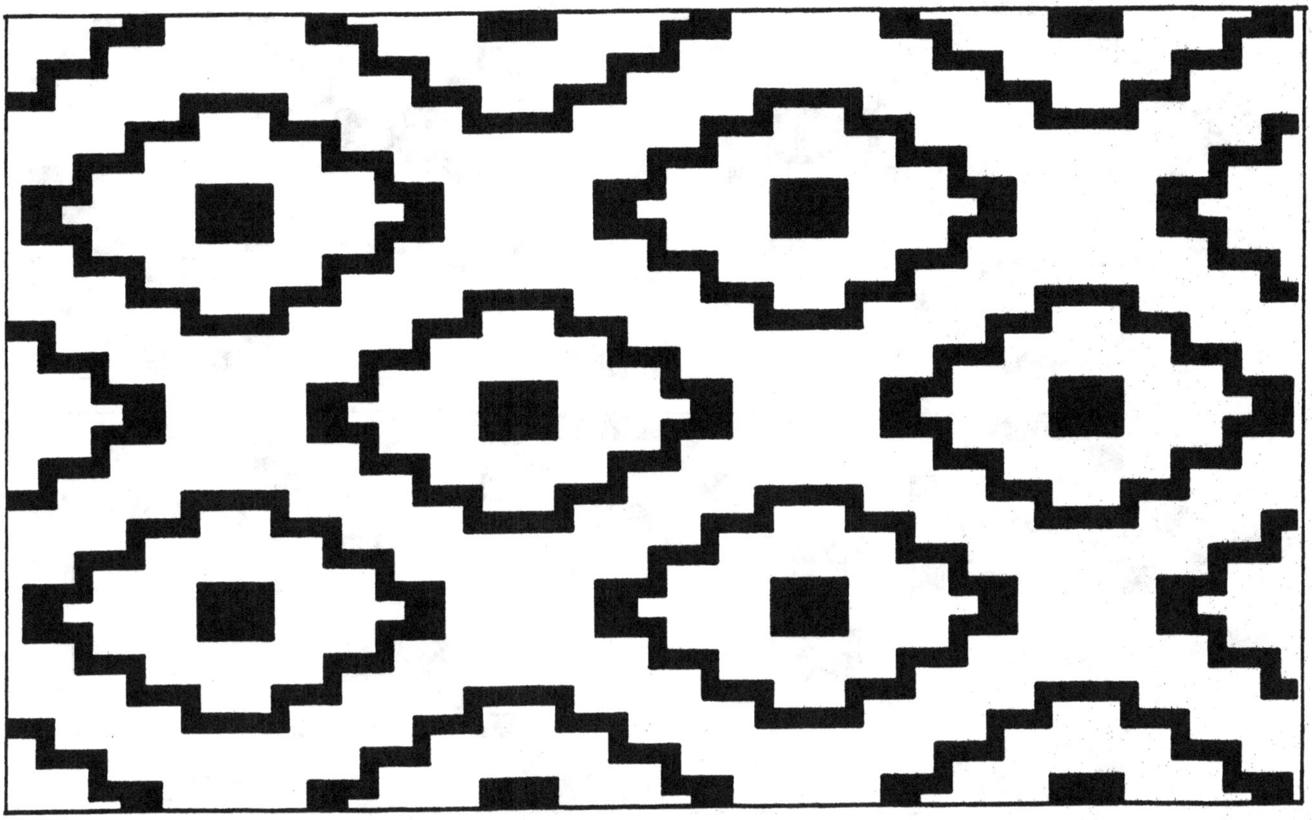

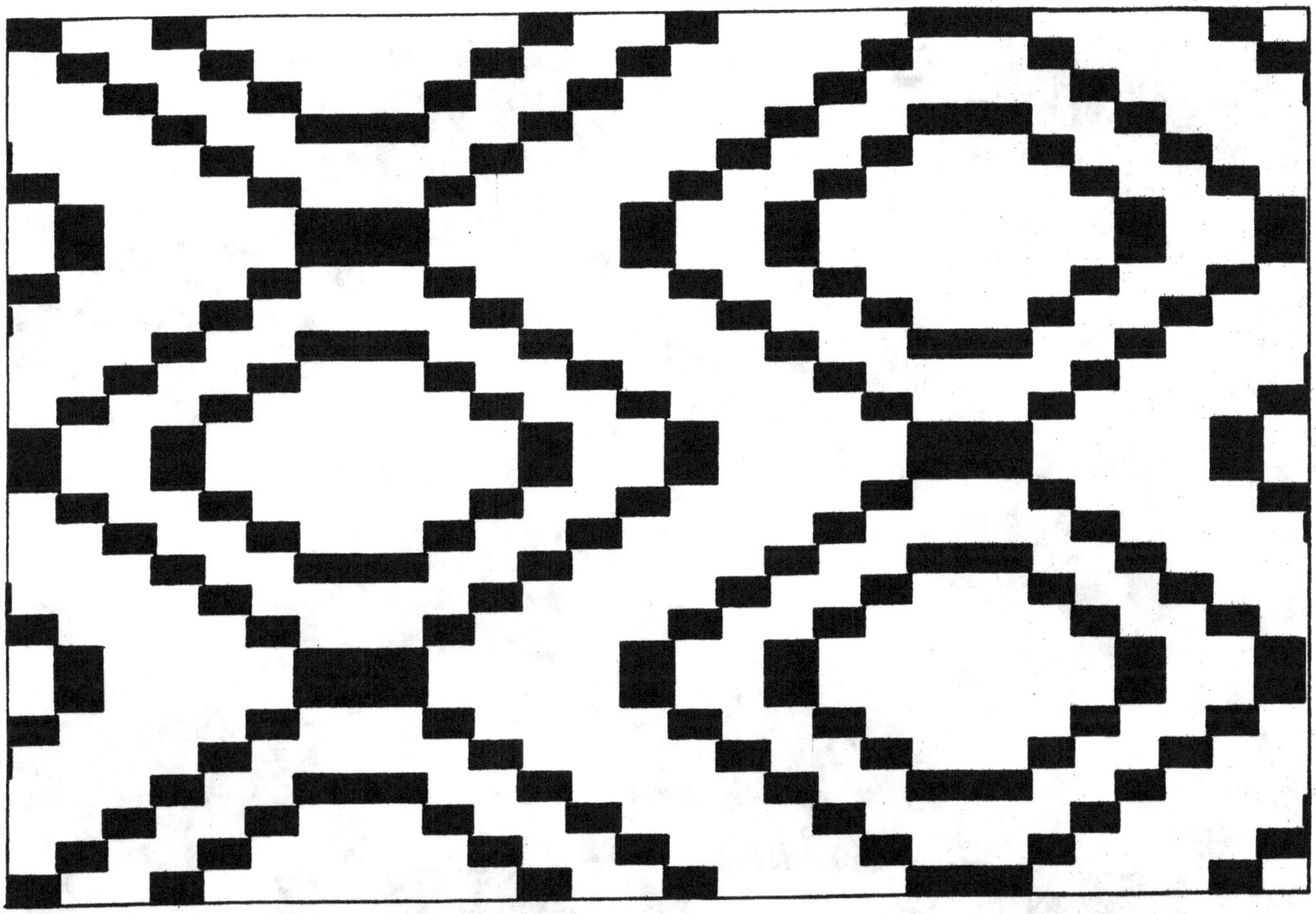

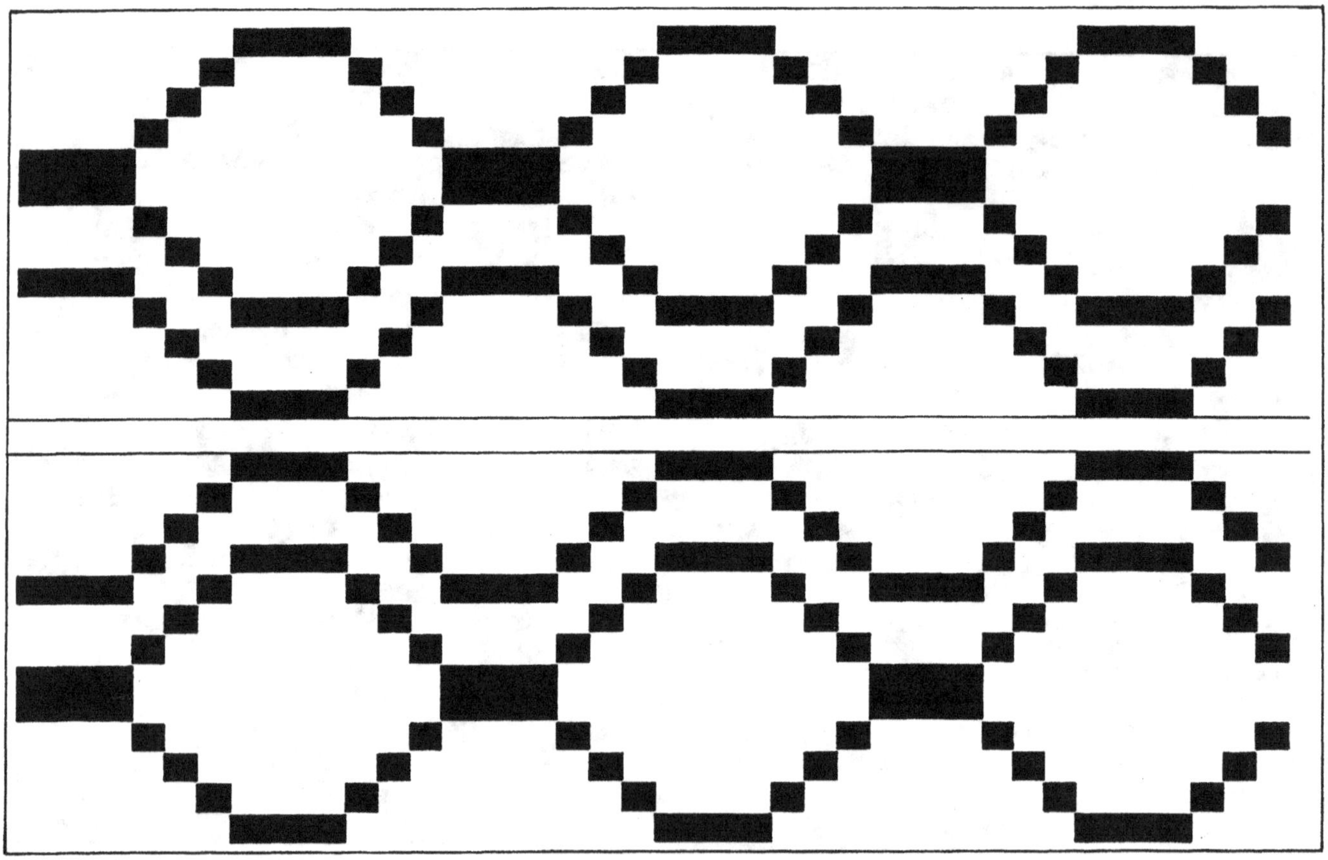

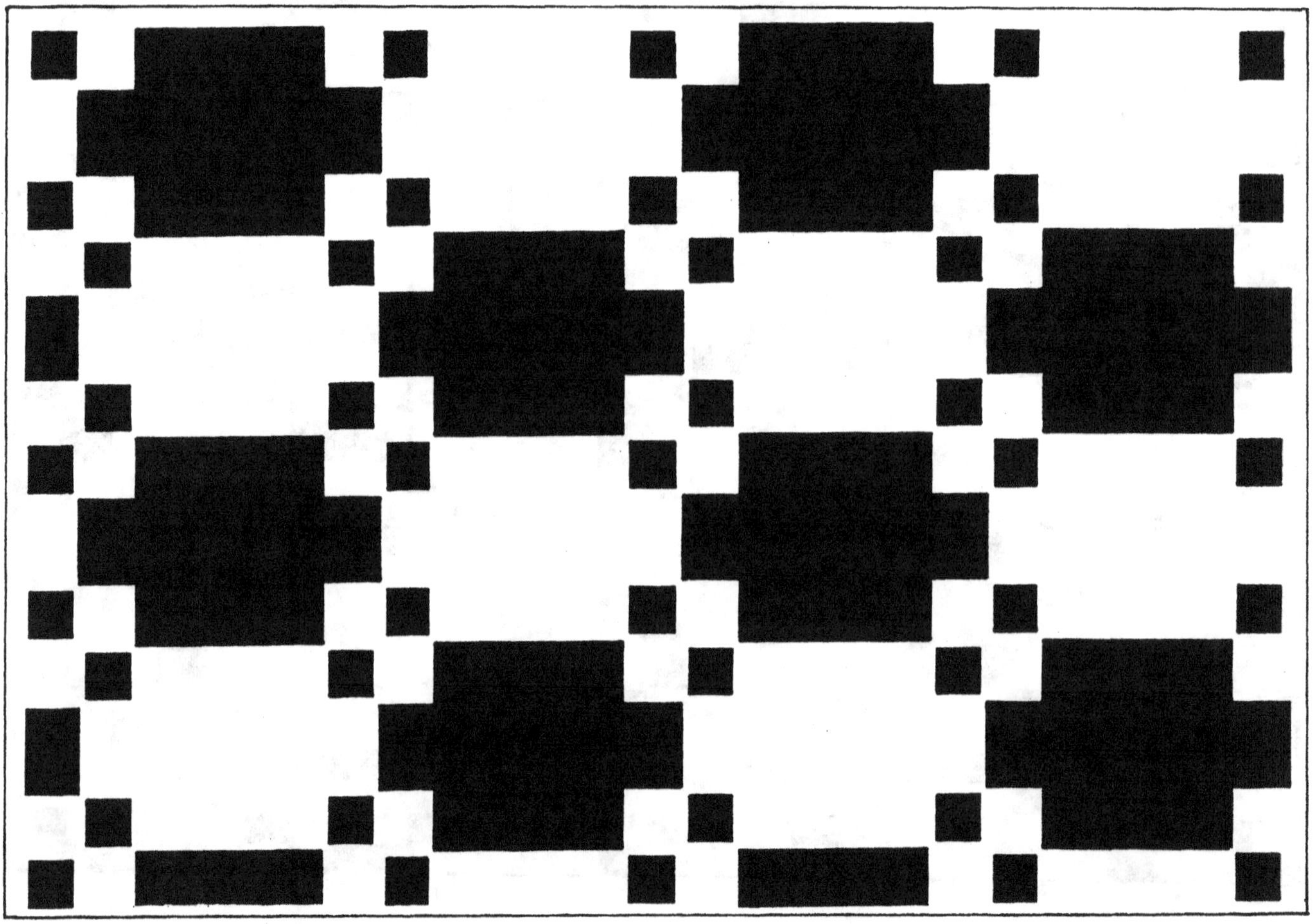

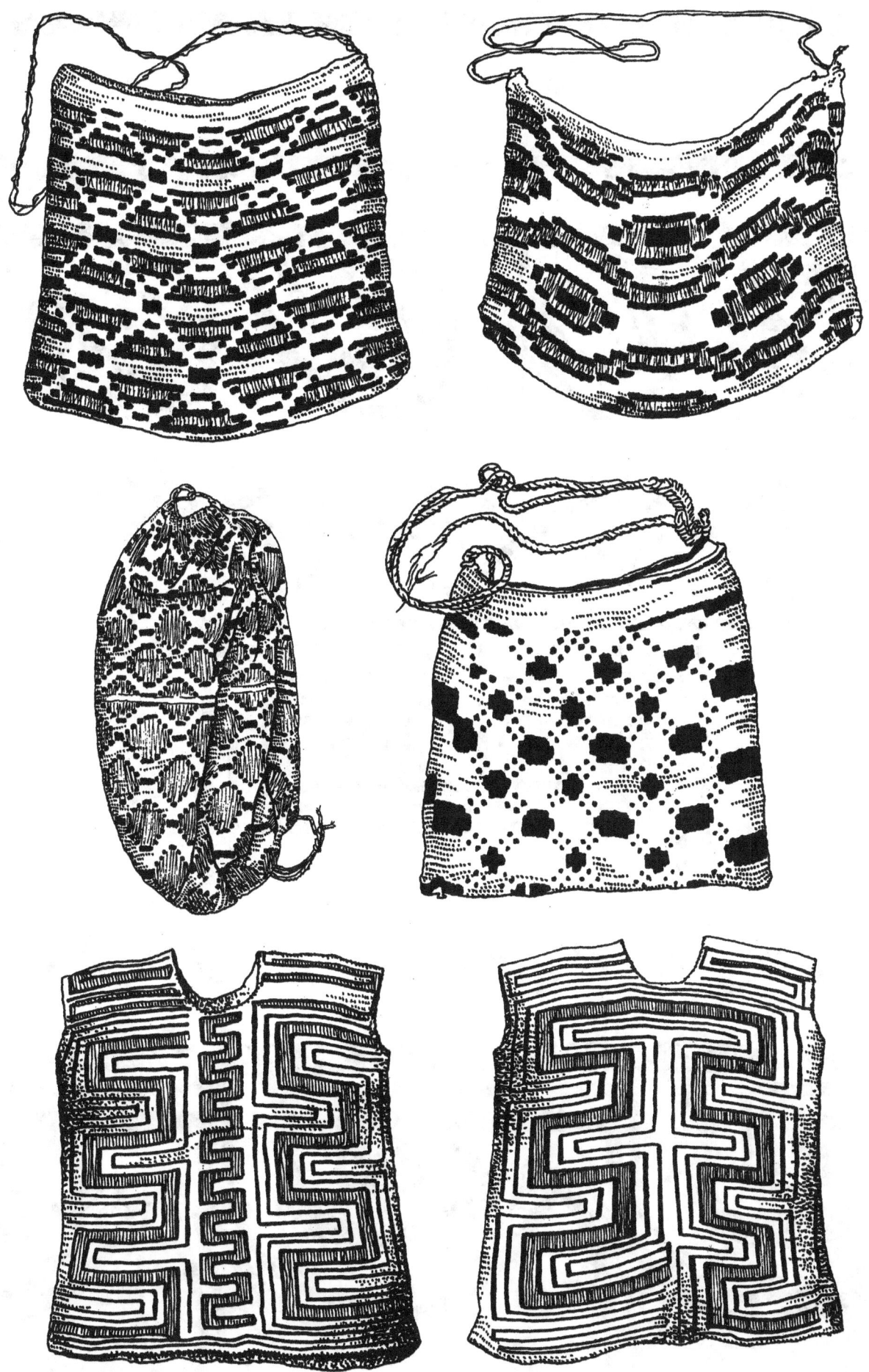

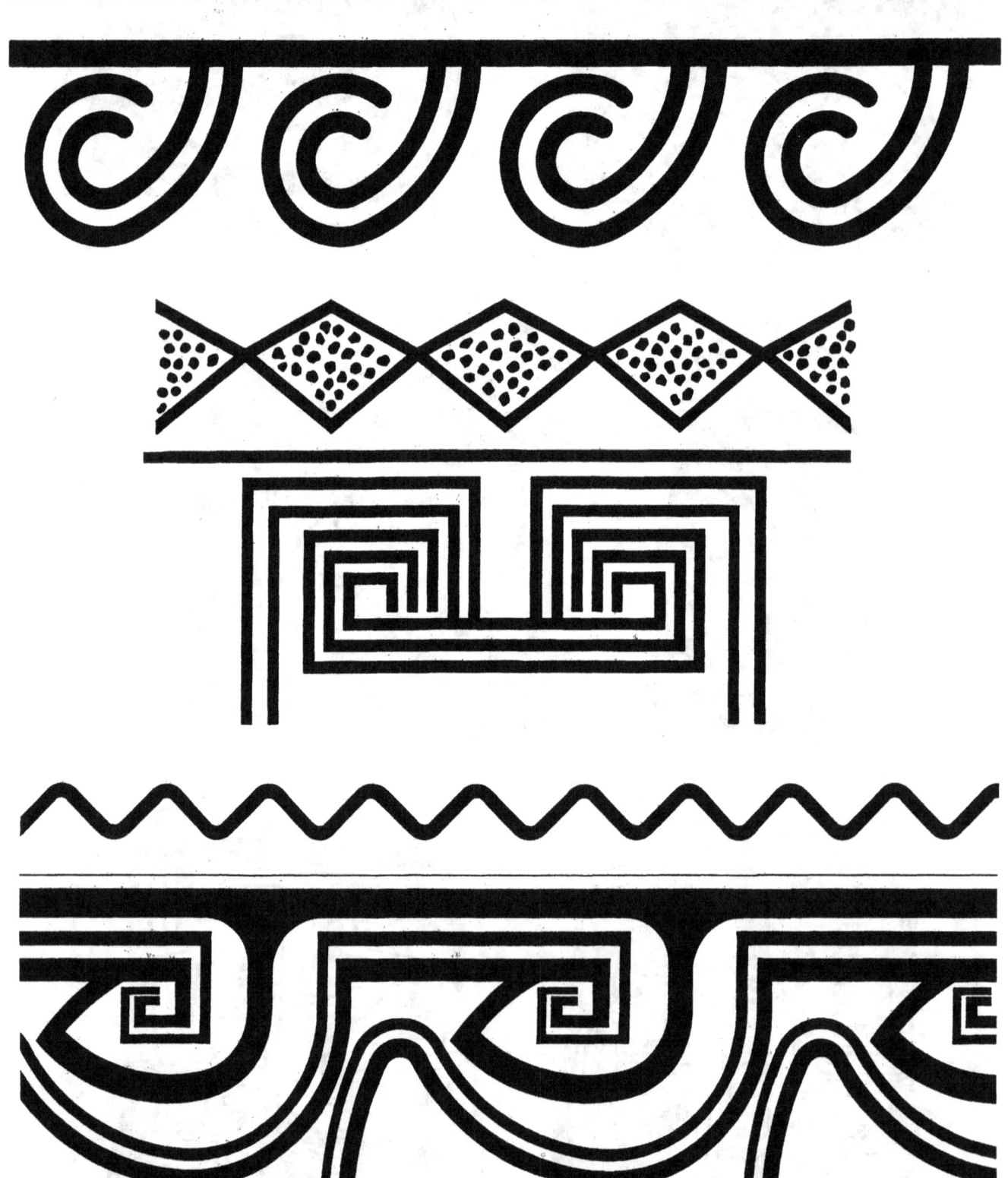

Corner for the design above (created by the author)

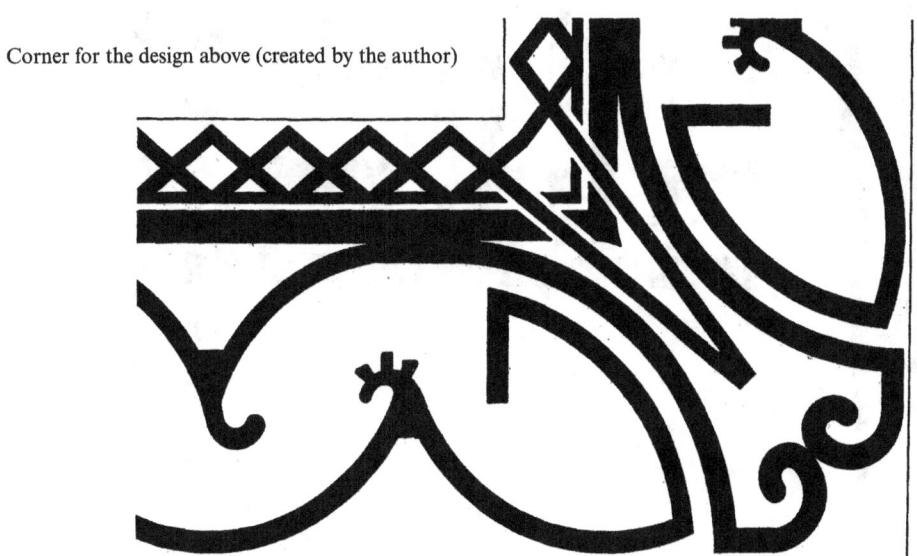

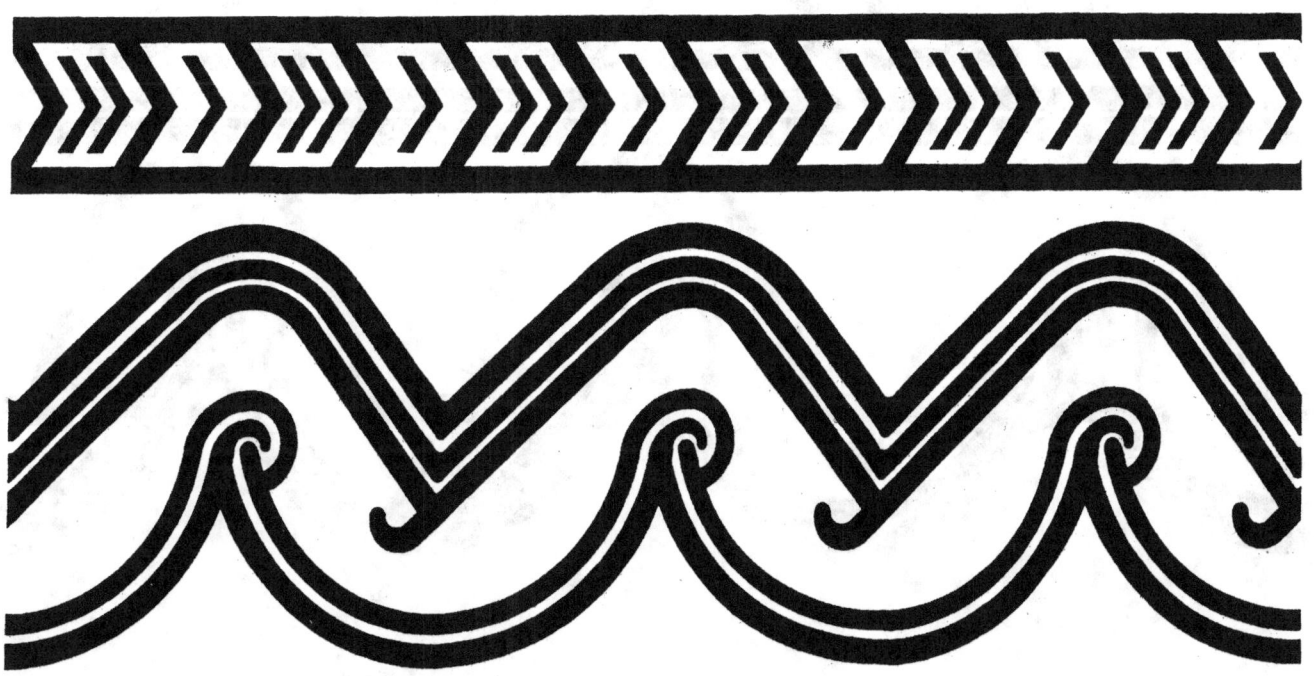

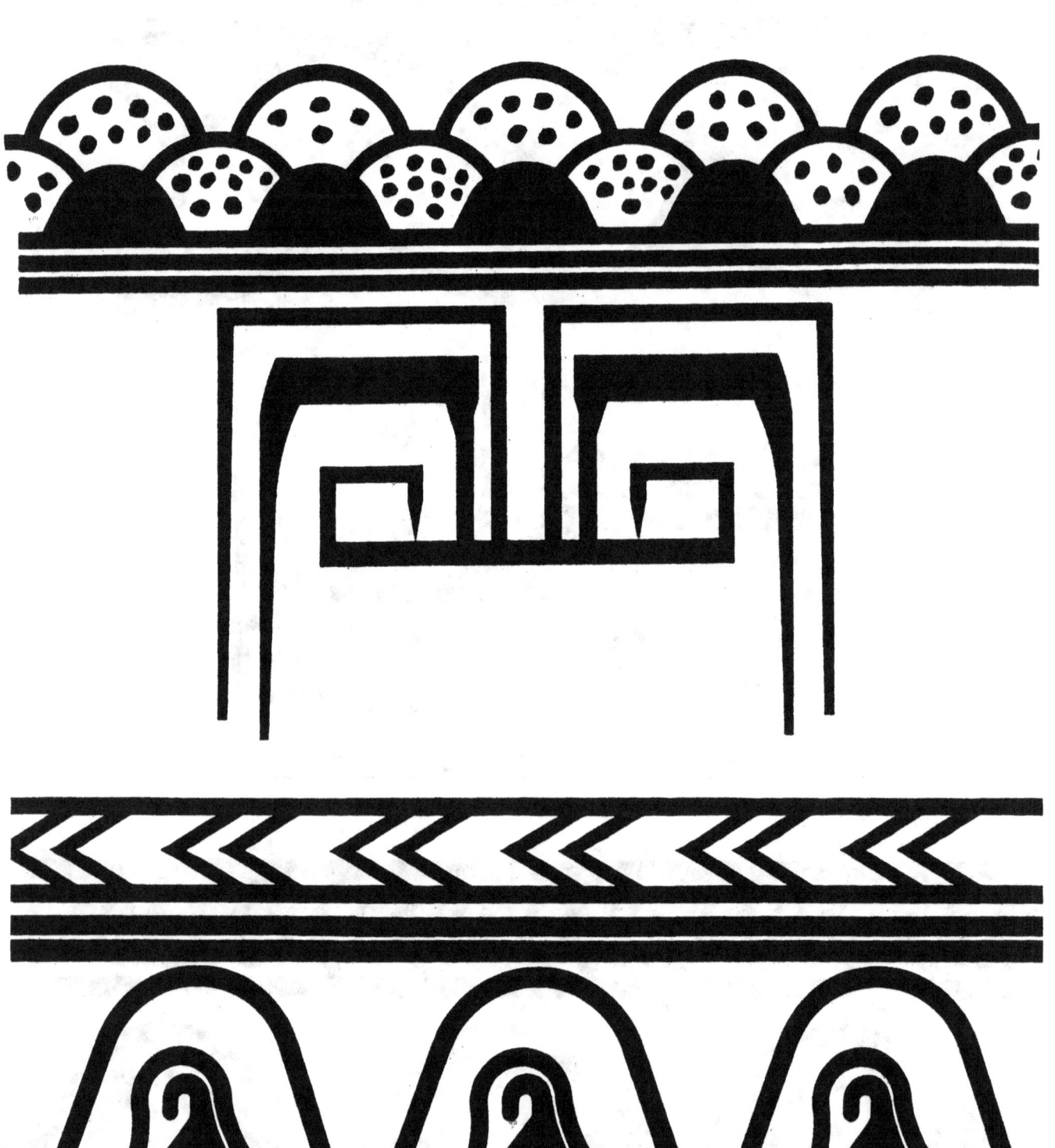

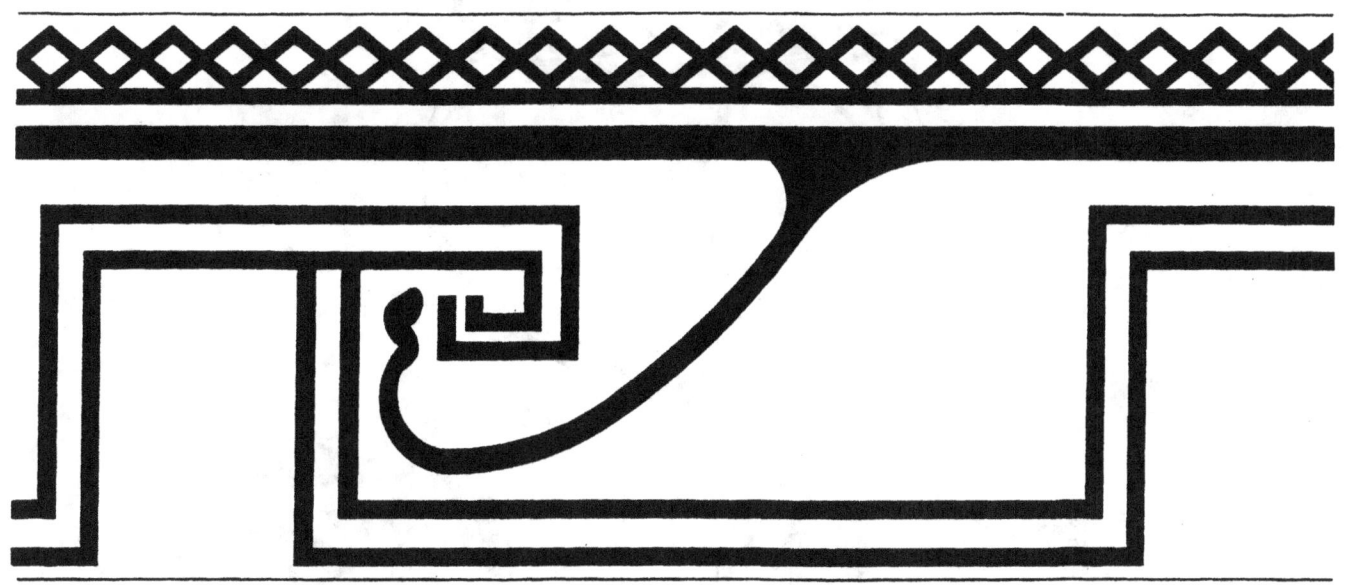

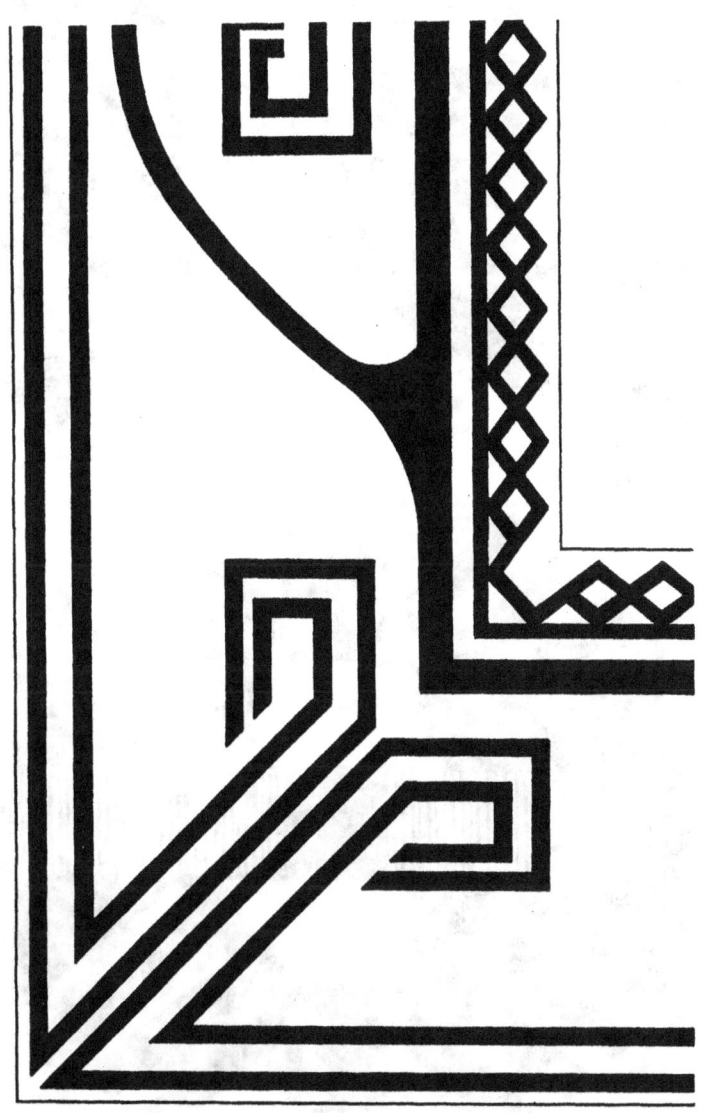

Corner for the design above (created by the author)

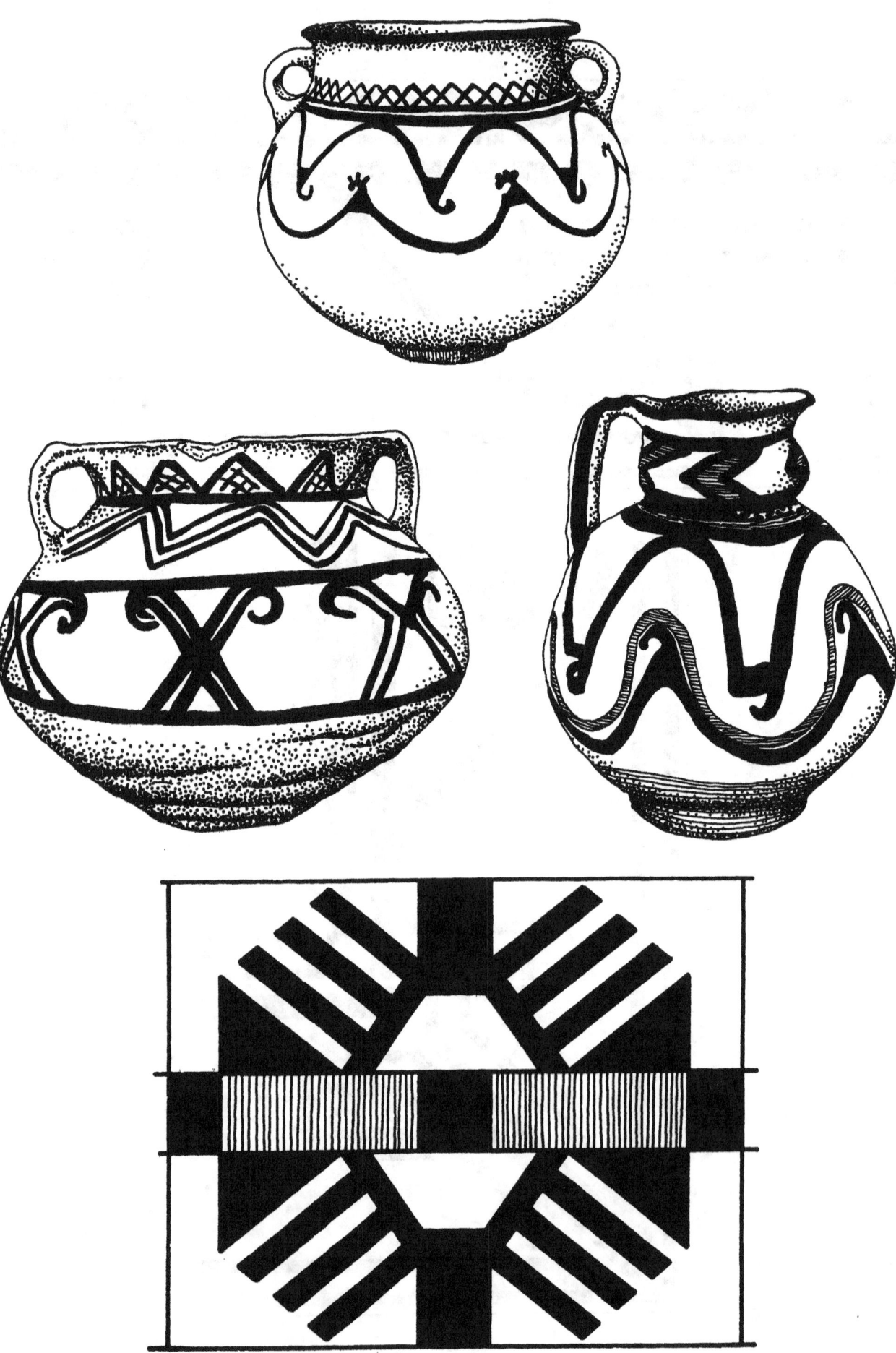

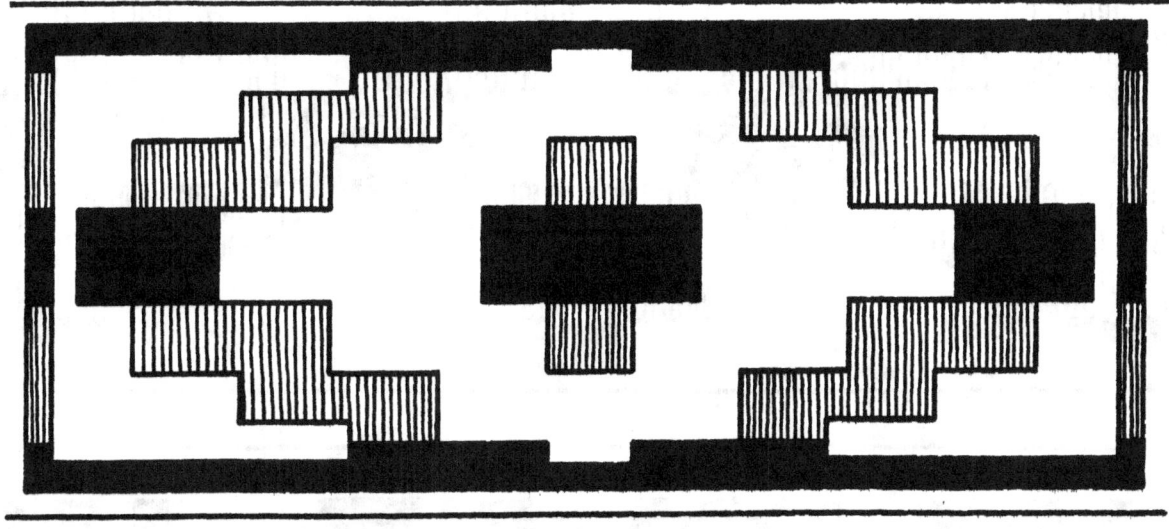

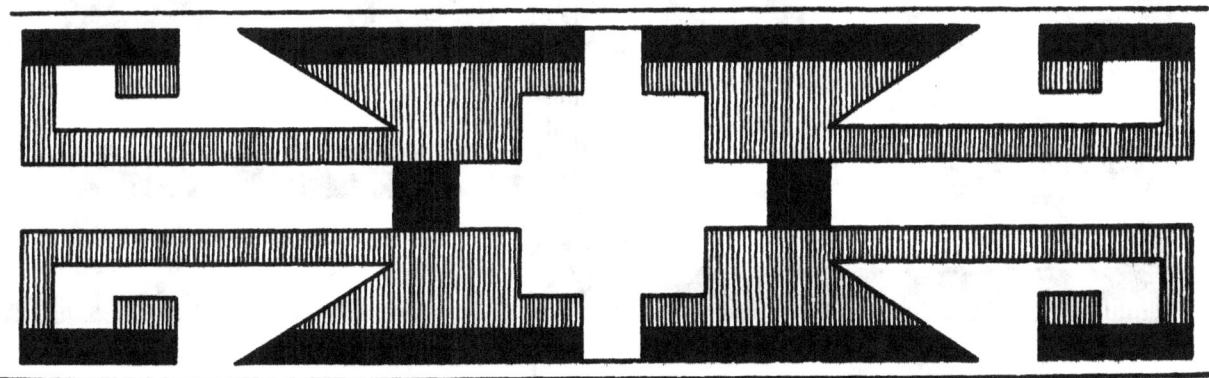

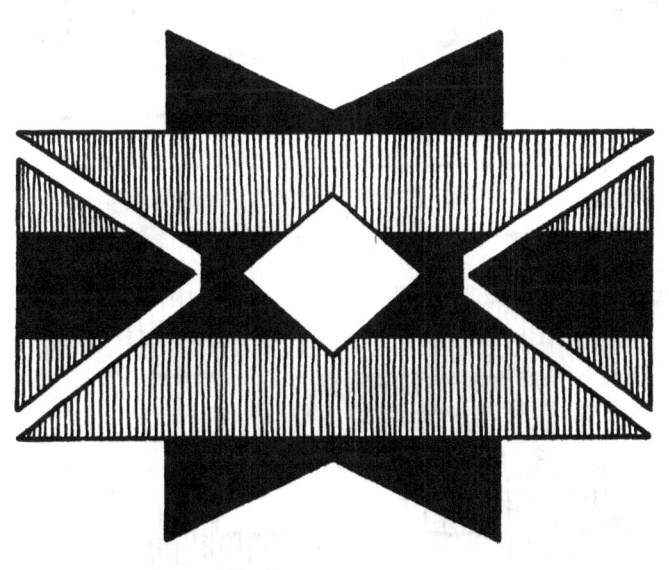

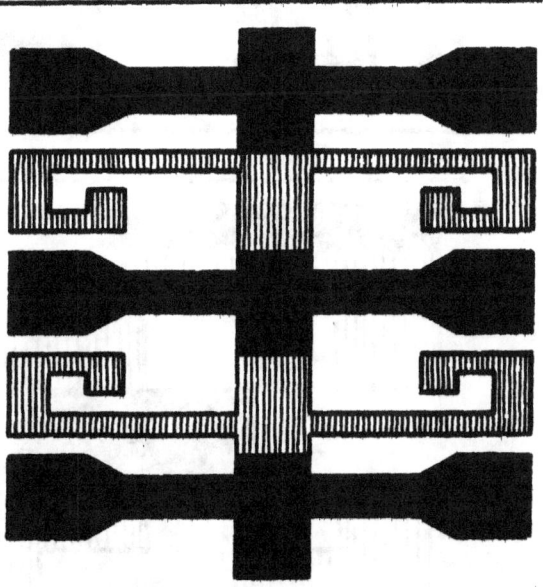

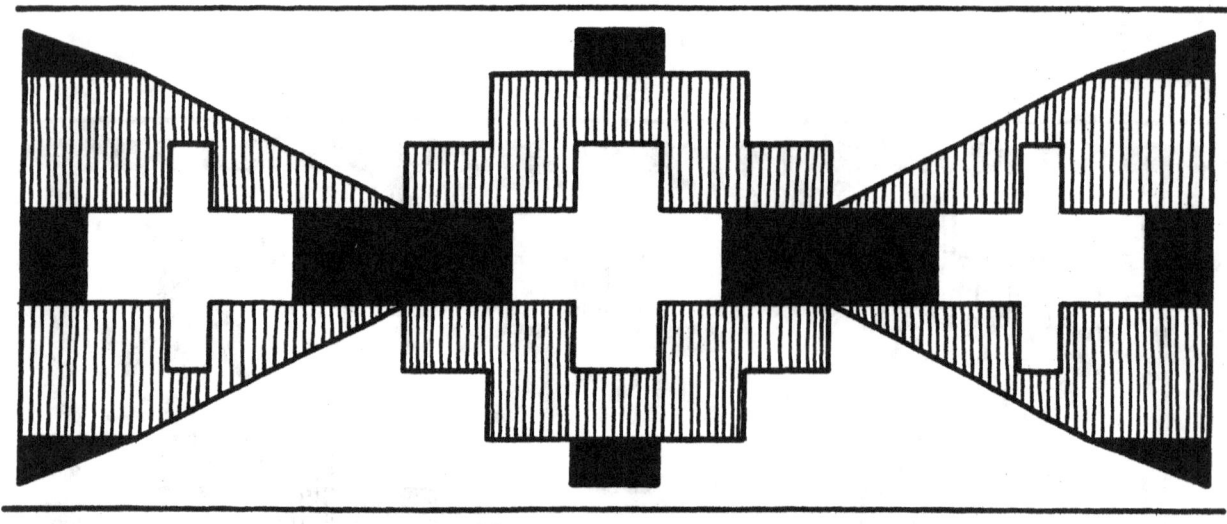

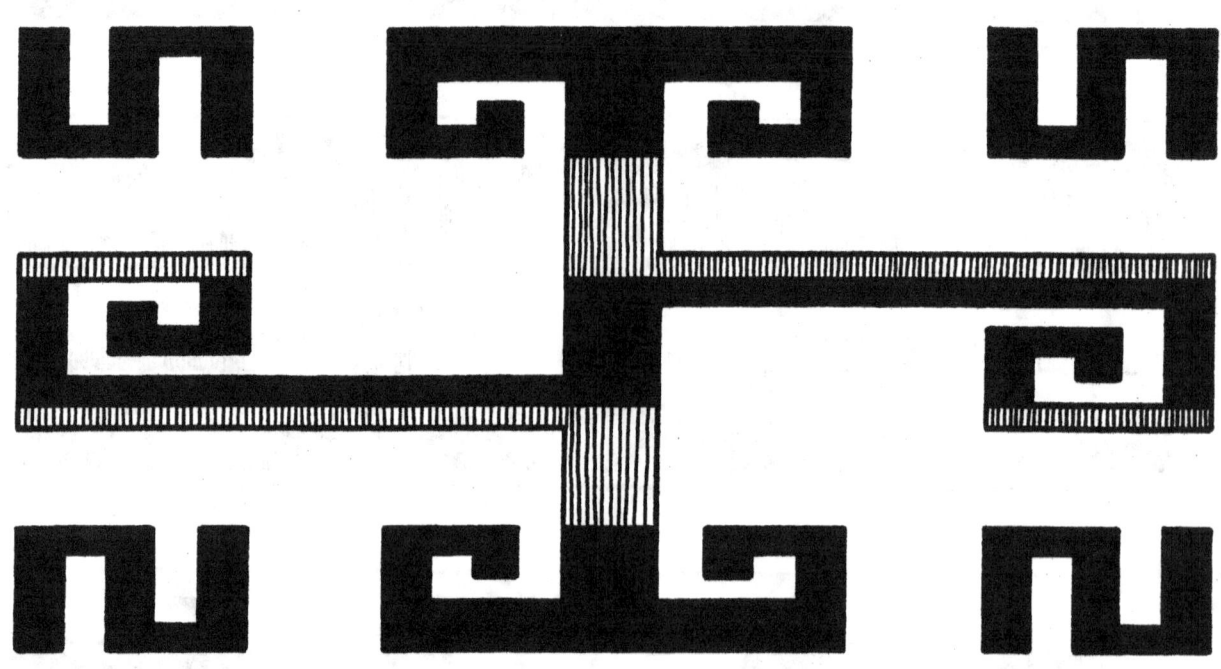

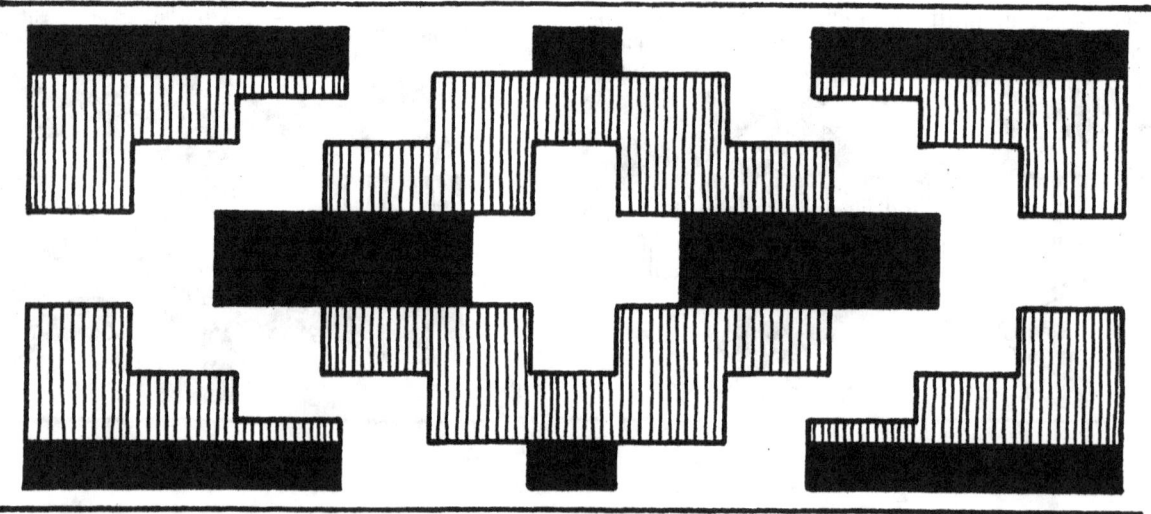

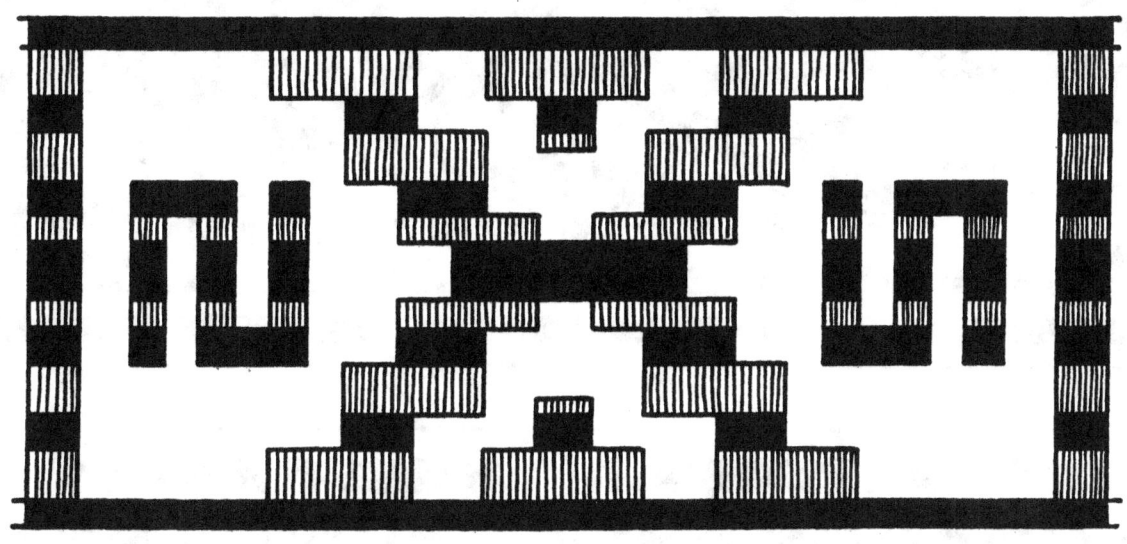

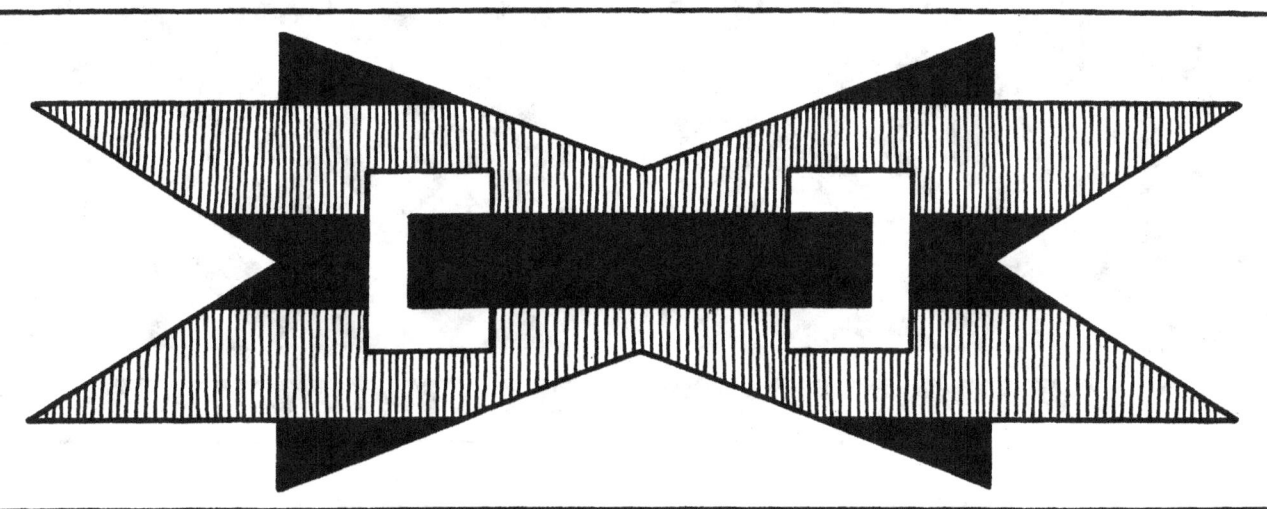

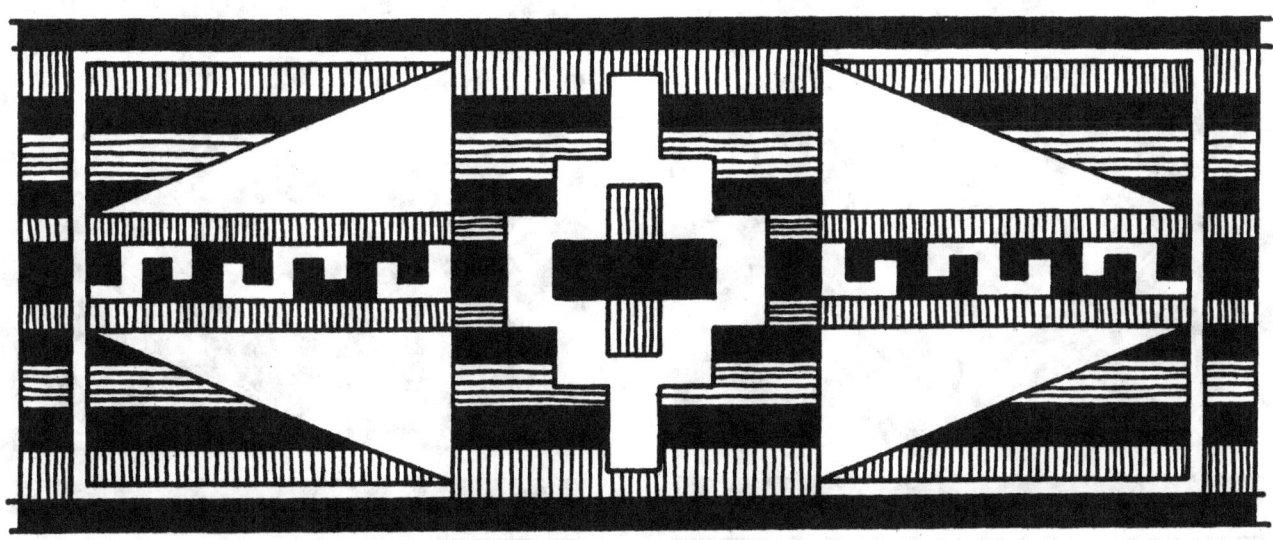

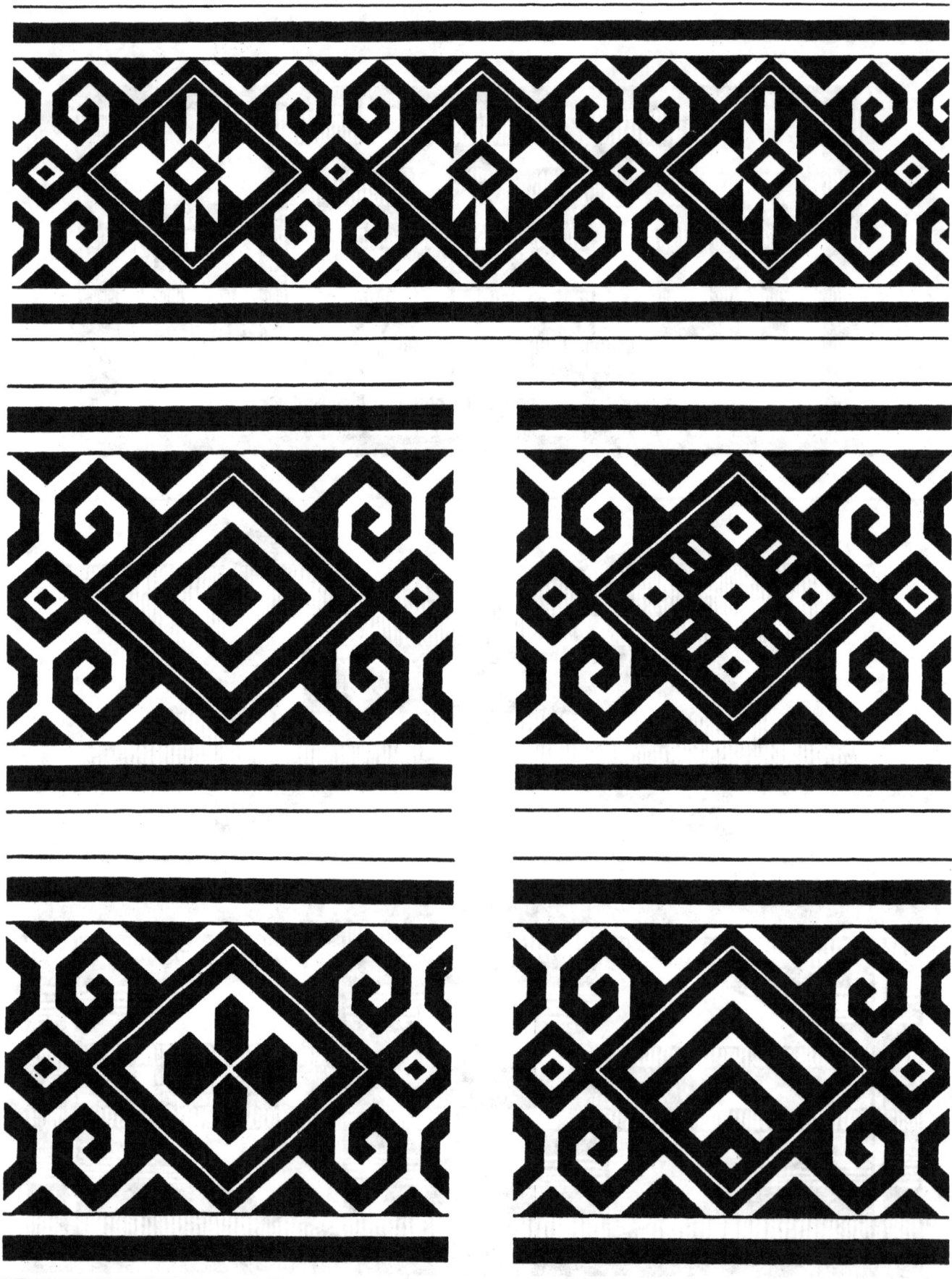

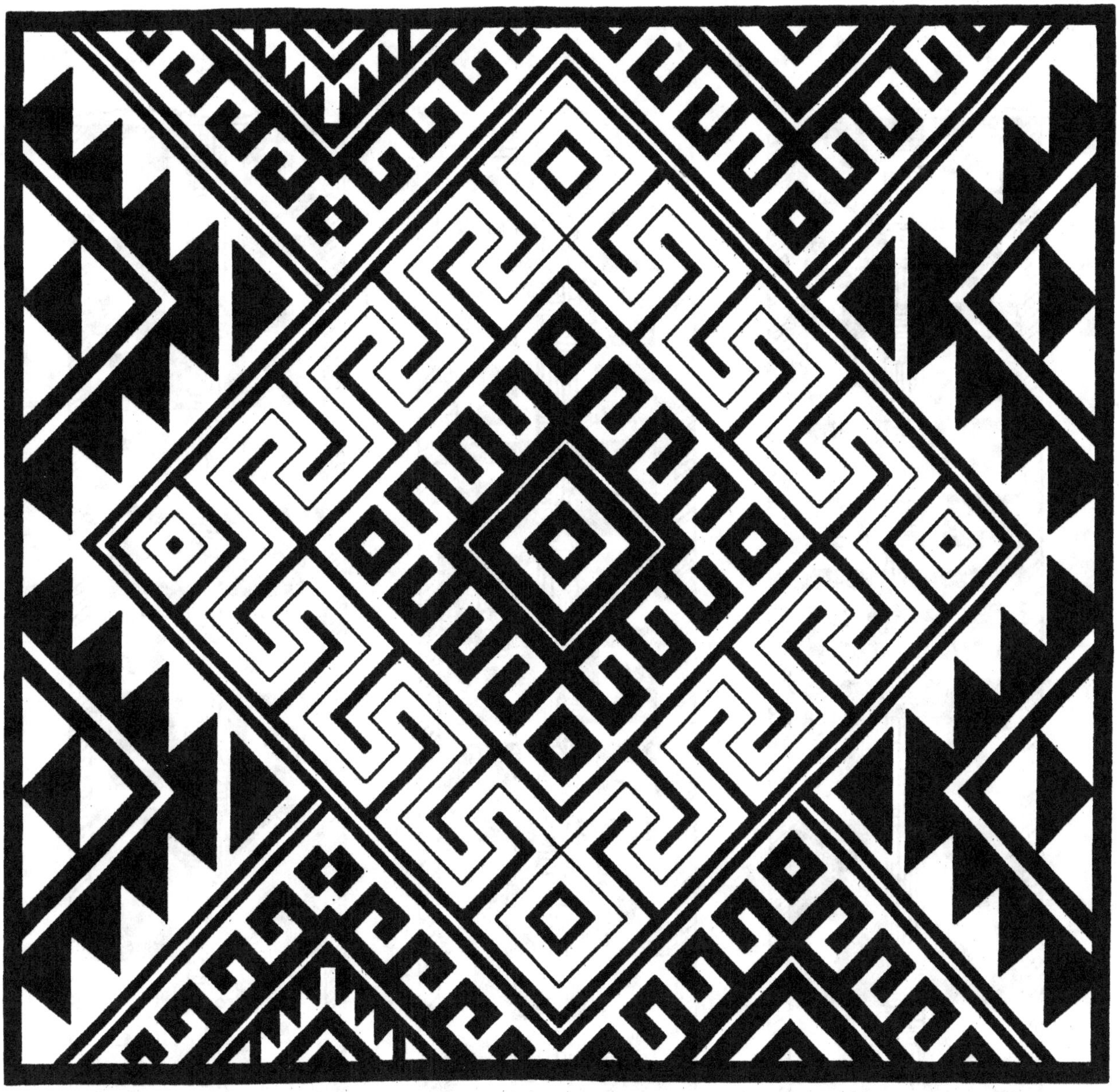

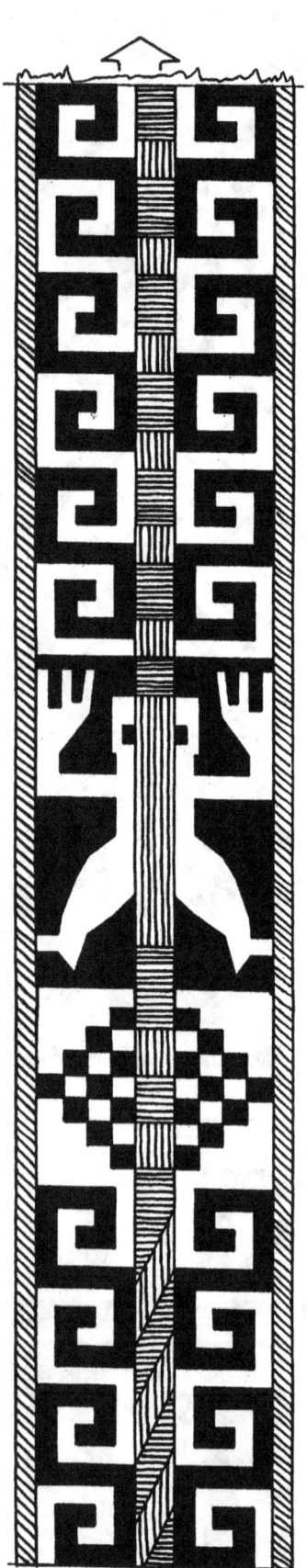

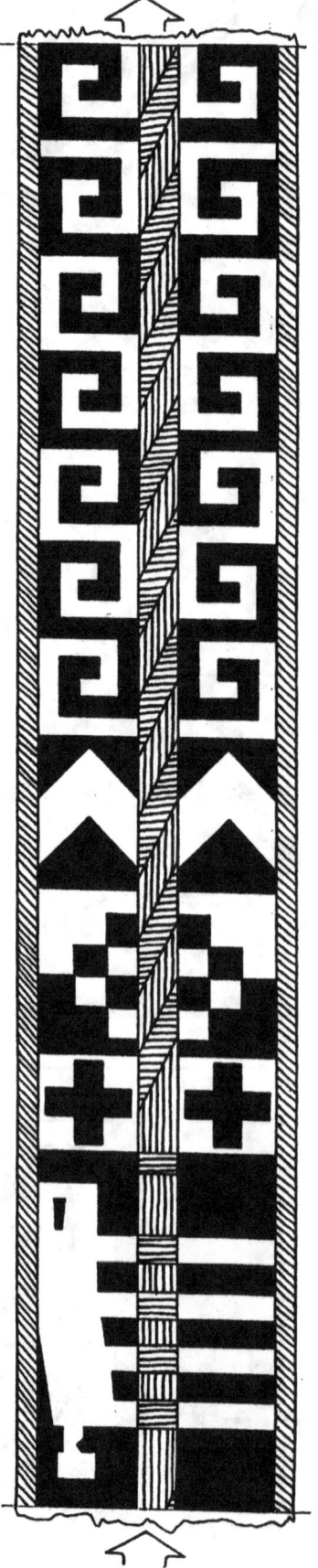

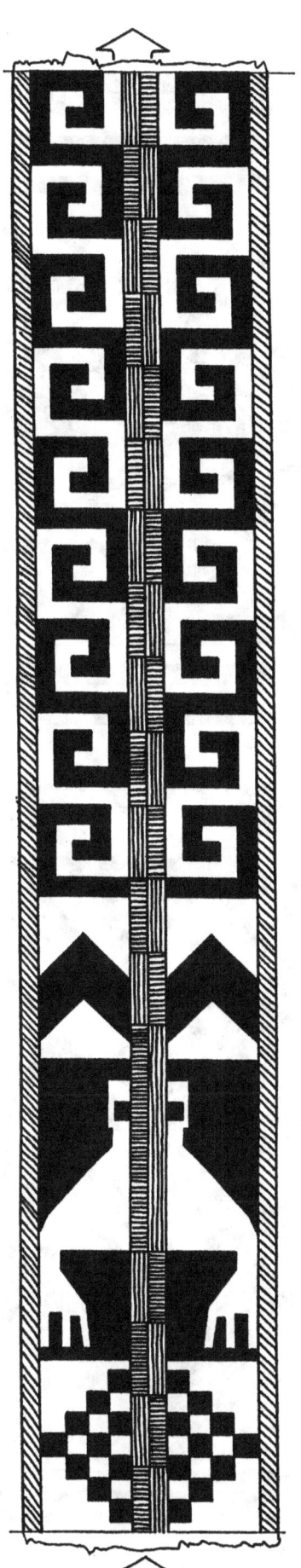
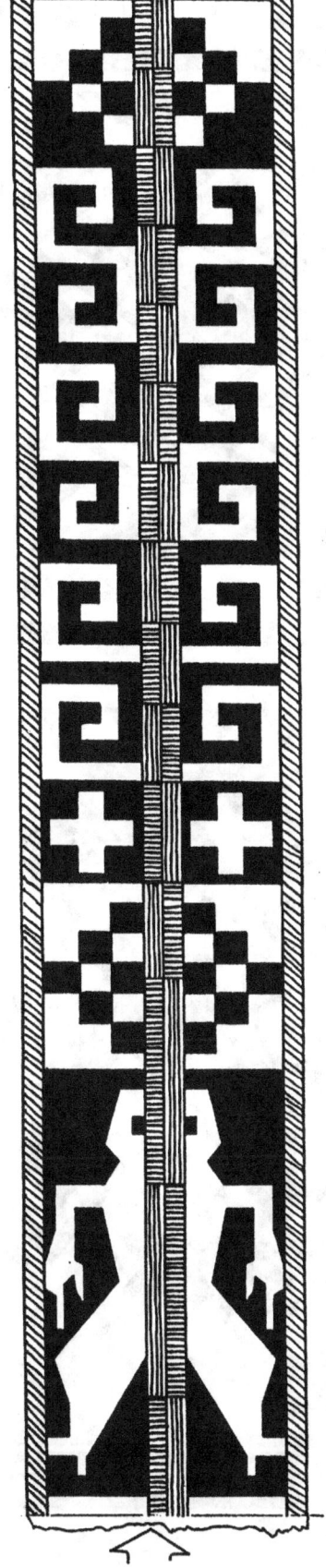
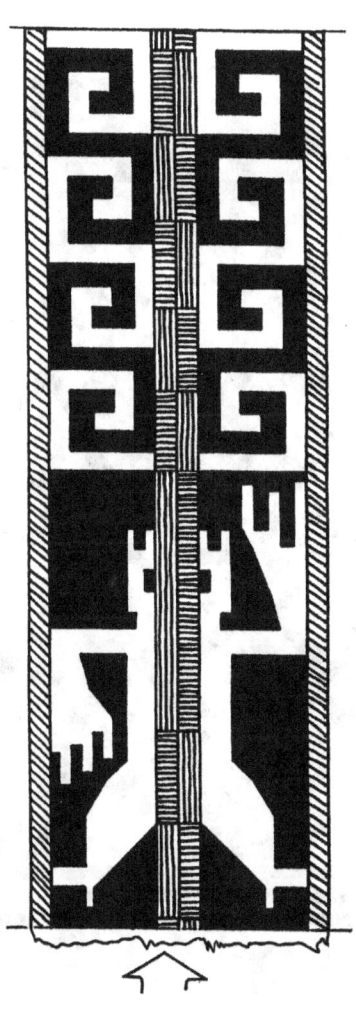

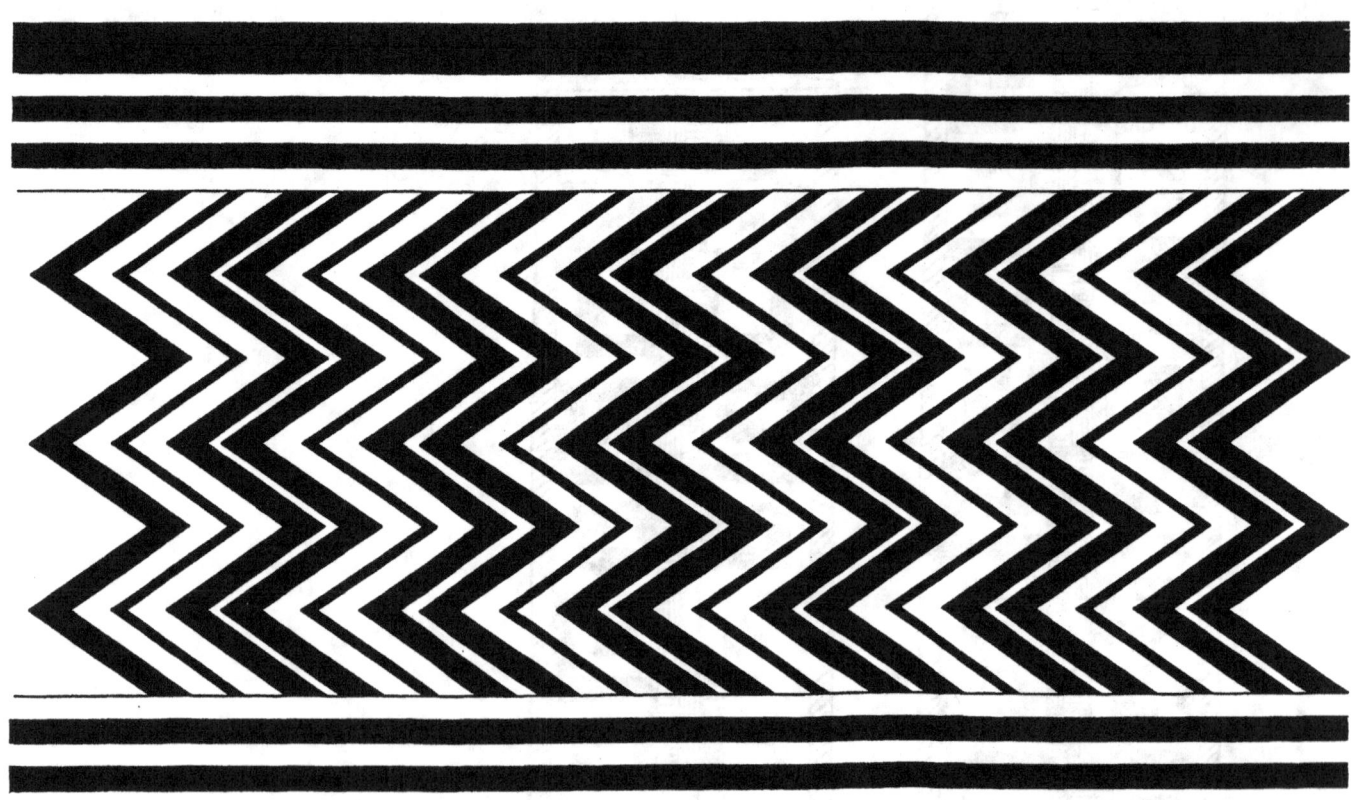

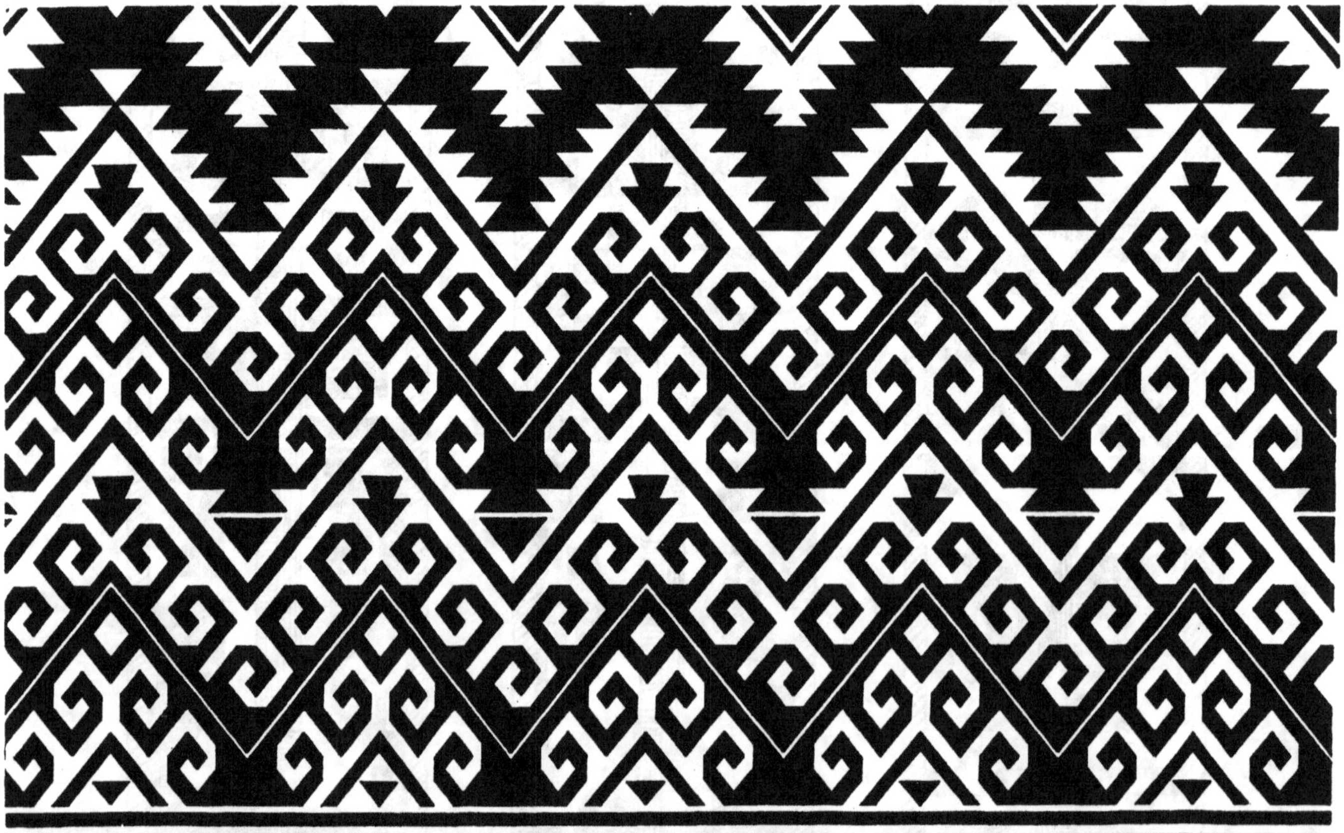

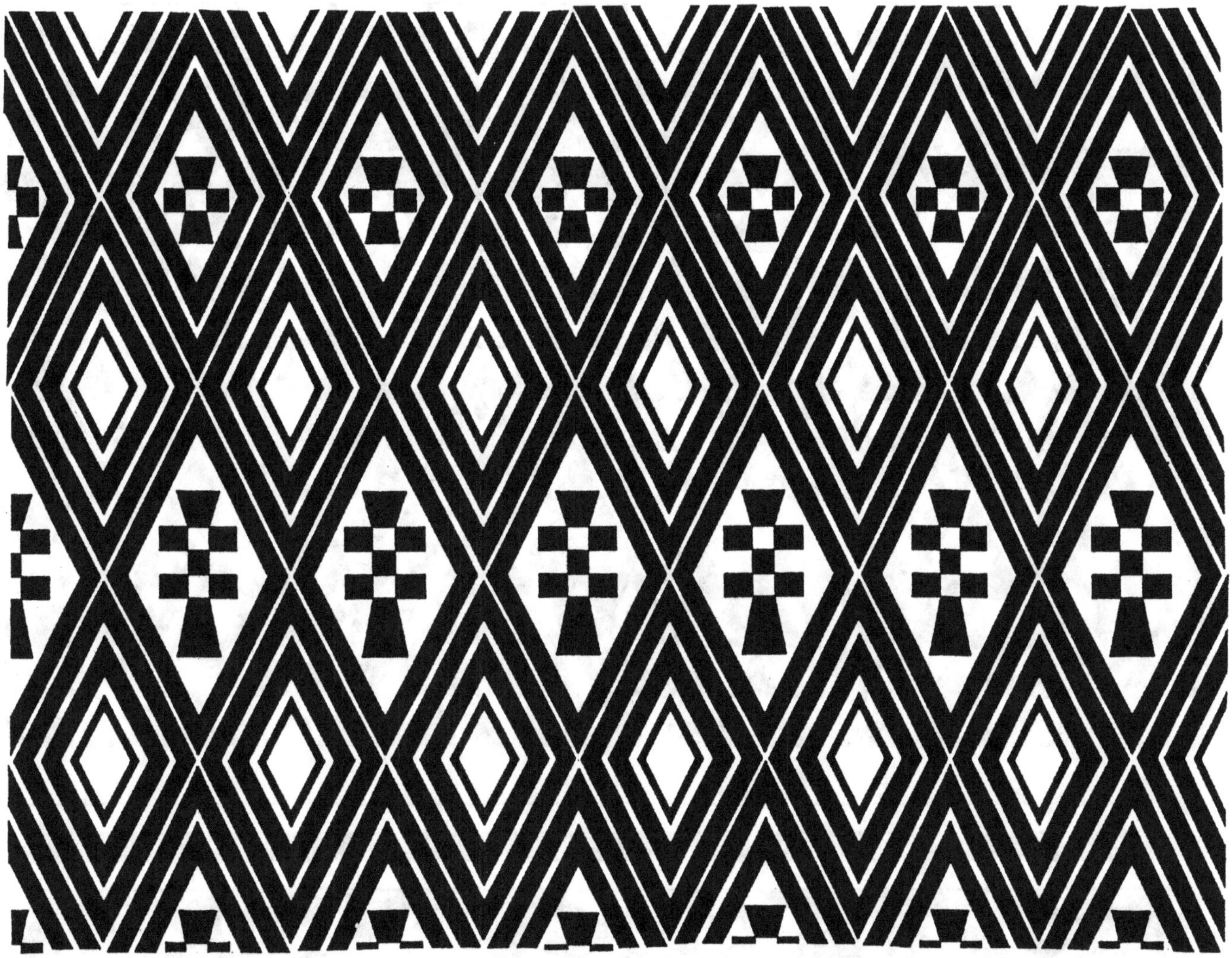

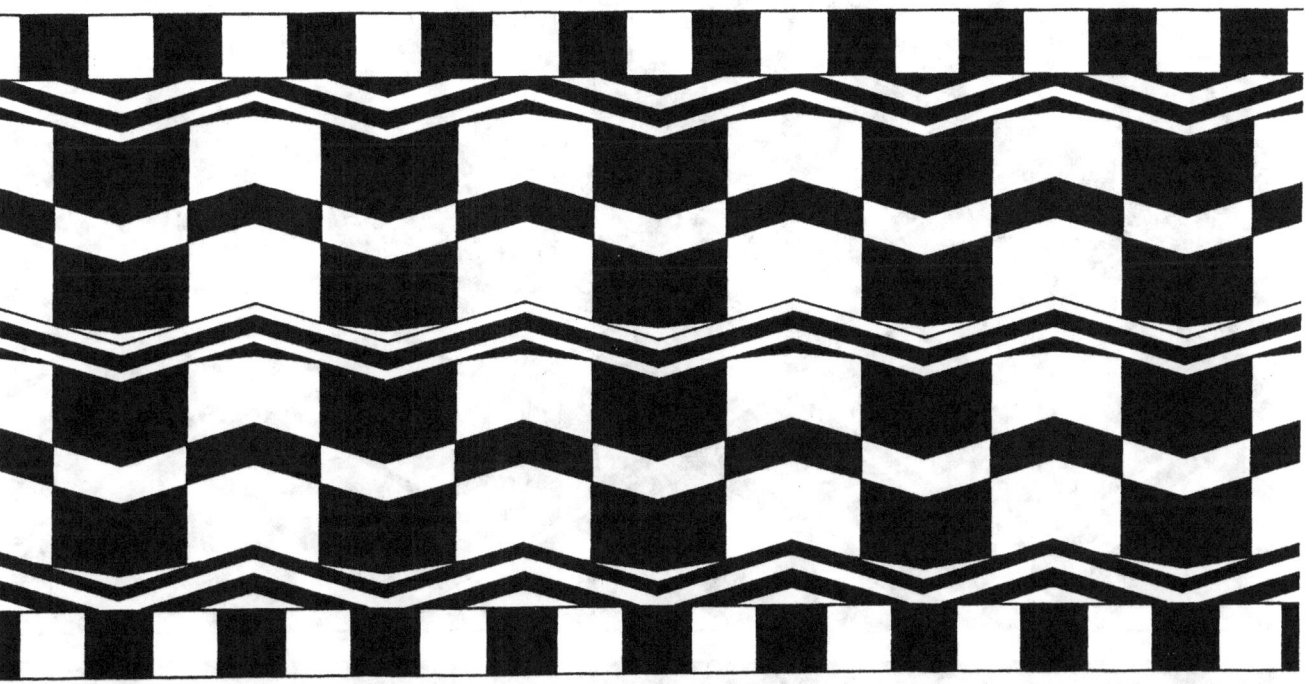

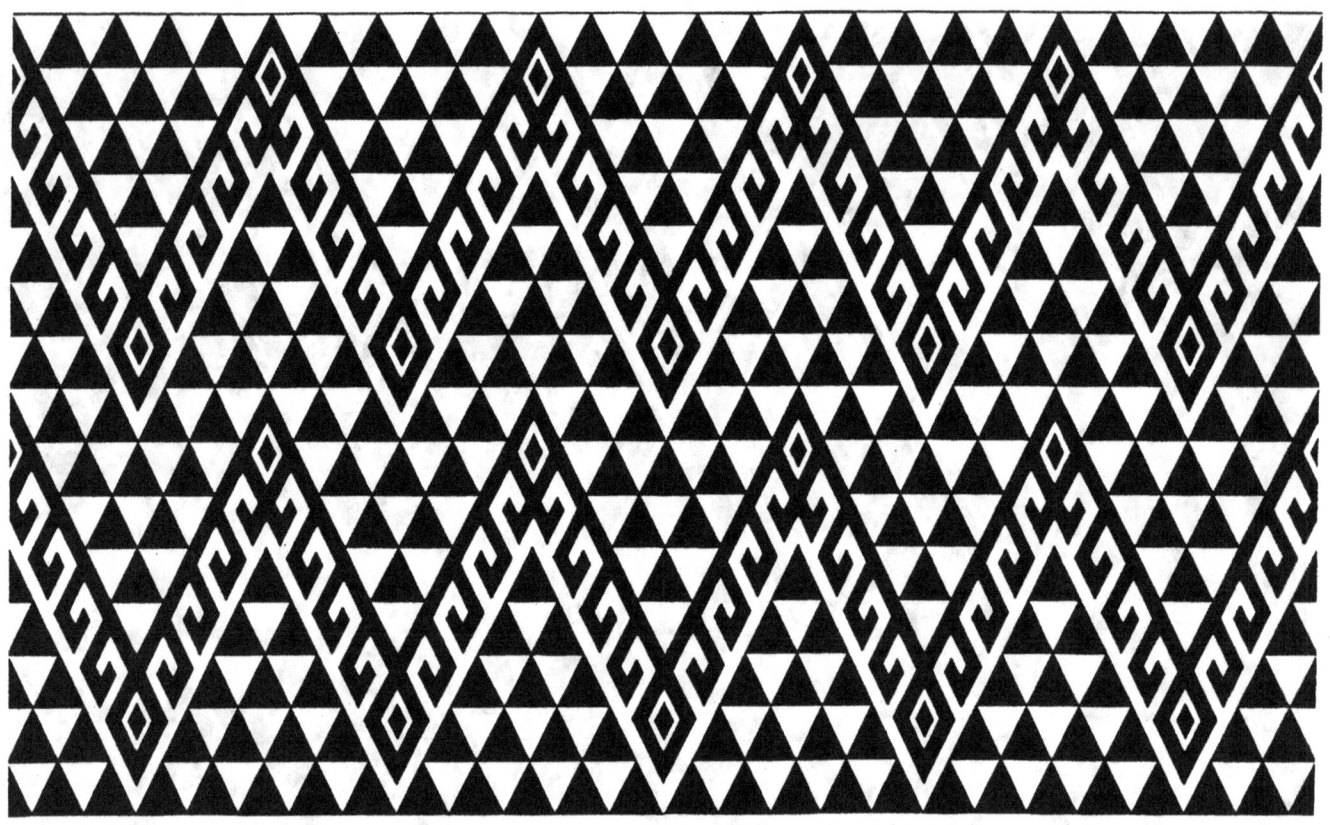

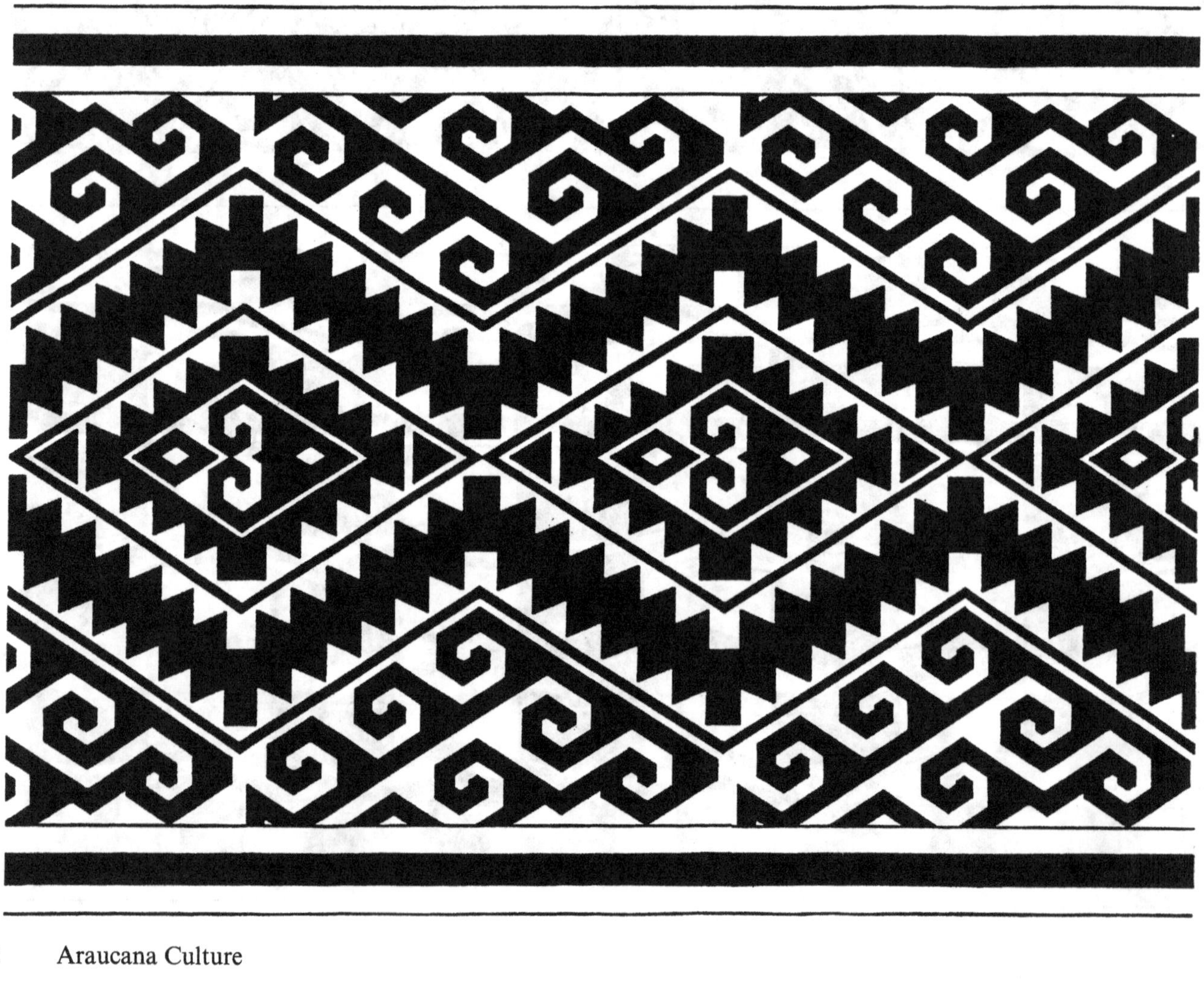

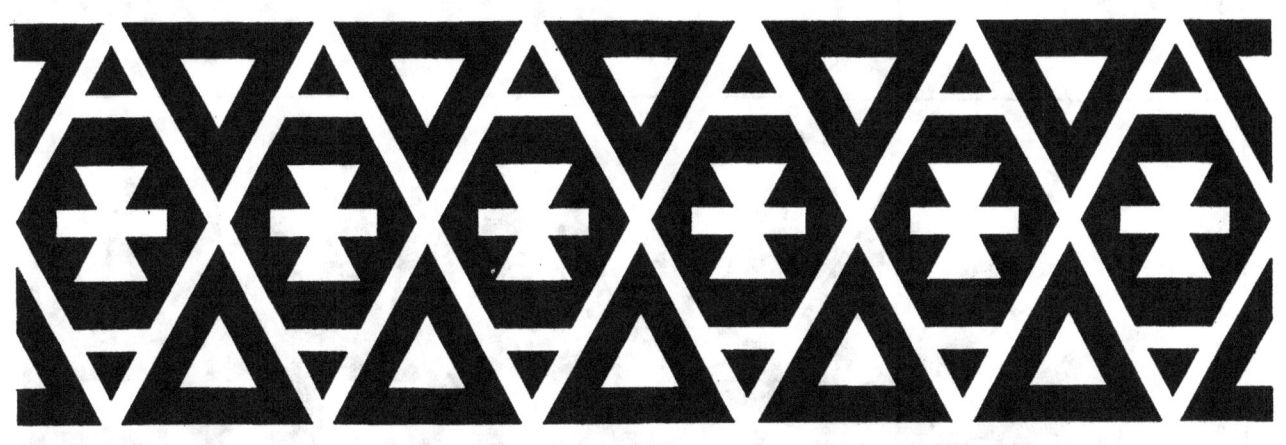

Corner for the design above (created by the author)

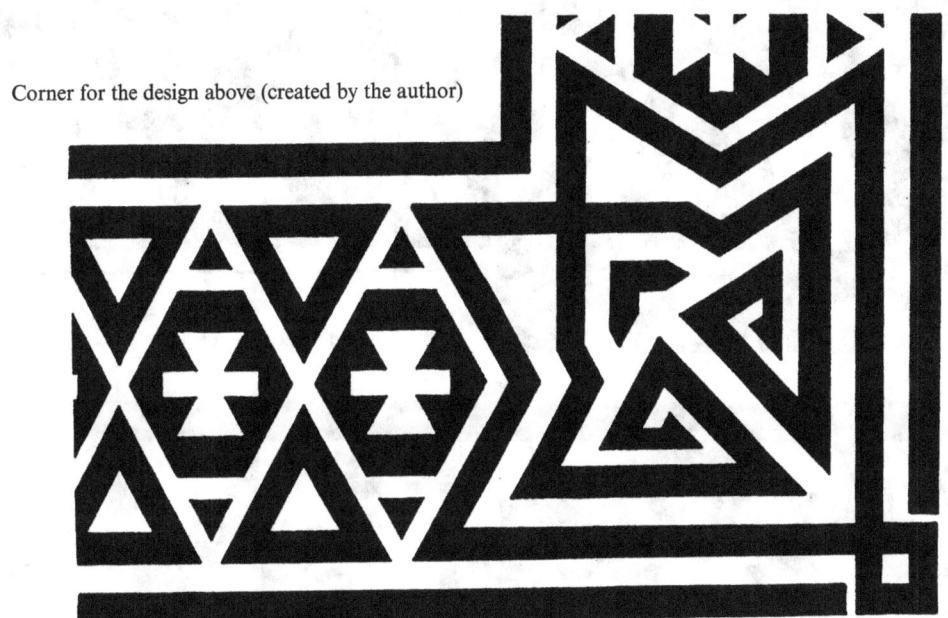

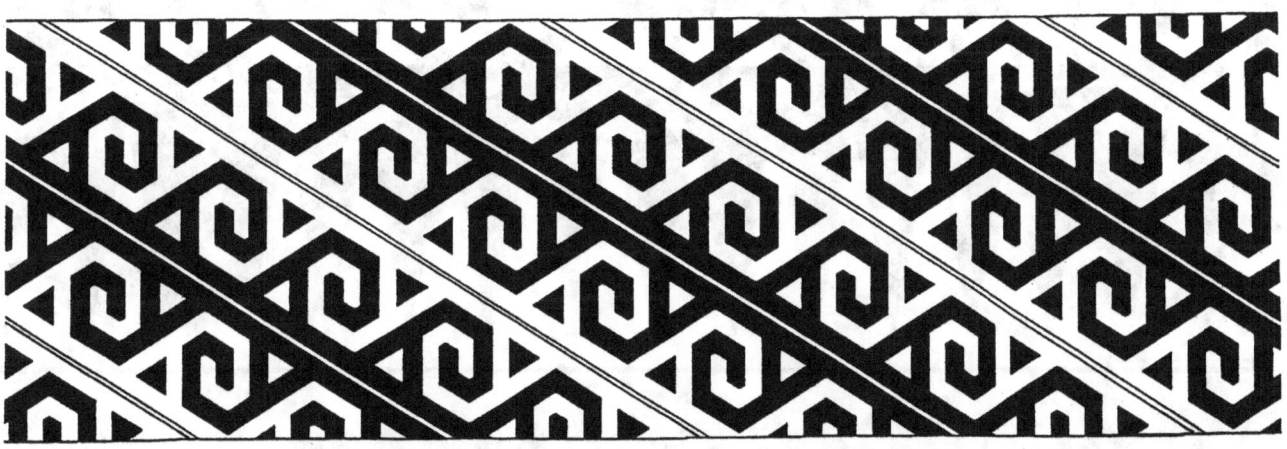

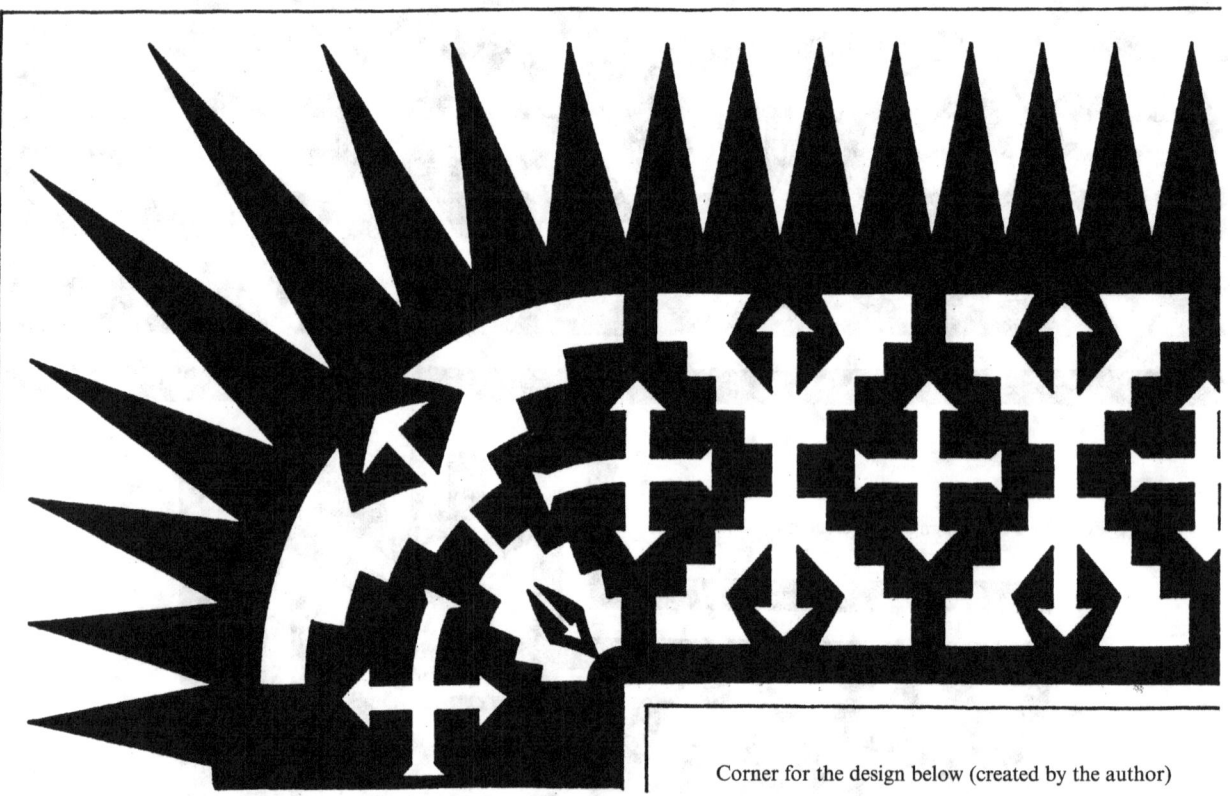

Corner for the design below (created by the author)

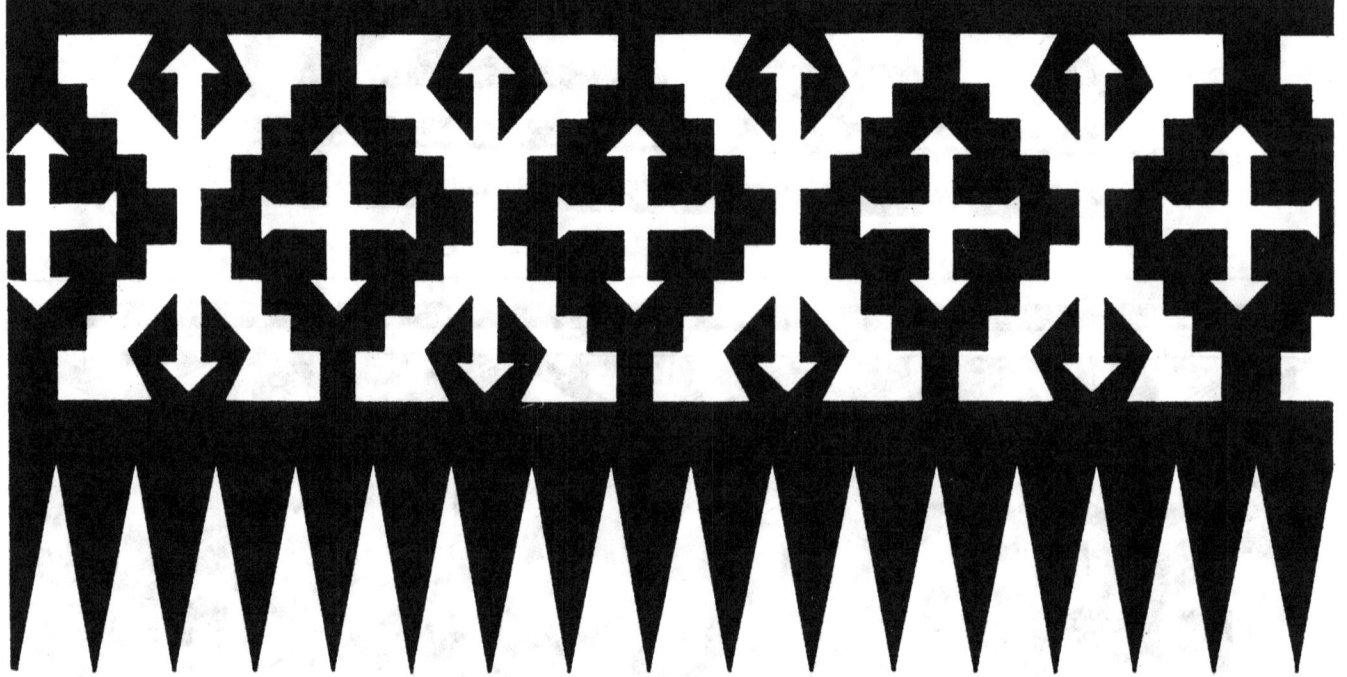

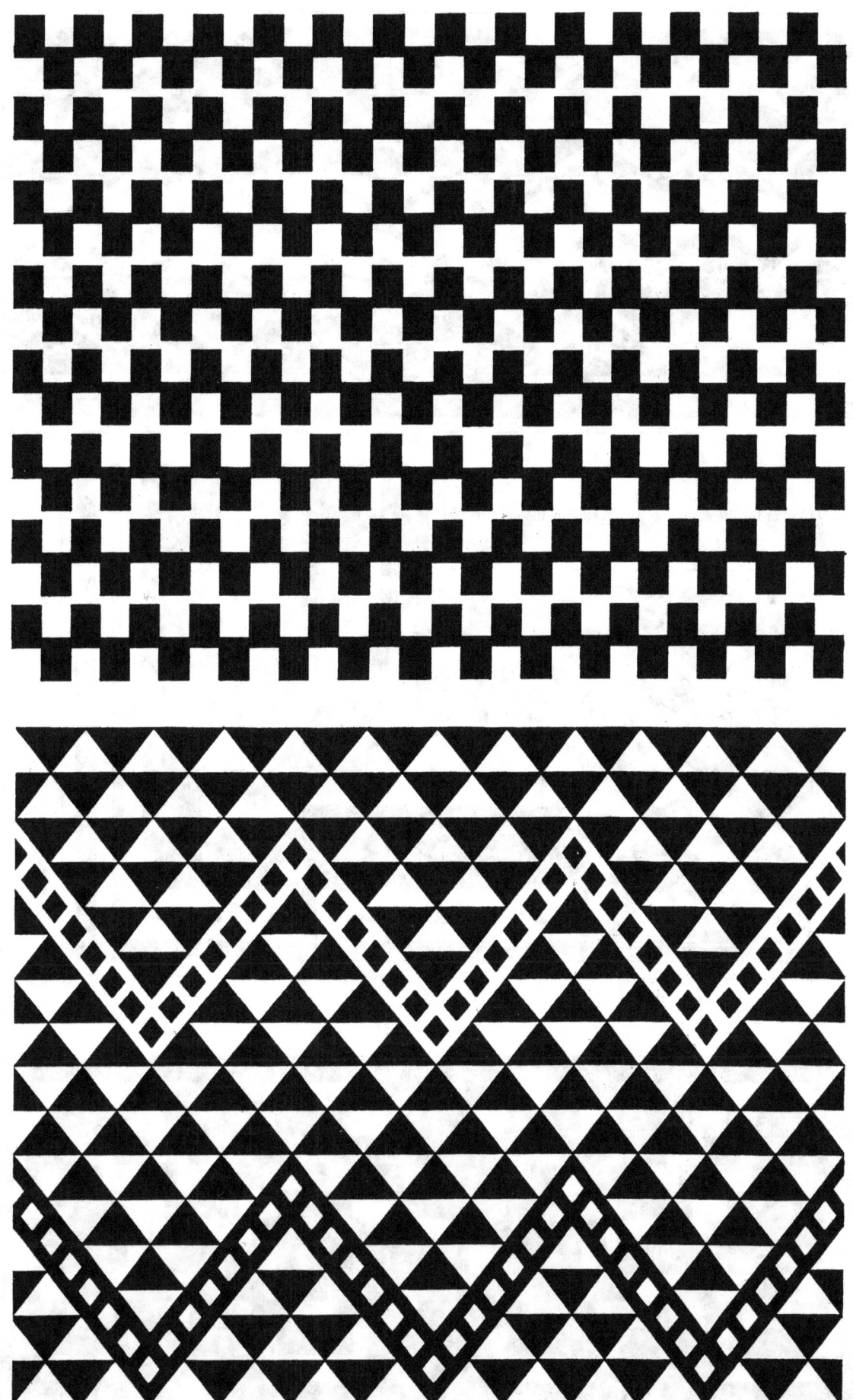

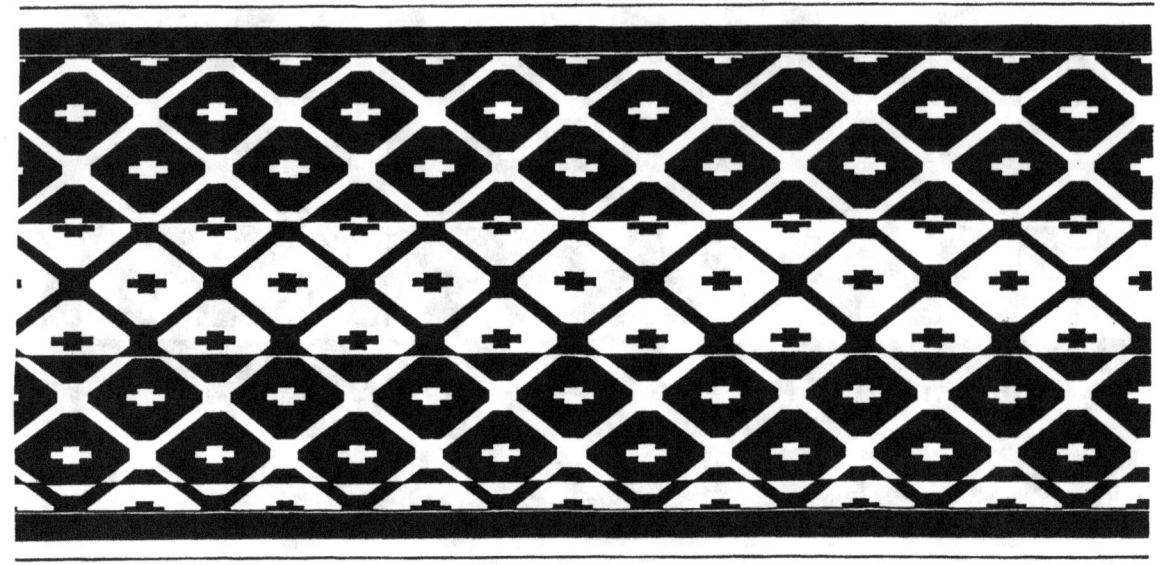

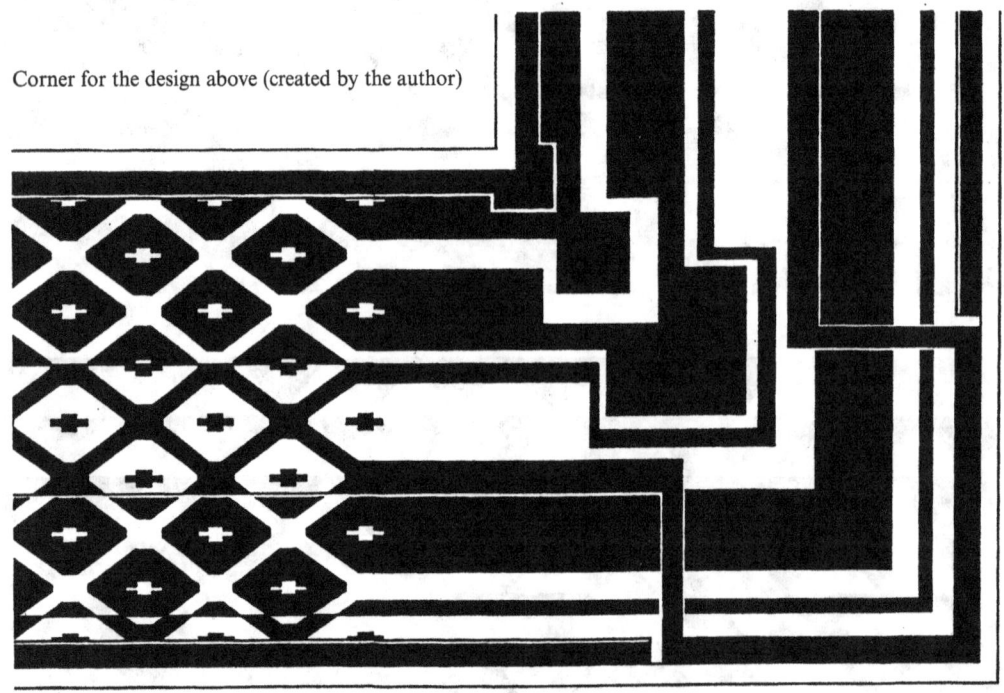

Corner for the design above (created by the author)

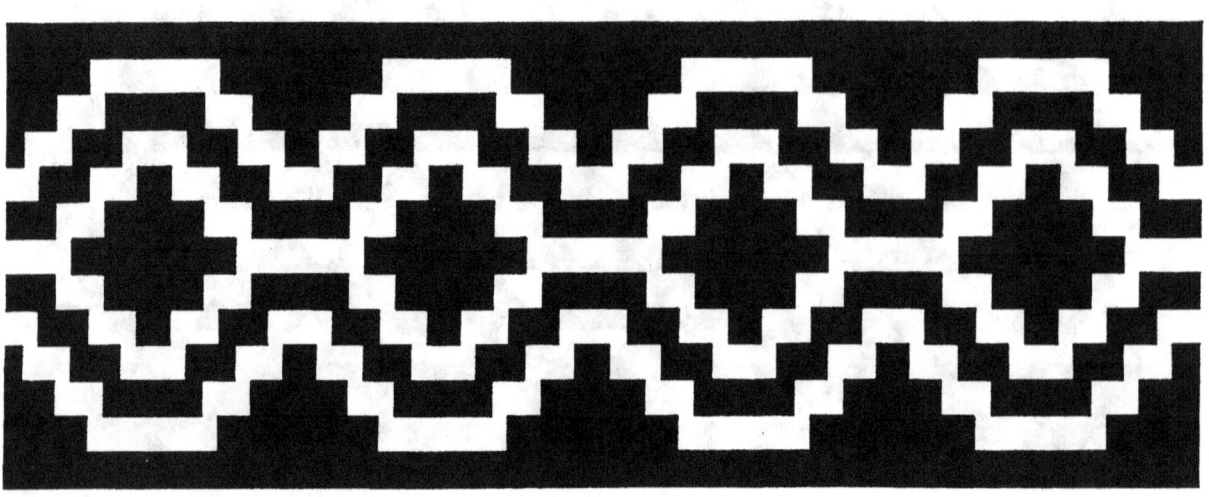

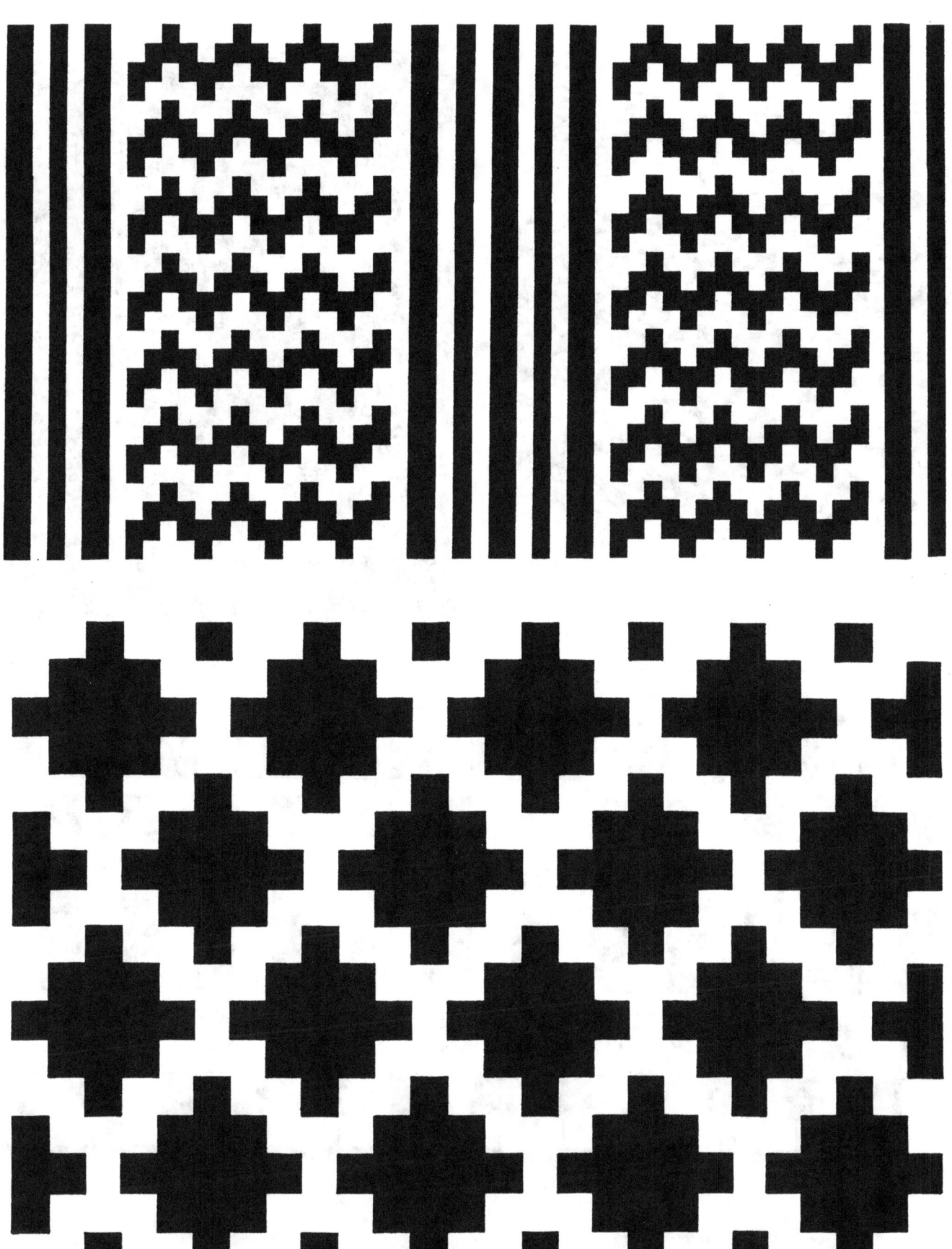

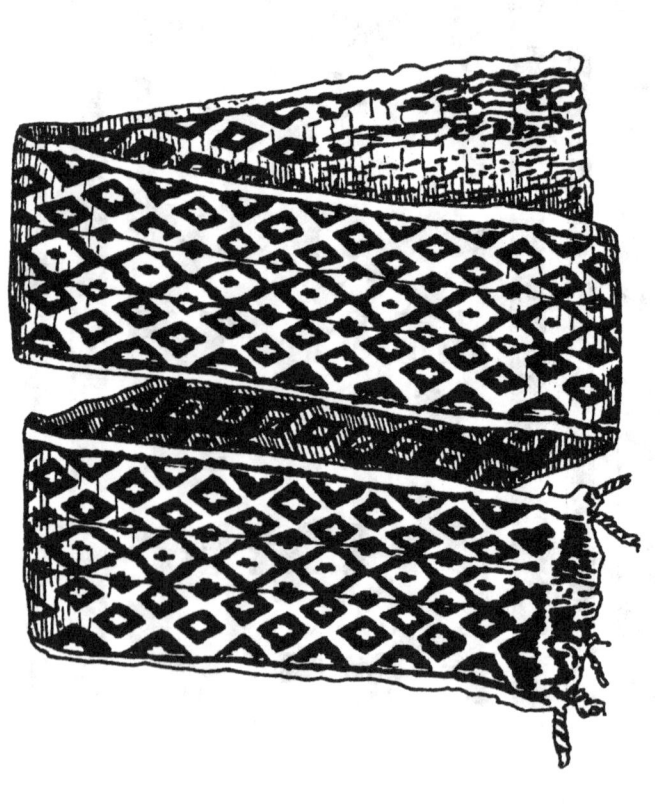

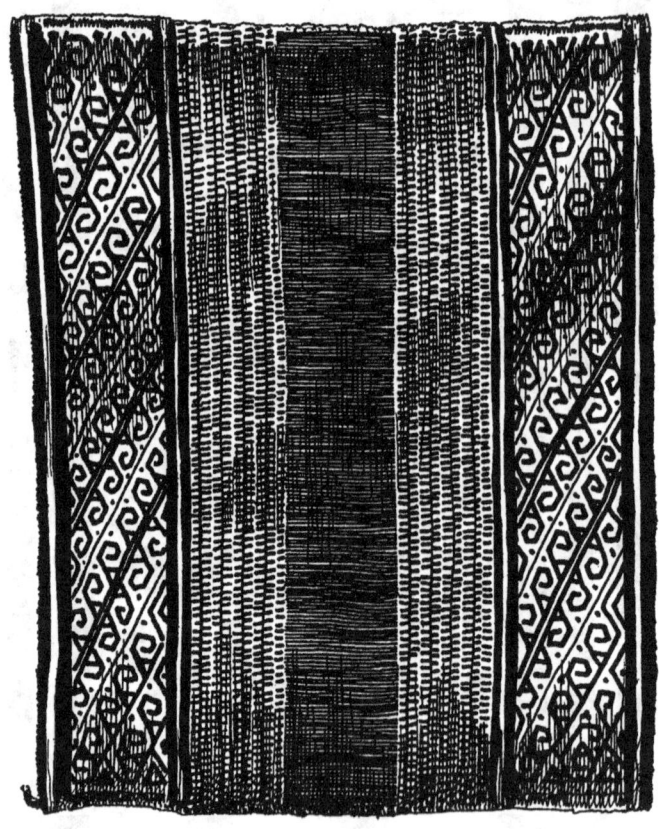

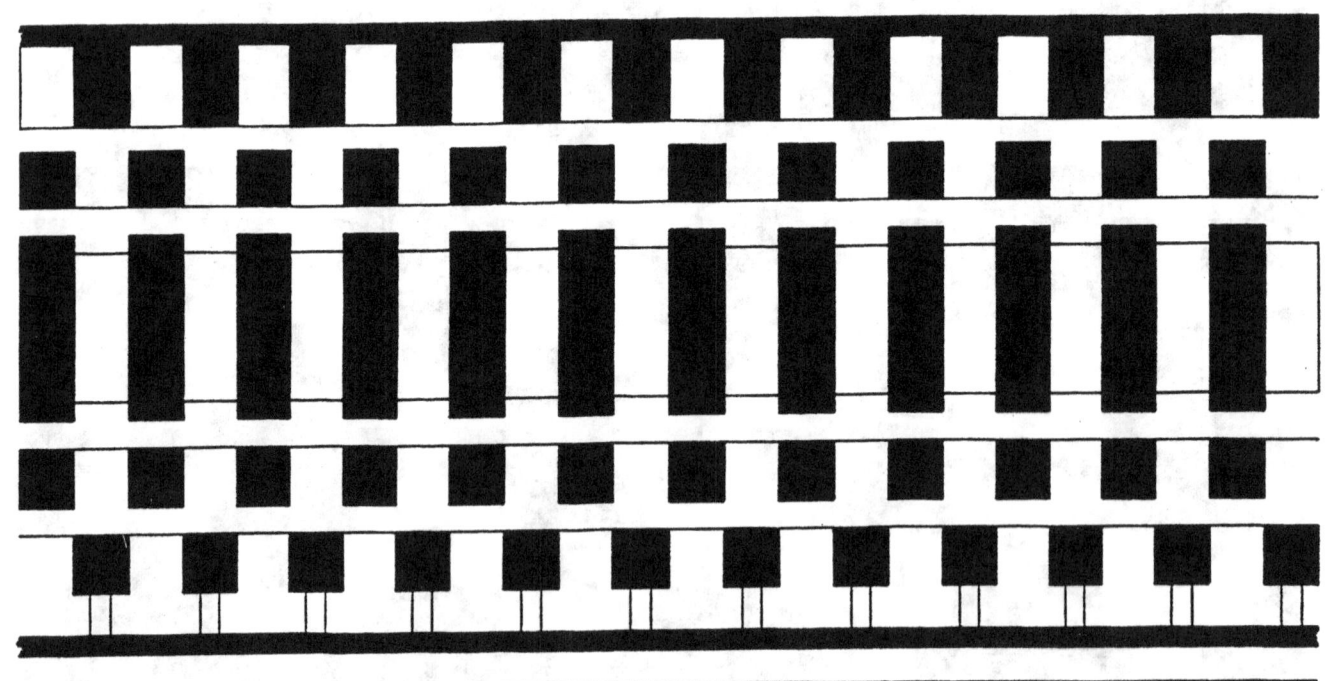

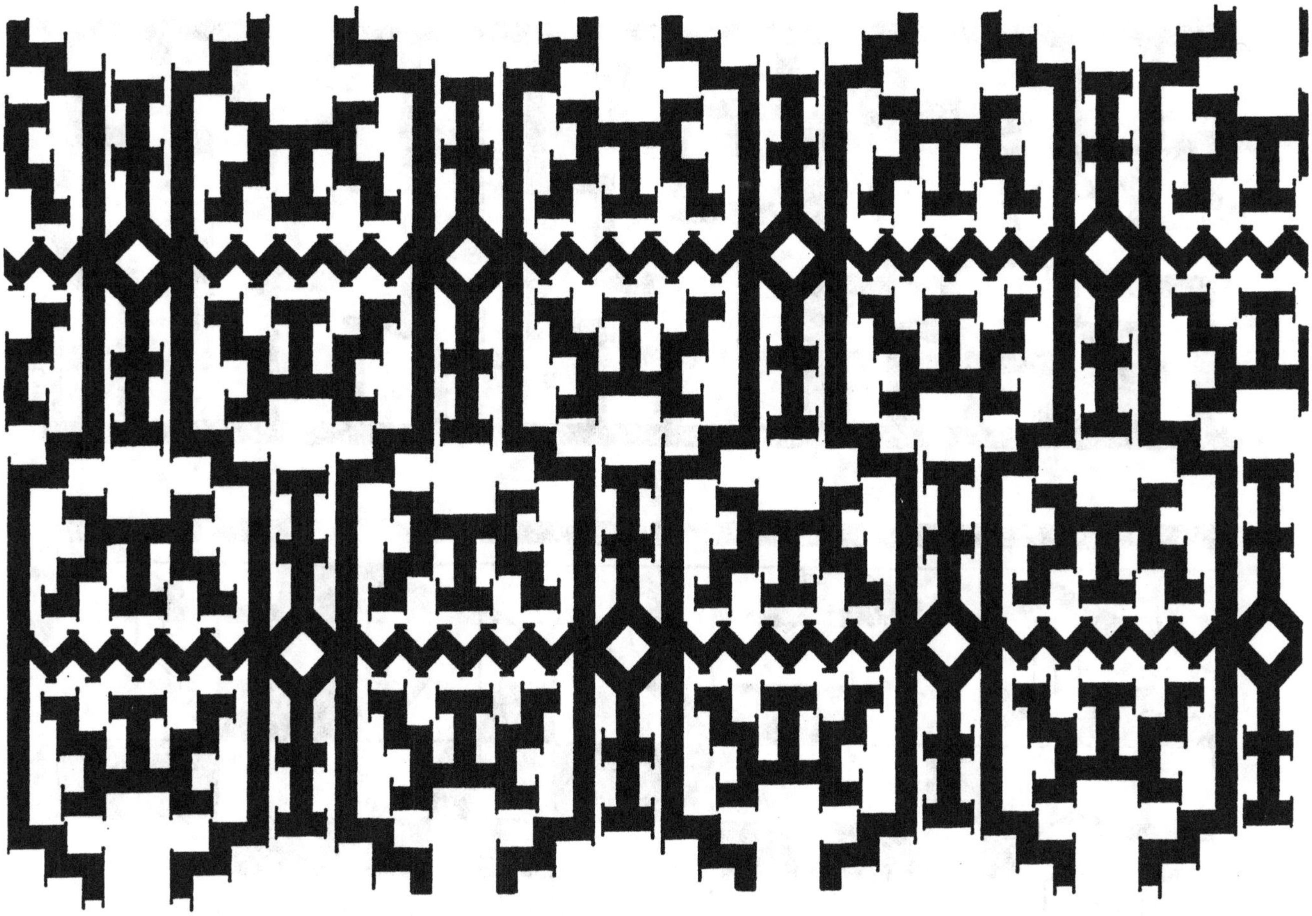

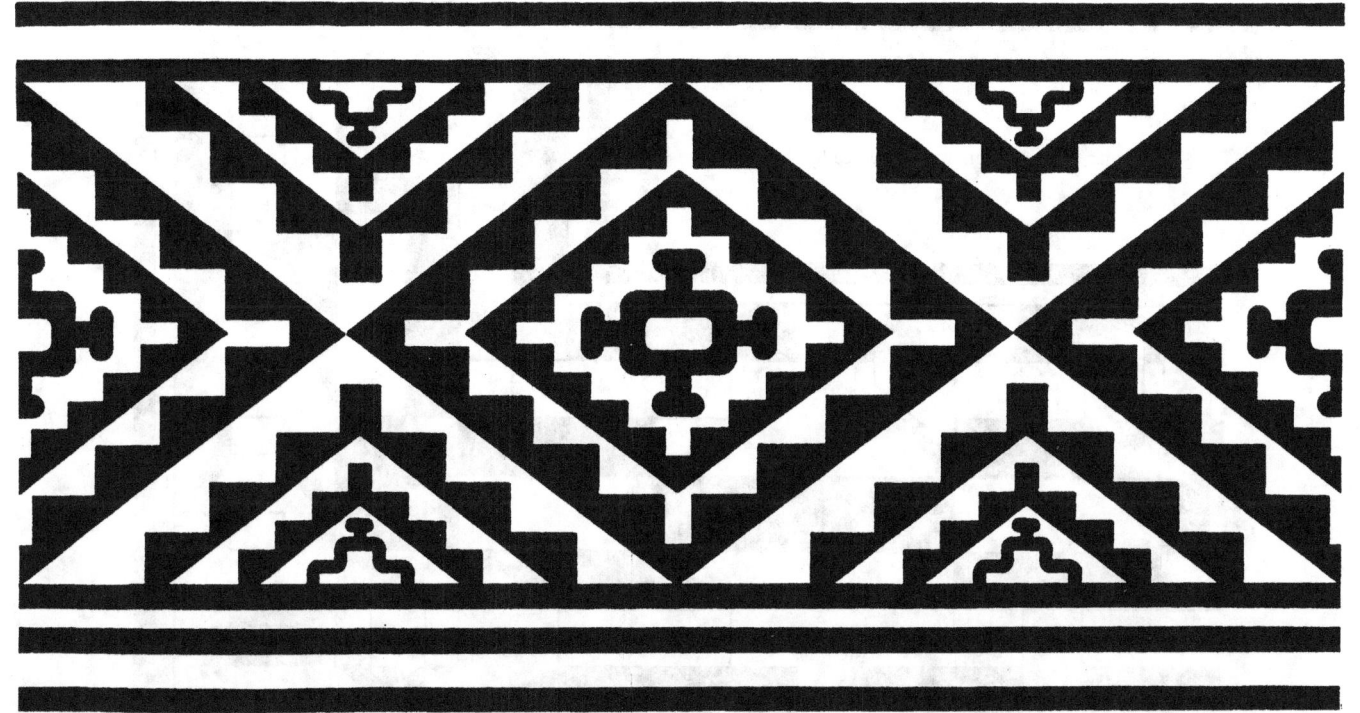

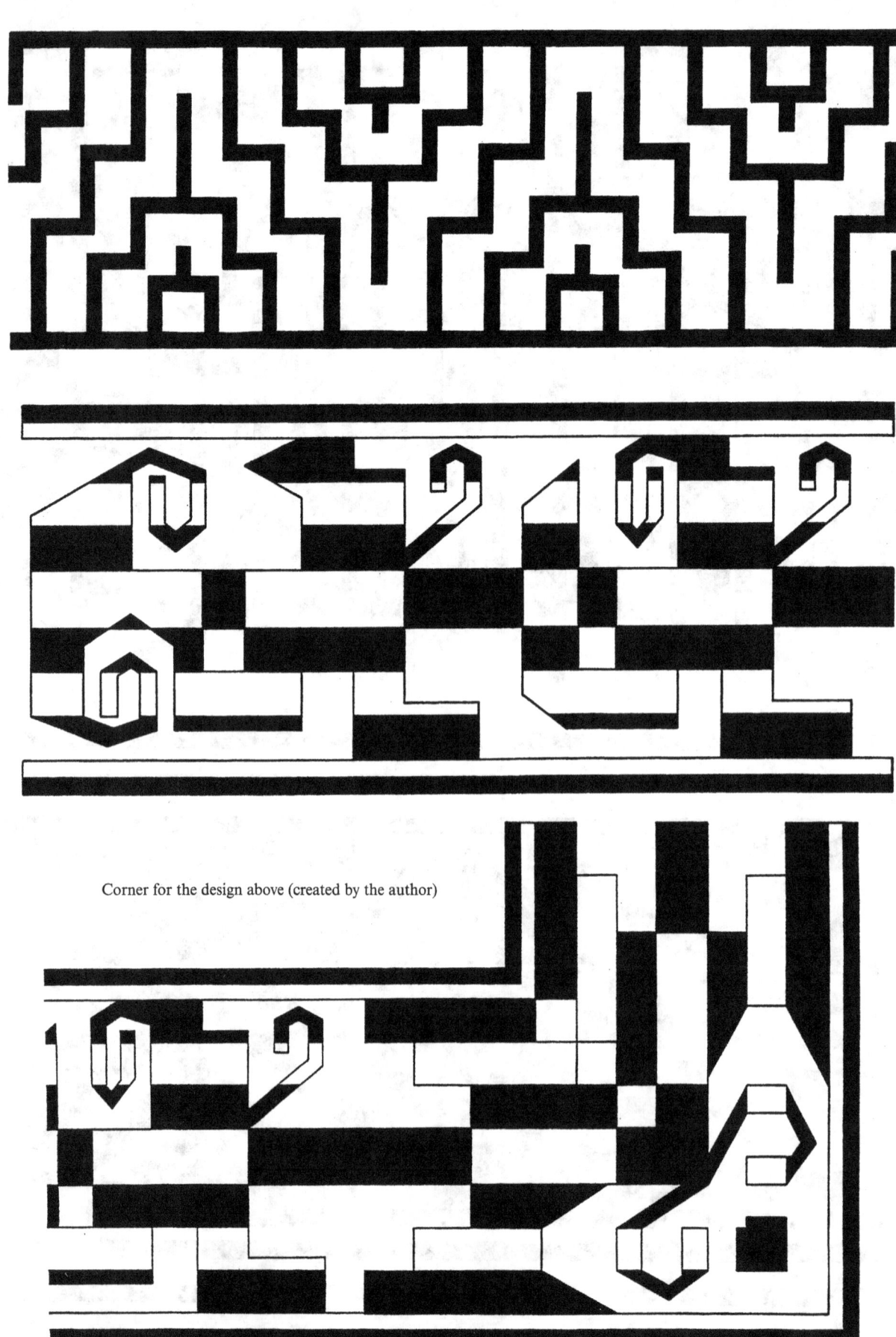

Corner for the design above (created by the author)